Philosophy of Ecology and Capitalism

The True New Green Deal

By

Jacques Richard

Philosophy of Ecology and Capitalism: The True New Green Deal

By Jacques Richard

This book first published 2023

Ethics International Press Ltd, UK

British Library Cataloguing in Publication Data

A catalogue record for this book is available from the British Library

Print Book ISBN: 978-1-80441-338-8

eBook ISBN: 978-1-80441-339-5

Table of Contents

Introduction

This book offers an approach to the philosophies and politics of nature based on a reinterpretation of the history of capitalism, in particular its concept of capital. It makes it possible to present a new complete theory of capital, different from that which Marx had proposed, in an erroneous way. It leads to a new anti-capitalist conception of the philosophy of ecology which takes into account at the same time history, ethics, politics, law and economics. The *first part* is dedicated to the notion of modernity and its history, based in particular on a historical study of the development of capitalism from ancient civilizations to the particular form of capitalism that arose at the end of the Middle Ages. It allows us to conclude that there is a close link between modernity and capitalism, at least one of its forms.

A *second part* shows why civilizations before the end of the Middle Ages were not modern and what role notably the ideas on the economy of the ancient Greeks and the ancient Latins played.

A *third part* is devoted to the review of the main positions of economists and philosophers faced with the problem of the degradations of nature which arise with modernity. The positions of economists are first examined with, to begin with, those of forest economists (in the 16th and 17th centuries), then those defended by certain neoclassicals such as the promoters of the concepts of "externalities" and of" existence value." The approaches defended by the philosophers of nature who claim to be Environmental Ethics will then be discussed, in particular those who founded the schools of Pathocentrism, Biocentrism and Ecocentrism. To conclude on this third part, we will show that all these approaches, whether of an economic or philosophical nature, remain influenced by modernity and do not allow us to leave it to move towards a true ecological economy.

A *fourth part* demonstrates that to truly break with capitalist modernity, two conditions must imperatively be respected. Firstly, to rely on the philosophical principles defended by the supporters of "Relational Ecology" but also, secondly, to go beyond the framework of this school by developing a new ecological economy based on a drastic expansion of the concept of capital-debt used by capitalists to conserve their financial capital. In a way, it is a matter of turning the weapon of capitalism against it to completely transform the systems of private management and national accounts that currently dominate global economic policies and, more broadly, the lives of all human beings.

By linking philosophy, law, economics and management, this work seeks to go beyond the mono-disciplinary and purely theoretical approaches which often characterize works devoted to the philosophy of nature or the philosophy of ecology. It is a question of proposing a concrete philosophical alternative to modern capitalism which leads to ecological co-management and care at all levels of society, including that of political bodies, and the reform of constitutions and parliaments. It is thus a book for a theory and a practice of environmental action in the broad sense within the framework of an institutional revolution passing in particular through the heart of the capitalist system: "its" corporate law and "its" accounting law. In short a concrete guide for a true green new deal.

Part One
History, Distinctive Features, and Relations Between Modernity and Modern Capitalism

In this first part we will successively address the history of the appearance of modernity, the birth of modern capitalist management in the Middle Ages, the ignorance of this modern capitalist management by most economists and philosophers, the evolution of modern capitalism towards financial capitalism and the diversity of points of view on the reality and scope of capitalism.

Chapter 1
A brief history of the emergence of modernity and its concepts

This chapter will deal with the notion of modernity in the frame of ecological philosophy and with the controversies about its emergence.

The notion of modernity and ecological philosophy

Flipo (2014a, 15-17), shows, based on Afeissa (2007), that there are two traditional currents of ecological philosophy: the "Anglo-American" current, which focuses on questions of environmental ethics, and the "continental" current which, for its part, is more interested in technological questions of the struggle for the conservation of nature. He rightly underlines that these two currents both leave aside the fundamental question of "the questioning of modernity. [1] For our part, we make modernity a central question of our reasoning. But this question is not obvious, if not because the definition of modernity is problematic. A large number of dictionaries refer to generalities encompassing several very broad concepts. Thus the Dictionnaire des Sciences Humaines (Editions Sciences Humaines, 2004, 563) affirms that "we agree to identify modernity with the historical period which opens in the West with the Renaissance (15th century). This new era is marked by large-scale transformations which have affected both social structures (urbanization, birth of capitalism), ways of life and values (individualism, advent of public freedoms, equal rights), rise of rational thought, sciences and politics (democratization)" ..."Reason, the individual, progress, equality, freedom: these would be the key words of modernity."

But, contrary to these very general visions, we find much more targeted approaches. Thus, according to the Romantic movement, notably with

[1] He notably evokes the positions of Catherine and Raphaël Larrère (Du bon usage de la nature, p.175) who consider that there is no fundamental problem of conflict between environmental ethics and modernity.

Rousseau, modernity would be defined as a taint caused by men of an intact, beautiful nature, without cities, in which man could go and dream as a solitary walker. However this is a nostalgia for a bygone past that hardly interests us, especially since it only really existed before the early days of agriculture, in the Neolithic (see below).

Another conception of modernity is more interesting. This is the one proposed by Lévi-Strauss (1962) and Viveiros De Castro (2009). According to them, while the pre-moderns, like the Amerindians, based their conception of the world on interrelational approaches and saw their universe populated by human and non-human subjective agents with a "similar soul," the moderns put an end to this view of the world to impose a reality that suits them. With them nature, that is to say everything that surrounds man, is populated only by objects to be used, the subject, man, being external to them and seeking to dominate them. This conception of modernity, which is based primarily on the subject / object dichotomy, is also that of Descola (2005), Moscovici (1968, 1972) and Latour (2014). The main question, within the framework of this reasoning, is to know what is raised to the rank of subject who has the power and what is lowered to that of pure object subject to the wills of the subject.

But we can oppose this vision centered on the subject-object distinction and power relations with more complex, if not different, visions, such as that of Norgaard (1994). According to this author, the modern approach is characterized by five constitutive elements: objectivism, mechanism, atomism, nominalism and monism. The criterion of objectivism, based on the ability of a subject to stand apart from what one wants to understand, can, to a certain extent, correspond to that retained by Lévi-Strauss and De Castro if one adds the question of power, in particular of abstraction of the object concerned. The mechanism, according to Norgaard, developed from the 18th century with Descartes (1637). It refers to the claim to know how to represent objects faithfully as pure homogeneous forms, with predictable behavior:[2] in these conditions nature can be captured by deterministic and predictable Laws. Atomism, on the other hand, is based

[2] Descartes (1637) asserts that "earth and heaven are made of the same matter" and that this physical world behaves "in a predictable way."

on the thesis that any system is composed of invariable parts, which again constitutes an element of determinism. Nominalism adds the idea that systems are objectively determined by their elements, and not the other way around. As for monism, linked to nominalism, it makes it possible to move from individual positions to an objectification of the whole, a coherent universal whole: it is an epistemological nominalism. We find in Gladwin et alii (1995) and their "technocentrism" similar notions to characterize modernism, with however a particular focus on the faith of the moderns in technology, a technological optimism which allows limitless possibilities of the exercise of the human power over objects, so much so that the modern world is perceived as a "vast machine."[3]

As can be seen, depending on whether one emphasizes the subject-object relationship and power as do Levi-Strauss, Viveiros de Castro, and even, to some extent, Gladwin et alii or that we add other criteria like those proposed by Norgaard, we end up with various definitions, if not very different, of modernity which will in particular pose problems for its identification and its historical location. For example, if we stick to the definitions formulated by Norgaard and the precisions he gives, modernism could not really begin[4] until the 17th century with Descartes (1637) and the "development of the mechanism." Likewise, even if the Middle Ages saw a notorious capacity for technological innovation (see below), it is clear that Gladwin et alii refer to the technological and industrial revolution of the 19th century rather than to the time of Leonardo da Vinci.

In this study we will not retain all of the criteria proposed by the various authors. We will consider that the criterion of the subject-object distinction is the determining criterion of modernity because it is the basis of the other criteria, as we will see later. We will therefore seek the first traces of this modernity in the appearance of a systematic partition between men (or

---

[3] We gloss over even broader and more imprecise definitions that incorporate allusions to 'dynamic', 'democratic' and 'economically advanced' attitudes. We also reject, for reasons that will be seen later, the criterion of the quest for productivity as the basis of Modernity.

[4] We will see that already among the ancient Greeks certain authors like Democritus announce the theories of Descartes. But the latter is generally considered the father of "mechanism."

certain men) who are the subjects and nature which is the object. We will come back to the rationale for this position later, especially when studying the history of ancient civilizations, particularly that of Greek philosophies. We are also leaving aside for the moment the fact that, with regard to the subject-object relationship, modernity cannot rest on a total objectification because it is obliged to interpret the phenomena that it claims to observe "scientifically": it cannot reveal all the objective elements of this complex reality. Furthermore, we underline that the notion of the subject, as composed of absolute freedom and will, corresponds to an ethereal, purely theoretical vision of the reality of modernity. As Latour (1997,2014,) shows, the purification of objects has its limits: the world is populated by new hybrids, partially unpredictable, that the modern approach will try to objectify but still with the limits inherent in the subjectivity of humans in their efforts to interpret the realities of a constantly changing world. This is also what Bouriau underlines in 2000: "the object of [modern] science is no longer the object itself (the thing in itself) but the implementation of objectivity, id est the mind taking itself for the first object." Thus science reasons on and from the representations that the subjects have of the world, [5] themselves based on supposedly objective intermediaries. However, for us, these attenuations do not call into question the fundamental subject / object separation that we will find in many modern practices. This type of separation is of great benefit to modern humans. It gives them the possibility of splitting the complexity of reality into two distinct ontological zones: one, the object, intended to be controlled and supposed to be controllable and the other, the subject, intended to control and supposed to have the qualities for doing it and thus simplify the problems. One of the examples of these simplifications consists in particular in considering that the world is probabilizable and can even be aligned with what the ideal man expects from it. A world without surprise, purified where, as Latour (1997) says, "subjects win every time." From the beginnings of modernity they therefore had absolute rights over objects, such as forests, expressed by "scientific" representations supposed to provide a faithful description of them. But to justify these statements we

[5] Utilitarianism, in particular, seeks to objectify this subjectivity by measuring the objective consequences of the manifestations of subjectivity, such as happiness, for example.

must now identify the existence and the novelty of modernity by historical arguments.

The controversial history of the emergence of modernity

The appearance of the concept of modernity and its justification are closely linked to the observation of a destructive action of man on nature, nature being understood here in the restrictive sense of the term which is that of modernity: including everything that exists on earth except humans. Although, as Flipo (2014a, 11) rightly puts it, "the culprit is not well identified,"[6] the general thesis is that as "modern man"[7] treats this "nature" as an object, a simple resource to meet its objectives, it destroys it systematically and progressively whereas the pre-moderns tended rather to preserve it because, in particular, of their relations of equality and respect towards the other living beings. If this thesis is correct, we should be able to date the emergence of modern man by the observation of massive phenomena of destruction of nature, especially forests, which are the most favorable places for biodiversity. But serious difficulties arise when it comes to verifying this hypothesis. Indeed, from the Neolithic period (9000 BC), during the birth of agriculture and breeding, and the sedentarization of human beings (Ponting, 2007), the area of forests near the territories of humans decreases very significantly (Groombridge and Jenkins 2002),which affects ecosystems, even sometimes until today (Olivier, 2006). We would then be led to consider that our neolithic ancestors would already be moderns. However, these ancient phenomena of mass destruction must be put into perspective both in their impact and also above all in their frequency: these are still localized and non-regular phenomena. On the other hand, in the opinion of specialists in the matter, a change in the scale of the level of deforestation appears in the Middle Ages, leading to effects out of all proportion to previous impacts. These effects would herald the contemporary ecological crisis (Williams, 2006). We are then led to seek the birth of modern man in this historical period.

---

[6] This author shows that the authors evoke in particular "humanity, western man, the West, homo faber, or even homo economicus."

[7] Next we will clarify what we call "modern man." We show that only a certain category of human beings deserve, historically, to be called modern.

But two main explanations oppose the cause of this appearance of modernity in the Middle Ages: that of Lynn White Junior (1967) and that of Renouard (1949). The first defends the thesis that the reason for the appearance of this new situation would be due solely to Christian thought: it would have gradually established a conception of the world at odds with most religious systems, this because of two new principles. The first is that man is separate from nature inasmuch as he was created in the image of God, and the second is that it is God's will that he exploits nature for his own ends.[8] Thus, according to this thesis, the catholic religion, the most "anthropocentric" of all, man being at the center of the universe, would be the cause of the emergence of modernity. According to White, too, the development of techniques arose as early as the 7th century, but it was its progression from the early Middle Ages to the 11th century that was the reason for the systematic destruction of our environment. The interest of this thesis is to highlight that the questions of the ecological crisis and sustainability (particularly of forest and climate) are linked above all to thought patterns concerning the relationship between man and nature, even if they are connected to practices. These are fundamentally neither questions of equity (such as that of inter- and intra-generational relations), nor even questions of rational management of natural resources. In short, above all, questions of culture and politics: in the broad sense of the term[9] cosmograms, that is to say problems of articulations between humans and non-humans in order to build a world (Latour, 2007a). But Lynn White's thesis is very controversial (Minteer and Manning, 2005; Afeissa, 2012,97[10]), for two main reasons. The first is that a serious reading and interpretation of the biblical texts does not mean that these texts make of man a subject who is the measure of all things and that nature can be exploited as he pleases. The first account of Genesis certainly states that "God made the beasts and the earth after their kind, and the cattle after their kind, and God

[8] The text classically invoked is that of Genesis (I, 26-29) which commands man to "rule over the fish of the sea, the birds of the sky, the cattle, all the wild beasts and all the creatures that crawl on earth."

[9] In contrast to this broad sense, politics, in the restricted and pragmatic sense of Dewey (1930), is the science of solving concrete problems, within the framework of politics in the broad sense.

[10] This author rightly underlines "the profound ambiguity of the Judeo-Christian heritage" (97).

saw that it was good" (Gn 1, 24-25). But, as underlined by Callicott (2009,21), one of the creators of the current of environmental ethics, in this text, "God represents an objective and independent axiological point of reference" and thus, we humans, "we have the right to the usufruct of our possession of nature as long as we govern it with benevolence and do not draw on its main reserves." This interpretation of Callicott, among others by the same author,[11] is that of man as steward or guardian of nature entrusted to him by God. It corresponds exactly to the one recalled very recently by Pope François in his encyclical Laudato Si (2015), a text that we will examine in more detail later. The second reason is that there have always been different currents on the problem of relationship of man and nature within the Catholic Church: thus the (true) followers of the ideas of Saint Francis of Assisi were active defenders of the protection of animals. If we admit that it is more than simplistic to place the weight of the cause of the emergence of modernity on the Christian religion, and in particular the Catholic religion, then other avenues must be found to explain this appearance.

In fact, another factor, not inherently religious, may have played a very important role. One can indeed oppose, with Yves Renouard (1949), a theoretical framework other than that of the religious cause: that of a modernity which would be founded on the emergence of "modern" capitalism and its concepts. Within this framework of thought we then trace modernity back to at least the 14th-15th centuries to extend it to the present day without interruption.[12] We then consider the emergence of this modern capitalism as a break with all the traditions of the past (including religions) due to human reason, or at least a certain human rationality linked to this type of capitalism: being human is then judged free, able to master his future, to control it and to constantly make it better. It is the idea of a continuous progress of the free subject or more exactly of a certain free

---

[11] Callicott (2009, 61-62) will have another interpretation of the relationship of man with nature from the second story of Genesis according to Yahwist sources: for him, in this second story, man would no longer be only a simple steward of God but a conscious actor of the protection of nature with which he is in collusion.

[12] Contra, it seems, Pelluchon (2011, 103), building on Chakrabarty (2010), who believes that "we are collectively a geological agent." We will come back later to this highly debatable "collectivist" thesis of modernity.

subject, capable of distinguishing facts and values, which is a major characteristic of this modernity against an authoritarian traditional, subject to laws immutable. Indeed, as Renouard shows, the development of "modern" capitalism is giving rise to new capitalists who want to dominate nature, in particular thanks to their scientific and technical knowledge.[13] This historian also underlines that these newcomers have an ambition to dominate the world with their companies of international dimensions and their very active participation in political life. This new type of capitalist will, of course, be supported by certain currents of Catholicism, but it will also run up against certain principles of this religion (see below). It can be considered as the prototype of the new "modern subject" which makes nature a simple object to be dominated, which leads to the new geological stage of the "Anthropocene"[14] or rather, as we will demonstrate, of the Capitalocene. Let us underline in this regard that this capitalism is not only a commercial capitalism: it is also a devastating industrial capitalism, like many of these capitalists of Florence who practiced the wool industry (see in particular Piper, 1978, and, on this basis, Richard and Rambaud, 2020; 2022a).[15] More generally, as Gimpel (1975) has clearly shown, the Middle Ages were already the scene of a first industrial revolution. It would therefore be this triple crucible, first and foremost capitalist, but also industrial and, in part, religious, which would gradually lead, according to this thesis, to new massive environmental impacts, especially forest ones, over the following centuries. Of course, as already noted, the degradation of nature did not begin at the end of the Middle Ages. Despite controversies they are often traced back to the beginning of the agriculture, around 10,000 years ago, with massive changes due to human action. But, as Jones (2004) underlines, towards the end of the Middle Ages, changes in the scale, rhythm and nature of environmental impacts, linked in particular to new types of "modern" management of companies, potentially lead to a new geological era: we enter the era of the "modern" capitalist enterprise with a *permanent,*[we underline this adjective], rational calculation adapted to

---

[13] Which does not mean that this knowledge is the dominant factor: it is only part of the question.

[14] A term coined by the Nobel Prize in Chemistry Crutzen (2002).

[15] Grange (2012,124-127) also rightly shows that this type of capitalist is a special man, but she does not agree on the date of its appearance: she shifts it to the 17th and 18th centuries, at the time of what is commonly called the "industrial revolution."

the ambitions of this new type of capitalist.[16] Of course, business and profit were not born with "modern" capitalism (Hudson, 2010; Wunsch, 2010). Assyriologists, in particular, show that Assyria and the kingdom of Babylon experienced a structured economy with companies seeking a surplus, a private profit (see below). But, on the one hand, these companies had very strong relations with the public institutions that were the temples and the Government Palace, in particular to avoid excessive fluctuations in prices. On the other hand, their management was based on calculations of results in terms of cash flows that have nothing to do with those that will develop the Italian merchants and industrialists promoters of the modern capitalist enterprise. As we will then show in more detail these types of ancestral capitalist calculations, which are also found in ancient Greece and Rome, could not allow a permanent and efficient rational management of the resources to be used. For the most part, economic activity was concentrated in the hands of small farmers who had little in common with the spirit and the means of the large industrial and commercial capitalist enterprises that we see appearing at the end of the Middle Ages, particularly in northern Italy (see below). We therefore note, from the start of the history of companies, that we cannot speak in the abstract of the firm, including capitalist one, as a single model but rather of various modalities of the firm with different types of management. The new modern capitalist enterprise of the late Middle Ages is truly a revolution. Thus, as Sombart (1902), then Renouard (1949), Robertson (1959), Castoriadis (1976, 2013), Moscovici (1972, 1977), Goody (2004), Nitzan and Bichler (2012) have already pointed out, birth of modern capitalism and modernity are intimately linked, if only from a temporal point of view: it is indeed Italian merchants and industrialists who are the founders of modern capitalism at the end of the Middle Ages. Max Weber (1920) links capitalism and its new spirit above all to the Reformation (in the 16th century), therefore to problems of religious ethics, which in our opinion is a major error. However, he clearly recognizes that "it would seem that the development of the 'capitalist spirit' is to be regarded quite simply as a specific phenomenon within the general evolution of rationalism and that it is the

[16] Our thesis is therefore opposed to that of Pelluchon (2011, 22) who sees, relying on Grinevald, the emergence of a break only in the 18th century with the "thermo-industrial revolution."

result of certain positions taken of the latter rationalism on the ultimate problems of existence." He therefore nevertheless connects capitalism and rationalism, while making it a certain form of the latter. Weber is thus led to distinguish various forms of rationality, including an instrumental rationality that he attributes to modern capitalism. It is this thesis that Castoriadis (1976) clearly adopts. For him, modernity appears as the observation of a "[…] convergence that we see from […] the fourteenth century, between the birth and the expansion of the bourgeoisie, the obsessive and growing interest in inventions and to the discoveries, the progressive collapse of the medieval representation of the world and of society, the Reformation, the passage from the closed world to the infinite Universe, the mathematization of the sciences, the prospect of an indefinite progress of knowledge and the idea that the proper use of reason is the necessary and sufficient condition for us to become masters and owners of Nature (Descartes 1637)." Later in another writing (2013) Castoriadis makes instrumental rationality one of the two fundamental traits of capitalism.[17] For him, this second characteristic "is obviously that the push towards mastery gives itself new means, and means of a special rational character [...] - to be accomplished. It is no longer magic or victory in battles that is the means, but precisely rationalization."

The capitalism that emerges in the Middle Ages is thus a particular attitude to the world characterized by a rational control of certain subjects (the capitalists) over objects (nature and certain humans). It already corresponds to the modern "orthodox" view. The period of the early Middle Ages is therefore, in our opinion, that of the true birth of Modernity and of one of its fundamental characteristics: an unprecedented type of business management. This does not mean, as we will show later, that all the characteristics of this modernity appear at this time. But that does mean, on the other hand, that before that time it was difficult to be able to talk about modernity. Let us underline, in this regard, two last points relating to this analysis which rests the transition to what we have called modernity on the

[17] The other feature being the aim of a total mastery of society (including education and politics), not only of production and the economy.

shoulders of modern capitalists which leads to speak of Capitalocene rather than Anthropocene to name this new era.

First, there is no question for us to consider that all human beings in this period of the High Middle Ages were modern subjects: only a very specific segment of the population were. From that time on, therefore, we cannot speak of "Modern Human Nature" but of various "human natures," some of which are modern and others not. Most of the people of the time were farmers or small artisans who behaved more like the ancient Greeks and Latins than the new modern capitalists. This situation will largely continue until the 20th century (see below). Second, as we will show, these new capitalists, with the support first of princes or kings, then of all the republican governments of Western Europe and America, will, over the centuries, considerably increase their wealth and their power and dominate the economic and political scene to the present day. Therefore, even today, one cannot consider that the modern cause is that of human beings as a whole: the capitalists in question are "more modern" than the other layers of the population, in the sense that this it is they who are “at the helm” of this modernity.[18] We cannot therefore put in the same basket the leaders of modernity and those who are practically obliged to follow it, even if, in theory, they have the power to change things within the framework of parliamentary systems. If this thesis of the primacy of the influence of modern capitalism in the responsibility for the degradations of nature is correct then our position according to which the role of Descartes and his mechanistic philosophy is a secondary element, or even irrelevant in the treatment of this question, will be justified. This man of science is not fundamentally responsible for the current ecological disasters. So now, to consolidate our position, we need to analyze in depth what are the major characteristics of this modern capitalism which was born towards the end of the Middle Ages. We will be particularly interested in what, according to the meritorious and precursor works of Sombart and Weber,[19] made the fundamental mark of this type of unprecedented capitalism: its accounting

[18] Descartes' general split between things that think (human beings as a whole) and matter (res extensa) is therefore irrelevant to our analysis.

[19] Even if they could not perceive the essence of modern capitalist accounting (see below) we must pay homage to these two sociologists for having understood the importance of this discipline: it is a rarity.

system. Without this presentation it is impossible to understand not only what capitalism really is but also modernity.[20] We can then explain why the ancient Greeks and the ancient Latins practically did not enter modernity despite the considerable progress of their scientific and technical knowledge.

[20] For more details on this complex issue see Richard and Rambaud (2020 and 2022ac).

Chapter 2
The Birth of modern capitalism and modernity in the 14th century in Italy

The modern capitalist firm is a company that Christophe (2007) designates as "promethean." Indeed this type of company is characterized by the modern subject / object divide: the subject(s) (mainly capitalists) appear on the liabilities side[1] of its balance sheet in very peculiar capital accounts while the objects (or resources to be used, or more precisely their cost of use), as nature and certain human beings, are registered on the opposite side of the balance sheet into its assets, this term referring to simple means of action (from the Latin verb agere, to act). The bases of the future "denaturation" or "dehumanization" or of "disenchantment" of certain human beings and the systematic destruction of nature are already anchored in this accounting system which is still rife at the time of writing of this book. In his analysis of the disenchantment with the world, Gauchet (1985, 20) considers that the source of this state lies in the "quest for added value" and "economic gain" [which] is not a matter of opinion but of calculation which is imposed on all and all." He is right to link the source of this disenchantment to calculation problems, but he is wrong to think that these calculations are not a "matter of opinion." On the contrary, it is the totally selfish and perverse opinion of a group of individuals who, from the Middle Ages, will begin to conquer the world thanks to their very particular rationality and gradually make it a rationality which dominates the world, all the peoples of the earth. From this point of view, because of the lasting victory of these capitalists, it can be said that theorists and practitioners of human rights have never put their rhetoric into full practice. The famous Kantian principle of classical ethics that one should do for others what we want them to do for us has never concerned the accounting law of modern capitalists. To verify the validity of these assertions it is first of all imperative to thoroughly analyze this terrible type of management by distinguishing notably two of its major

---

[1] The words "passif or Passiva" which design the liabilities in French and German accounting comes from the Greek verb pateiv which means "to bear," in particular weights which can be physical but also relational, such as debts.

innovations: double-entry accounting and the principle of prudence. Once this task is accomplished we will conclude this chapter by showing that in most cases these major innovations and their consequences have been largely neglected by philosophers.

The invention of modern double-entry subject/object accounting.

The mode of calculation of the modern capitalists, as it appears in northern Italy at the end of the Middle Ages, is marked by the use of a particular accounting device, completely unknown before: double-entry accounting (DEA). As we have said, Sombart (1902), the first, long before Weber (1920), whom he strongly inspired, rightly made it the major characteristic of "modern capitalism" to the study of which he dedicated an important part of its work. Even if he did not understand its mechanism and in particular its concept of capital (Rambaud and Richard, 2020,2022ac), he had the immense merit of emphasizing the importance of this technique which is very difficult to interpret, in particular for who is not a practitioner of accounting and does not know its historical evolution.[2]

Indeed, the complex problem that arises is to know what exactly is meant by modern capitalist double-entry bookkeeping (DEB). Some Chinese historical studies argue that this use of the double entry technique, it means the simultaneous recording of a single given transaction in two different accounts,[3] appeared in China around the sixteenth century (Aiken and Lu, 1998). Moreover, other historians even believe that double entry accounting was already used in the year 100 BC among the Romans for planning and administrative control tasks: "double entry was used in Roman governmental planning and control as early as 100 B.C. (Most 1976 and, on this basis, Strachan 1984). But, in fact, these types of so-called "double-entry" accounting differ fundamentally from the double-entry accounting invented by the Italian capitalists, in two main respects, the second being

---

[2] To tell the truth, even many accountants, who often have no historical training, also have difficulty in identifying the originality and the salient features of this invention. They learn accounting by heart as a simple technique without perceiving its ethical and ideological underpinnings.

[3] For example a purchase of goods.

fundamental. Firstly, they only deal with cash movements (outflow of money from one account and inflow of money into another account) while the Italian DEB, with a universal vocation, also concerns other types of movements such as purchases or sales on credit, operations without any cash consideration.[4] Second, and above all, these ancient types of accounts never considered the capitalist subject as a creditor of his own enterprise, whereas it is this duplication of the personality of the capitalist that will found the modern capitalist accounting system from the end of the Middle Ages.[5] Indeed, from the birth of modern capitalism, in the Florence of the 13th and 14th centuries, certain factories and capitalist commercial firms show on their balance sheet a cleavage between capitalist-subjects and objects subject to the will of these subjects.[6] The typical initial balance sheet (at the time of foundation) of this totally new business model is as follows (assuming that a private capitalist X has invested a sum of 100[7] from his personal savings):

Assets (resources to be used)	Liabilities (debts to be repaid)
Cash on hand 100	Capital due to X 100

Table 1.1 *Typical initial balance sheet*

[4] Typical examples are a purchase of a machine on credit and the depreciation (wear) of this machine as it is used. These types of neuralgic operations for modern capitalists absolutely cannot be recorded in a simple "cash" accounting of the Greeks and Latins insofar as they do not involve any movement of cash. In this respect, the invention, in particular, of the concept of depreciation (even in a rudimentary version) was a major innovation in management. Economists traditionally attribute this invention to Quesnay, but the truth is that this concept was discovered and used by Italian accountants more than three centuries before the "discovery" of the famous author of the "economic circuit" who, moreover, did'nt understand it (Richard and Rambaud 2022ac).

[5] Rambaud (2015, 143) points out that "the Chinese double-entry accounting described above does not personalize the accounts; it only aims at simple inscriptions of flows and therefore of interrelations of hybrids, being in this perhaps close to pre-Modern thought.

[6] We will of course find these characteristics again later, particularly during the industrial revolution: see in particular the case of the Oberkampf firm described by Briot (2014). But it was not this industrial revolution that created modern capitalist management: it only applied the invention of the capitalists of the late Middle Ages.

[7] The monetary units are not specified to remain within the framework of an abstract reasoning and to shorten the figures.

In this modern accounting vision which "sees double," which one can notably observe concretely in the balance sheet of the capitalist Datini of January 31, 1399 (De Roover (1956), two striking elements appear.

First, contrary to what the quasi- all economists, whether classical, Marxist or neoclassical will think thereafter, the capital of the capitalist (the modern capitalist as a practitioner, not the capitalist in the imagination of economists[8]) is absolutely not an asset (or a resource, or a means) to be used but a debt towards the capitalist, a debt which appears on the liabilities side of his own company's balance sheet. At the same time, the means to be used are never named "capital" by these accountants, as economists do, but "assets."

Second, although from the founding of this company employees could be hired they do not appear as capital in this accounting: we will show subsequently they are treated as simple objects. The capitalism which was born at this time is therefore a "mono capitalism," in the sense that only one type of capital is strictly preserved thanks to its recording in the liabilities 'side as a debt to be entirely repaid to the capitalist.

Normally, the study of any phenomenon begins with its detailed description to show its appearance, then the nature, the concepts and the laws which govern it: all science consists first in giving an account of experience, of real practice. But economists, with very, very rare exceptions, have never wanted to respect these principles when it comes to the case of capitalism. In particular, they were unable or, more generally, unwilling to seriously study its actual practice, especially its heart, accounting. Even Marx, who nevertheless spent a lot of time in the study of capital (to put it mildly), and who was interested in certain accounting concepts, notably that of depreciation (Chiapello, 2007), was unable to see how (and why) capital, in the practice of capitalism, is not a means of action or a resource,[9] but a thing to be conserved.[10] Marx's goal was above all to demonstrate that

---

[8] See for more detail on this specific point Richard and Rambaud (2022ac).

[9] Marx's famous cycle of the circulation of capital in the form of money-commodity-money (MCM') is well known. For a classical capitalist accountant, capital is not something that circulates: it is assets that circulate.

[10] We are aware of the heated terminological debate between "conservationists" and "preservationists." For our part, we will not make a state affair of these terms. The

the accumulation of wealth by the capitalists in the framework of the expansion of the productive forces would inevitably lead to the destruction of capitalism. This very Hegelian position would even lead him to be a "free trader." As he says in Misère de la Philosophie (1847, ed 2002 p.197, 212) "the system of commercial freedom hastens the social revolution. It is only in this revolutionary sense, Gentlemen, that I vote in favor of free trade." Why then bother studying thoroughly the capitalist accounting and inventing a counter accounting model when the dynamics of the system being criticized is leading it to death?

After him the other economists, especially the neoclassics, will develop an economic theory that has nothing to do with the real functioning of capitalism. This statement may seem provocative, but it is also that of a few rare economists and not the least ones: thus, for example, Stiglitz (2010) comes to say that "economic theory has become a self-sufficient world, a false representation of reality." Neither did Marx's successors rectify the situation, including those who had an ecological "touch" (see below).

Two conclusions on these developments can then be drawn. First, we can only speak validly of capitalism by making a phenomenology of its real practices. Secondly, this type of modern capitalism does not date from the 20th century with what is called financial capitalism, nor even from industrial capitalism of the 19th century: it appears long before, at the end of the Middle Ages, and this not only under a commercial form (that of simple merchants) but also in industrial form with large factories, especially wool manufacturing. Meiksin Wood's (2002) thesis, inspired by the writings of Marx, that the capitalism of northern Italy in the 14th and 15th centuries was mere capitalism of merchants who bought for resale is unfounded. The concept of modern capitalism should therefore not be confused with a type of activity: its major innovation, modern double entry accounting, and its economic and social consequences already concern at its birth, in the Middle Ages, all types of activity. Let us underline, in this regard, that even Polanyi is also mistaken when he affirms in his "Great Transformation" (1944) that the labor market and the class struggle only

main thing, as with "sustainable development," is the philosophy (anthropocentric or not) that is associated with them. The reader will judge what it is by reading the entirety of this work.

really existed from 1834. He lacks knowledge of social and accounting history, at least those aspects concerning modern double-entry capitalist accounting at the time of the great Italian cities of the end of the Middle Ages.[11]

To return to this event and to the conditions and means of its birth during this period, we see that we are dealing here with an extraordinary duplication of personality which anticipates by nearly five centuries the development of types of companies having a legal person: the private person X who founds a capitalist company 'lends' a sum of money to this company which, as a fictitious capitalist business person, must reimburse him this sum. We will show that this major innovation of a remarkable fiction[12] allows the capitalist to use his money (and more broadly his various types of assets) while conserving his capital, that is to say a sum of abstract mone[13] that must be refunded to him. In other words, the accountants of modern Italian capitalists have discovered that in order to be able to ensure a systematic and permanent conservation of the financial capital invested by their masters, it is necessary to consider this capital not as a means of action (an asset) but as a debt or liability. In a certain sense, we can say that these capitalists have "sanctified" their capital: we must not touch it.[14] We can also say that they have invented a principle of absolute

[11] It is symptomatic that in his famous article on "socialist accounting" (1922) he does not use this concept of double entry at all.

[12] Harari (2019),in his magnificent fresco on a "brief history of humanity," rightly points out that fictions have played a major role in this adventure. But he did not see the major role of the fiction wrought by double-entry accounting, although he has a keen interest in capitalism, which is to his credit.

[13] This sum of money is abstract because it is independent of the concrete form of the resource that corresponds to the assets. If our capitalist had brought at the time of the foundation of his firm a building of value 100 instead of currency the capital in both cases would have been 100 in liabilities.

[14] The fact that nowadays a private capitalist makes the decision to risk his personal wealth by gambling on the stock market and thus to make a commodity of it does not imply a commodification of the global capital of the capitalists: it is a game between them in which there are winners and losers which does not prevent this global capital from being "normally" subject to systematic preservation thanks in particular to the double-entry technique. Of course, this type of conservation does not protect against social revolutions or ecological crises that can arise at any time but, for the moment, it ensures, as history has proven (see in particular the works de Piketty, 2012 and 2019) a

prevention in this regard, as opposed to a principle of precaution (see below for more details). In another sense, we can also say that they made themselves morally responsible for the conservation of their capital, this before, much later, in the 19th century, this responsibility was sanctioned by law and therefore became legal(see below).

It has often been said, notably with the famous Meadows report (1972) that modern (capitalist) society is characterized by a society of "unlimited growth" but this is not correct. The capitalists have imposed certain (very specific) limits on their growth. In particular, there is a sacrosanct limit that these capitalists will never cross: it is the destruction of their capital of their own fault. To this end, the type of management that they will use involves a particular concept of capital to be conserved which we will call capital-debt. This capital-debt, although within the framework of capitalism and commodification, is not an object or a commodity at all.

In a founding text of bio-centrism and even eco-centrism (insofar as it is particularly interested in soil protection) Routley (1973[15]) asserts, (referring to Barkley and Seckler: economic growth and environmental decay), that "the liberal philosophy of the western world defends the idea that everyone should be free to do what he wants as long as he does not harm other people and that he does not harm him in an irreversible way."[16] In fact this conception of liberalism, which they qualify as "chauvinist" (power of men in general over other living beings and things), seems questionable in view of modern accounting law which will develop on the basis of the accounts practiced in northern Italy at the end of the Middle Ages, and that this liberalism, over the centuries, allowed and even made compulsory by laws (see below). This for two main reasons. First, as we will see in more detail, this accounting law practically endorses an objectification of certain humans, those who are under the domination of capitalist subjects. Secondly, it obliges on the contrary to systematically conserve certain material things, mainly the money invested by the capitalist, but not only:

---

great ability to overcome hazards and therefore the possibility of enormous enrichment in the medium or long term.

[15] Text reproduced by Afeissa (2007,31-49).

[16] This last point clearly refers to the ban on the sale of certain organs and, in some countries, suicide.

in fact certain modern capitalist accounts which aim at the maintenance of physical capital can ensure, for example, the conservation of machines.[17] We can then consider, in this regard, that these capitalists, no doubt in a more or less conscious manner, inaugurate, for the protection of their financial capital, a concept of intrinsic value, this insofar as they consider this type of capital as must be systematically conserved:[18] it is for them an end in itself because before being able to accumulate wealth, they must first conserve the capital they have invested, as Monsieur de la Palisse would say. It is traditional, when we talk about capitalism, to focus on its desire for accumulation, but we neglect the fundamental problem of conservation. In fact, the concrete realization of this conservation, especially if it must be a permanent one, is not at all obvious: it took the "brilliant" invention of the double entry accounting, dixit Goethe,[19] and of a certain concept of cost of conservation to put it into practice. We will show later that this cost of conservation, after certain corrections, corresponds well to the famous intrinsic value, the quest for the Grail of environmental ethicists. For the moment, let us be content to insist again on this accounting revolution which will continue and will eventually lead to the catastrophic ecological and human consequences that we are experiencing today. Before being characterized by relations of production, modern capitalism is first of all by relations of conservation which condition the relations of production. We can even see in this focus on issues of conservation and preservation a kind of "good use" of certain things on the part of the founders of modern capitalism.

---

[17] When it comes to machines, capitalism does not hesitate to check, with the help of experts, whether their conservation is not endangered by abusive exploitation (problems of overheating, speeding, risk machinery breakdown, etc).

[18] This proves that, contrary to what Routley (1973,45) says, the concept of conservation is not necessarily the prerogative of environmental ethics: capitalist law is also a follower of conservation, which is moreover actually practiced. But obviously not of the conservation of the same things the Routleys are aiming for.

[19] Most accounting teachers know this astonishing sentence from Goethe which appears in his novel devoted to the suffering of young Werther: "double-entry accounting, one of the most beautiful inventions in the world" (Sic!).

The 'good use' of the first modern capitalists

Aristotle, as Aubenque (1963) has shown, recommended acting in such a way as to ensure the conservation of things used, notably through what he calls "good use" of things. He added that this good practice had to go hand in hand with a principle of "prudence." It is interesting to compare these good "Aristotelian" principles with those which animate modern capitalists from the end of the Middle Ages until around 1980.[20] We will start by dealing with good practice before addressing the issue of prudence. As far as good use is concerned, we will show that the principles of "good use" of which Aristotle speaks remain only vague and inefficient words, at least in a monetary market economy based on the regular measurement of profit, if they are not associated with precise accounting rules for the conservation of capital. It is precisely these accounting rules that modern capitalists in medieval Italy had to invent to properly manage their businesses in this modern context. Let us take again to explain precisely this hotspot but little known, especially by economists, the fictitious example of the founding of a modern capitalist enterprise that we presented previously. Here is again his initial accounting statement after the foundation by the capitalist X:

Assets to be used (resources)		Liabilities	
Cash on hand	100	Capital due to X	100

Table 2.1 *Initial balance sheet*

We see that in this practice of modern capitalism the same sum of 100 appears both as an asset and as a liability. At first glance, this double entry seems odd: with the sole entry of money "capital" in the assets, we are already very well informed about the means available to the company or firm. Suppose that this firm, with the money it has in hand, buys, for the first period, a commodity for 100 and then resells it for 320. Suppose also that this capitalist has employees, responsible in particular for handling and transport of goods, which he pays according to the labor market of the place and the time, admit for 50. After payment of this salary, he will therefore only have 270 left in the cash box and it is this concrete sum of

[20] See below for this temporal nuance.

money that will appear in the assets of the final balance sheet for the first period after the resale of the goods. This capitalist enterprise thus realizes a profit[21] of 170 which will be entered in the liabilities of its balance sheet as an amount due to the capitalist, which gives the following balance sheet at the end of the first period:

Assets (resources to be used)	Liabilities (debts to be repaid)	
Cash on hand 270	Capital due at X	100
	Profit due to X	170

Table 2.2 *Balance sheet at the end of the first period*

Let us underline in passing that if the profit of 170 is indeed also a sum owed to the capitalist it is not a capital-debt because it is, as a general rule in accounting, *potentially consumable* whereas capital is not:[22] all debts are therefore not capital debts. Note also that, in our case of positive earnings, the equity of (170), which takes into account the profits accumulated (registered in retained earnings) by the capitalist, is not to be confused with its capital either: the profits placed in retained earnings can also be consumed while the capital cannot be.[23]

But back to the double entry system. An attentive and critical reader could very well object that the initial double entry of the sum of 100 in the assets and in the liabilities seems redundant and that one could be satisfied with a "simple " single entry system in which one would only use the asset column. Indeed, in this case, it is apparently sufficient to compare the final sum of money of 270 with the initial sum of 100 in the assets 'side to know immediately that there has been a profit of 170. The passive column and notably the capital item would therefore be perfectly useless and, at the

---

[21] This profit is not necessarily the real profit because from that time there were taxes to pay and various taxes. We disregard these elements so as not to complicate.

[22] If our capitalist had made losses of 60, the amount of his capital would however remain equal to 100 to clearly show that his repayment remains to be made. The loss would appear in a separate negative account, the capital remaining equal to 100. On the other hand, its equity, a different concept to measure the total wealth of the capitalist, would amount to 40. Always the same logic which makes capital an intangible amount except with the explicit agreement of the capitalist.

[23] Thus not only the dimension of capital is generally totally different from that of equity but its nature is also very different.

same time, the famous double entry, which would duplicate use. In fact this reasoning is simplistic. For two main reasons. The first, and most important, is that it does not distinguish between an asset to be used and a capital to be conserved. Let us return to the previous example by supposing that in the first period considered the capitalist has given up buying the commodity under consideration because its purchase price has increased to 200 and that he had to take the time to raise new family funds in order to make a new capital contribution of 100 at the end of this first period, this before carrying out the commercial operation, which is postponed to the following period. In this case, at the end of the first period (before any purchase and resale operation) the balance sheet established by the modern capitalist according to the double entry would be as follows:

Assets (resources to be used)		Liabilities (debts to be repaid)	
Cash on hand	200	Capital due at X	200
		Profit due to X	0

Table 2.3 *Balance sheet in the case of the new capital contribution*

In this accounting system, no profit appears because the increase in capital on the liabilities side counterbalances the increase in assets that took place after the first stake.[24] On the other hand, if we used only the assets as a basis for information, we should then recognize a profit of 100 corresponding to the difference between the final asset (200) and the initial asset (100), which is an aberration.[25] Note that taking into account changes in capital is not limited to problems of increasing capital. It can obviously relate to withdrawals of capital and other eminently more complex problems, in particular the taking into account of inflation. Let us also add that the problem of capital conservation is linked to that of depreciation. As we have seen, as part of their conservative management, modern capitalists have invented the concept of depreciation of long-term invested assets

[24] The change in final and initial assets equal to 100 (200-100) is not a profit because it only corresponds to an increase in capital, that is, to the new loan of the capitalist as a private person.

[25] Of course the reader could object that it suffices to correct the figures obtained by simple variation of the assets to take account of the capital increase which took place during the period: but it is exactly this objective that the double entry pursues, and this in a systematic way. This is why this system has imposed itself.

which allows them to take into account the periodic wear and tear of these types of assets by reducing their distributable profit or recording losses of capital to be compensated as quickly as possible to ensure the real conservation of this capital. We can conclude on this point that a double-entry accounting which differentiates the concepts of capital (thing to preserve) and asset (thing to use) is absolutely essential to ensure *permanent* good management, good use of things in a conservation perspective would say Aristotle. To use an expression of Stengers (2013,51) these capitalists have the art of "being careful" with their capital. We can characterize them, with their accountants, as great specialists in the permanent conservation of things, but, unfortunately reduced to only financial contributions. Their concept of capital is a remarkable invention.

To come back to Aristotle, the major conclusion that can be drawn from this development is that, in practice, there can be no "good management of the business," in the capitalist sense of the term, in a modern capitalist market economy in which the permanent control of profitability predominates, without a differentiation of the concepts of asset (or resource) and capital-debt. More generally, to permanently manage this particular type of business correctly, it is necessary to constantly consider both things to use (assets[26]) and things to keep (capital in the accounting sense of the term[27] in the context of the double entry system).

Aristotle certainly wanted a "good use" of things and, implicitly, a good conservation, but he could not give a concrete translation of it in his time: he contented himself with simple advice. In the context of a largely family and agricultural economy which did not reason in terms of permanent measurement of the profitability of invested capital but essentially in terms of values in use(for self-consumption) or exchanges of values in use[28] people had hardly any reason, moreover, to follow from day to day the conservation of their capital and the profits that could be drawn from it. To verify if the use had been really good they normally had to wait until the end of the life of the company or its resale, which could very well never happen (see after). For lack of knowledge of these difficult problems of

---

[26] Or patrimonium, to use a term of lawyers.

[27] It means capital-debt.

[28] In the case of markets.

measuring the conservation of capital, Aristotle was therefore satisfied with general terms of expressions of desirable purposes such as the refusal of the use of money for money, which it calls the chrematistics. He was more interested in the good life than in concrete problems of conservation of goods. However, he was also talking about prudent management, which brings us to the second point.

The 'prudence' of the first modern capitalists

Bardout (2005) puts forward the thesis that while for Aristotle and then Thomas Aquinas prudence is linked to wisdom and allows a good integration of morality in acts, on the contrary, around the 12th century, prudence would have a negative connotation: it would no longer be a kind of wisdom but a calculation of interest, a ruse. This does not seem to concern the prudence of the capitalists of that time and of their successors. As a matter of fact, in addition to their "mania" for the systematic conservation of their financial capital, one can also undeniably attribute to modern classical capitalists great Aristotelian prudence in their management. Indeed, with regard to unsold assets that appear on their balance sheet these early modern capitalists refuse to value them at their potential selling price on the market: there is no question for them to anticipate mere hopes of profit.

More generally, even, unlike most economists, especially neo-classical economists who later proposed a theory of capitalist economy oriented towards the measurement of wealth, the goal of these entrepreneurial practitioners of classical modern capitalism, with this type accounting, is absolutely not to measure the value of their firm or their wealth on the basis of market prices, but to calculate their real profits, that is to say profits that can be consumed without putting their invested capital at risk. This is the reason why when they buy buildings, materials or goods they let them appear on the assets side of their balance sheet at their purchase cost as long as they have not resold them, even though they may have reliable information on their potential resale price on the markets. They then act in accordance with what will later be called in all accounting manuals, including still mostly today,[29] "the principle of realization or principle of prudence" (see for more details Richard 2001, 2005ab, 2012b, 2015a and Richard, Bensadon and Rambaud 2018).

Animated by this "phronêsis" dear to Aristotle, they therefore generally refuse to enter their unsold assets on the balance sheet at their potential resale value and even less to give an estimate of the overall value of their business.[30] Any registration of potential profits is therefore generally prohibited. Indeed the fundamental goal of these modern classical capitalists is not to resell their business on a market as is generally the case today with "financial capitalism" but on the contrary to keep it in order to pass it on to their families descendants, generally their sons, sexism obliges.

Let us underline this major fact of the systematic transmission of a human enterprise. The Greek philosophical doxa (see after), in particular that of the Epicureans, emphasizes the fact that after death there is nothing left of the body, nor of the soul and that, therefore, it is absurd to want to accumulate goods which, in any case, themselves will be lost, as they are subject to systematic degradation. It is therefore better to devote your life to living well quietly and modestly from your own productions to try and achieve ataraxia in the otium. But, with the discovery of the double-entry and the notion of permanently conserved abstract capital, modern capitalists, whether religious or not, are inaugurating a whole new type of reasoning. They can now believe that their creation will stand for eternity if their sons (sexism obliges) are as conservative and careful as they are. They will then consider them as their successors and their representatives on the earth that they must leave. We cannot therefore say about them that they produce only to produce, that they earn money to earn money. They also enjoy these men there. Not only the exercise of practically absolute power in their business (libido dominendi), but also the participation in constant technological innovations (libido scientiae[31]) as well as a pleasant life in beautiful homes (libido scienti) and even the satisfaction of being able

[29] See below for the nuance.

[30] Influenced by economists most philosophers believe that capitalist accounting serves to measure the wealth of capitalists. This is not true (if wealth means the resale value of the firm or of its assets).

[31] To borrow an expression from Serres (1990, 96).

to transmit all this to their sons (libido futurendi). Their life does have a meaning: you have to imagine these capitalists happy men. In a sense, they also care about future generations and conservation, more exactly, given their strictly family altruism, that of the generations they themselves have engendered. This, all with the absolution of religious authorities if they do a minimum of "social responsibility," which they usually manage by giving alms to the poor, by funding churches and even sometimes by associating God to their business![32]

Jonas (1979) is generally credited with discovering the principle of responsibility and conservation for the benefit of future generations. But these capitalists not only obeyed this principle but, unlike Jonas, extended it (logically) to their own generation and, in addition, invented a powerful means to put it into practice: double entry accounting. In short, we cannot consider that their life is reduced only to the search for profit for profit or to the use of endless means: it also has other purposes, in particular of transmission to their future generations, of accumulation of power and the search for pleasures, including intellectual or artistic ones. Indeed, they often rub shoulders with men of letters and artists (See Renouard, op cit).

Such is the new context which characterizes this "new human species" whose occurrence could not be anticipated neither by the ancient Greeks nor even by the ancient Latins: it is indeed kinds of accumulating demigods which appear and which will dominate the world scene until the present day. The central and striking point of their type of accounting management is therefore, fundamentally, that of the conservation of their invested capital, without taking exaggerated risks.

The desire for prudence of these capitalists is so developed that they even go, in the 19th century, accept two extraordinary principles.[33] The first is an even more "harsh" principle of prudence: not only to ignore the potential profits of their activity but to record any probable potential loss. It is a kind of precautionary principle, the one dear to environmental lawyers and to

[32] They sometimes go so far as to give a part of their capital to God in order to spare his graces: long before the Protestants of Weber (1920), these Catholics know how to do it to justify their activity as capitalists.

[33] We base ourselves on Richard (2015a) and Richard, Bensadon and Rambaud (2018).

the philosopher Jonas (1973) more than a century before. Indeed, according to a classic definition, this principle states that "the absence of certainties, given the current state of scientific and technical knowledge, must not delay the adoption of effective and adapted preventive measures aimed at preventing any risk of damage serious and irreversible... as long as the cost is economically acceptable "(Dupuy, 2010, 89). However, it appears that for these capitalists it is a question of cutting back on their profits in advance and therefore of limiting their means of action to preserve their capital, and this action on the grounds of probable losses, not certain ones.

But these capitalists will go even further with a second principle that already appears at the beginning of the 19th century: that of the valuation of their assets in the hypothesis of bankruptcy. It is then a question of considering the final catastrophe: the bankruptcy of the company, the blackest scenario for these businessmen. To this end, they imagine a fictitious liquidation each year of their firms and value their assets on the balance sheet as if they were sold at auction one by one. And so, with this principle of "early death," they systematically underestimate the value of their firm, already greatly reduced using the principles of realization and prudence. It is as if they took morbid pleasure in imagining the death of their firm. But this is to give even more the means to subsist, even in the worst of situations. We can say in this regard that they already apply the principle of "enlightened catastrophism" dear to Dupuy (ibid) and its fundamental rule: "adopt the most pessimistic scenario when two conditions are met: 1 / when the uncertainty is radical..2 / when the stakes are immense." In a "Tract" on the corona virus, the historian Jeanneney (2020, 38) relates how the French state allowed precious stocks of masks to be destroyed and qualifies this action as a "narrowly accountable vision." But the true classical accounting vision is precisely at the antipodes of this deplorable vision which is in fact that of financiers. Of course, for these traditional accountants, it is not a question of applying these good principles in environmental matters but obviously only to the salvation of their financial capital thanks, in particular, to the accumulation of so-called "secret" reserves which will allow them may be to face very serious situations. These capitalists therefore have an ethic of non-incantatory responsibility which does not push them to inaction but, on the contrary, to develop their businesses. Of course, within the framework of this modern capitalism, this moral responsibility always aims at protecting only the financial capital, and not the natural and human capitals, which remain simple objects. The fact remains that these capitalists, who seek to keep their business, have a "good management." They can therefore, to a certain extent, be compared with the artisans and farmers dear to the ancient Greeks and Latins. To a certain extent, however, because, as we will show in more detail later, the latter have never developed or wanted to develop such a modern weapon as capitalist double-entry accounting, due to very different goals. We are now going to show that this accounting weapon, for various reasons, has not been properly appreciated by most philosophers.

Chapter 3
The misunderstanding of the accounting realities of modern capitalism by most economists and philosophers

For all its importance, the "modern accounting revolution," which makes only financial capital an object of systematic conservation, has, to the great happiness of capitalists, gone largely unnoticed, including by environmental philosophers, yet particularly sensitive to everything that is harmful to nature and to human beings. Routley (1973), who, for example, obviously has no notion of what capitalism is, miss or do not want to hear about this major institution of liberalism. It is, moreover, symptomatic that he only refers in his text to what he calls "industrial society" (1973,43) and not to the concrete capitalist American society of his time. As we will show, this ideological drift is symptomatic of a frequent reluctance, or inability, to speak of the real existence of capitalism and in particular of its central concept of capital-debt.

Regarding the latter, let us make a final fundamental point to begin with this chapter: capital in accounting is indeed a debt, but it is not an ordinary debt. Indeed, this capital-debt is marked by a specificity compared to other debts, for example debts to banks or suppliers.[1] It is usually matched by the authorities of a very special quality: with it modern capitalists have permanent power over certain human and non-human objects. Thus, as Nitzan and Bichler (2012)rightly underline, drawing on the work of Castoriadis, "capital is not a means of production, [...] is not the capacity to produce hedonic pleasure and [...] is not a quantity of dead productive labor. Capital is power and nothing but power." "Nothing but power" is

[1] We also explain in more detail that the wages sometimes due to employees (not yet paid) although appearing on the liabilities side of the capitalist balance sheet as debts have nothing to do with capital-debts. The amount of the latter is never the subject of negotiation, whereas in essence even in the capitalist system the former are negotiated on the labor market. One should better speak with regard to them of provisions to be paid and not of real debts to be reimbursed.

not entirely correct, however. In fact, in accounting, the capital of capitalists on the liabilities side of the balance sheet is both a debt to be repaid and the basis of power of capitalist subjects over objects. With regard to the power linked to capital it is interesting to note that for centuries, until around 1930, most accounting books in practically all countries referred to this capital as the "boss" in the company, as if it was a real person: one could not better symbolize the presence and the domination of the capitalist subject in his enterprise (Richard and Rambaud, 2022c). Descartes certainly expressly formulated the radical distinction between the subjects and the objects as foundation of modernity but, in fact, it was preceded by the accountants of the Middle Ages who even imagined a new accounting system of capitalism based on this distinction. The capital of the Italian founders of capitalism must therefore be considered as a fundamental operational concept of modernity in the service of a particular group of subjects: modern capitalists. In this type of society some human subjects, from the Middle Ages to the present day, are therefore more modern than others because of their power over other men. In other words, to pastiche a well-known phrase from the French humorist Coluche, in the context of the liberal society inherited from the Enlightenment, some subjects are "more equal" than others.

Thus, while any business is necessarily dependent on three types of capital (natural, human and financial) these capitalists wanted to pose as a principle that they were, like Hobbes' Leviathan, but without any prior consultation, the person who will go and command, in an absolutist and authoritarian way, in the name of financial capital, over the other two type of capitals. We are therefore dealing with a "capital" concept of capital-debt-power, that is, a concept that is fundamentally a matter of social science. More specifically, despite its reputation of science of counting accounting, a fundamental branch of economics, is first and foremost a matter of ideology.

There is thus already a gap separating all those who want to make economic science a real (hard) science comparable to mathematics, [2]

[2] This is notably the opinion of the philosopher Comte-Sponville (see below).

physics,[3] or even biology,[4] from those who, like us, show its social bases, in particular the necessarily subjective choice of a type of capital to be preserved or conserved by humans. Advocates of modernity like Constant (1819) have argued that modernity is characterized by the consecration of the individual as a supreme value. But Constant's conception of modernity is purely theoretical and stems from a desire for manipulation: it does not take into account the reality of capitalist modernity, true modernity, forcibly imposed by subjects on objects.

Indeed, from the 14th century, in spite of numerous revolts, the new capitalist entrepreneurs will receive the support of the politicians of the time. It was the case, for example, of the Podesta in Florence, a group of politicians decided to repress the strikes and make work the workers of the wool from 16 to 18 hours per day, under the threat of corporal punishment (Piper 1978; Richard and Rambaud, 2020; Richard and Rambaud 2022a). These capitalists ignore the fragility of women and children and the harm they do to them: they treat them much worse than the farmers of the day considered their cattle. Already the company is seen not as an institution that brings together different providers of capital on an equal basis, as was often the case in ancient Rome (see below), but as the private matter of providers of financial capital. Under these conditions, the famous freedom of the moderns, which theoretically claims to make any subject a sovereign, will henceforth, concretely, differentiate these subjects in the company, and permanently endorse this differentiation in an accounting system serving the interests of the capitalists. It is thus misleading to assert, as is often done, that modern man in general is an empire within an empire: it suffices to consider objectively the social relations which emerge with modern capitalist firms. In this type of firms there is a fiction of freedom of private law relations: contracts between individual persons supposed to negotiate freely of their fate, although the power is in the hands of the capitalists. In fact, there has never been any real contractualism in this type of firm. Those who, from the 14th century onwards wanted to contest this new "contract"

---

[3] We can cite in this sense the (vain) attempt of Georgescu-Roegen (1971) This does not mean that his advice for a more sober economy, even for degrowth economics, is devoid of interest and that the use of information from the physical sciences is not necessary.

[4] This seems to be the case with Roddier (2013, 86-7).

often paid for it with their lives: thus Ciuto Brandini, who wanted to found a kind of union of woollen workers to protest against inhuman working conditions, was tried by the Podesta in Florence and hanged on May 24, 1345 (Piper, 1978). These workers, moreover, already not only challenge their working conditions but also want to take part in the responsibilities of management both in the companies where they work and at the political level. Following a terrible strike in 1378, they even manage to seize power in the City with the support of part of the bourgeoisie. But the capitalists allied with the nobles, with the help of the armed forces, block the city's supplies, especially wool, and the insurgents are forced to surrender.

Modern capitalism was therefore not born in the context of gentle contractual relations but in a context of fierce social struggle. From the start of its history, we can see that the capitalists reject any idea of co-management or the simple sharing of responsibilities in their firms and impose the wage system, at least in the large factories. They want to be the masters at home, the only "responsible" and themselves set the standards for the functioning of their firms. These are already the prototypes of the entrepreneur "free man" and "responsible" that Nietzsche, this reactionary, will propose as a model: "this freed man, who really dares to promise, this master of free will, this sovereign.. [to whom], with this mastery of himself,.. is also entrusted the mastery of circumstances, of nature and of all inconsistent creatures and of shorter wills "(Genealogy of Morality, 1996, 69- 70).[5] They alone, as an independent entrepreneurial elite, will be expected to take initiatives and risks and will therefore need to have power and responsibilities. They alone, therefore, will be expected to make mistakes and answer for their actions, if necessary. By contrast, their employees are already irresponsible and must therefore obey and, in the best case, rely on the benevolent protection of their bosses responsible for their fate. Subsequently these capitalists, modern heroes, will succeed in imposing their economic model until today: not by phenomena of duplicative mimesis (Girard, 1972) but well with the help of effective

---

[5] It is striking that for Nietzsche responsibility originates in the debtor-creditor legal relationship and rests on the right of the creditor to make the debtors suffer. Already in Florence in 1371 a decree of the Arte della Lana had stipulated that workers who could not pay their debts became de facto slave employees: Piper (1978) speaks of "Lohnsklaverei."

pressures: those of politicians and media, which they will generally succeed in bribing thanks to their increasingly considerable financial means (see below).

Beyond these social questions, this new modern capitalism is a revolution compared to the past. Aristotle, a long time ago, stigmatized chrematistics, that is to say the use of money for money. It has often been thought that he was one of the very first to denounce a form of capitalism. But the Academy philosopher, as we will see, lived in a world where modern capitalism did not exist. His criticism of chrematics was aimed primarily at the misuse of money for private activities and not at forms of power or domination by money as is the case in modern capitalism. The typical and extreme case referred to by Aristotle, it seems to us, was that of the miser, symbolized at the time of the ancient Greeks by Croesus (King of Lydia from 561 to 446): such people who accumulate heaps of gold for the love of money when they should use it to live like the philosophers, or, failing that, to finance the works and foundations of these philosophers. But these attitudes condemned by the founder of the Academy have nothing to do with those of modern capitalists like Datini: the latter, like later the Fugger who financed and dominated the Habsburg (Herre,1999), uses his money to develop his business and increasingly dominate his employees, his competitors and the princes, which does not can be equated with accumulating money for the pleasure of contemplating money. On the contrary, this type of accumulation of money is absurd for this modern capitalist: it is money which sleeps and which reduces its profits and therefore its power. For these actors of this type of modern capitalism, the full subject is indeed the one who has a capital which assures him of domination over the objects which work for him. Croesus too was very rich but, it seems, at least according to legend, was content, like Scrooge or any other miser, to contemplate his pile of gold, which made him happy, even his enjoyment. This type of capitalist is ridiculous in the eyes of ancient philosophers, but he is not inherently dangerous as long as he remains at this infantile stage. In a democracy people must be able to find their happiness as they want as long as they do not hamper that of others. If some people experience an orgasm from having gold bars under their beds without bugging their fellow citizens, let them do it! All this has nothing to do with a businessman like Datini who, like his capitalist "colleagues" at the time, was a tyrant in his companies: just read the descriptions that Piper gives (1978) of the management of factories in Florence in the 14th century and of the treatment of workers' revolts to be convinced of this (see Richard and Rambaud, 2022a). Of course, over the centuries, this situation will change, especially in the 20th century, thanks in particular to the action of trade unions. But even today the capitalists and their agents are the appointed leaders in the enterprise: they have a monopoly of economic power, backed by the law. Laborit (1974) generalizes the question of power too much when he says that "every isolated man is necessarily part of a hierarchy and within it adopts a paternalistic and domineering behavior towards his subordinates and a submissive and childish with regard to his superiors." In fact, he does not take into account the capitalist mode of management. Indeed, for us, there are conductors in this infinite succession of powers. Ferry (1992,33), to counter certain environmentalists, invokes in their regard that "the hatred of the artifices linked to our civilization of uprooting is also the hatred of humans as such": by this he aims in particular at the alleged hatred of these people ecologists with regard to homo oeconomicus. But these environmentalists have both a love for humans and nature and are right to attack homo oeconomicus capitalistus which is a destroyer of both. And Ferry (1992), who de facto supports the liberal capitalist model behind the facade of the defense of Man or industrial man, is indeed an antihumanist[6]. We can repeat these arguments against another author such as Gauchet (1990ab, Débat N ° 60) who, like Ferry, invokes against environmentalists, "hatred of men" and the risk of a return to enchanted primitive society, imprisoned in immutable religious rites.

All this does not come from a serious and in-depth analysis of modern capitalism. The emerging figure of the modern capitalist and his very particular mode of management testify to the birth of a separate subject: a veritable superpower of which a very good example is, towards 1490, Jakob Fugger der Reiche, the financier of Maximilian de Habsburg (Herre, 1999, 28). Nowadays, we also cannot decently put on an equal footing the exploiters of the big agricultural companies which are devastating the

[6] It must, however, be recognized that by accusing the industrial man or the homo oeconmicus in general many ecologists have opened a boulevard to Ferry, but that does not excuse his position.

Amazon, with the Indians of this region whose lands are threatened by these superpowers. Some authors like Doctor Marquis,(2022, 13-18) will point out that the influence of the ego is general among humans and that it is this which has caused the misfortunes of humanity, in particular the gap between the rich and the poor, the slavery, the black plague, and more recently the environmental crisis. But, in our opinion, in most humans this disease is hardly dangerous to the extent that their power of action is very limited. On the other hand, the ego of modern capitalists, armed with an accounting 'megamachine' and supported by alliances with other social fractions, notably the aristocrats, will play a role in history inconmensurate with that of most other humans. This is why, as it seems to us, the remedies that this doctor proposes in individual therapy for a decline in our self will not change much thing in the current social and ecological situation. The ego of capitalists is a superego and its effective treatment lies in political and social treatments that we will present later.

We can then, at this stage of reasoning, oppose two definitions of the modern subject. A broad definition according to which the subjects are all humans[7] (Latour, 1999) and a restrictive definition according to which the modern subject, the real one, is only the modern capitalist[8]: the one who from the early Middle Ages really has power in society and whose name appears on the liabilities side of the balance sheet of his company coupled with the debt owed to him. On the asset side of its balance sheet, on the other hand, simple objects or, more exactly, the cost of using these objects will appear: first, when the firm is founded, concrete money, then, at the as the operating cycle unfolds, buildings, machinery, materials (e.g. natural resources such as timber from forests), goods, slaves(registered at their purchase costs), and user costs of employees (purchases of labor power on markets) etc. Thus the balance sheet, according to this conception of the modern capitalist double entry accounting, conceptually and visually divides the world of humans between subjects who have the power, the

---

[7] This broad definition is generally retained by philosophers, especially those who, like Mill (1863), are inspired by utilitarianism.

[8] The bankers who lend to the company are certainly also subjects whose debt must also be repaid, but they do not have power in the company. They are capitalists of secondary rank in the firms which use their credits (except in the event of difficulties). But they are first-tier capitalists in their banks.

capitalists, on the liabilities' side, and the world of objects, included in the assets or treated as marketable things[9]. The subjects are on the side of obligations and dominants where ethical questions and management of accounts arise in particular. Objects are on the side of means, where technical issues and efficiency in their management emerge. The assets are therefore not only means but above all means in the modern and purified sense of the term, while the (true) liabilities refer to the purpose of the subjects, creditors and masters. The modern capitalist balance sheet therefore absolutely endorses the modern divide and makes it a major instrument of management, and more broadly, of regulation of the entire economy (see below): it is therefore not a simple technical instrument, as people believe generally, but the reflection of a vision of the world, a cosmology, a philosophy, but not wise. In short, modern capitalist accounting is a "political" institution, in the sense that it is based on a decision to choose the systematic conservation of a single type of capital to the detriment of the other types. Unfortunately, as we will show later in more detail, the current focus is on "economic" theories or models[10].The political character of accounting, and indeed of all type of accounting,[11] will subsequently be challenged by the defenders of the capitalist system who will try to pass it off as a simple neutral technique (see below). Just as neoclassical economists will want to remove the term "political" from "political economy," so the defenders of modern capitalist accounting will do their utmost to pass it off as a neutral tool. Notably the accounting choice of a capital to be conserved will generally not be seen by most critics of the capitalist system, in particular by structuralists like Marx, then, subsequently, also, even by ecologists like Dumont (1973-77): they will not see that the fundamental economic problem is not that of exchange (and exchange value), and of supply and demand curves, but that of the nature of the capital conserved.

---

[9] We will show that, on the other hand, employees are not part of this list of subjects.

[10] In the restricted sense of the term as a discipline specific to specialists who call themselves economists.

[11] We will show that any accounting that aims to recognize a result is based on a choice to conserve a type of capital, a decision that cannot be neutral.

Contrary also to the statements of the proponents of the "psychic" or "symbolic" thesis of modernity, such as Deleuze, Guattari (1972) and Lacan, the fundamental problem does not lie in the feelings or impulses of men in general, but in modes of management of certain subjects, modes ratified by laws which are favorable to them. Unfortunately, as we will show in more detail later, the current focus is on the attempts of economists to reform "economic" theories[12] and models and not on criticizing modern double-entry accounting, this "simple neutral technique" as many people believe. This "deviation" allows the capitalists to safeguard the essential: their accounting management system. Thus the difference in treatment, enshrined in a specific method of calculation, between the different capitals (capitals as subjects and "capitals" as objects), all of which are necessary for the activity of the entire company, is indeed the major mark of this modern capitalism which appears around the 14th century in northern Italy.

Subsequently most philosophers will not see at all the nature of this aberrant economic system. Thus Locke (1632-1704), who lived at a time when very large capitalist societies already existed, never took this into account in his most famous treatise devoted to "civil government" (1690). He will base his opinion on the question of property from a very particular, albeit widespread, form of private property. Not on that of the large capitalist companies of his time like the Joint Stock Companies of the "Dutch East India" type[13] (1602) or the "Compagnie des Indes Orientales" (1664) in France, companies which already have a legal personality but on the example of small farmers. So he's never going to deal with the capitalist world[14]. Locke is constantly immersed in a world of small farms where, of course, the problem of massive wage labor, as it already existed in Florence

---

[12] We will show that these economists will be helped in this attempt by all the philosophers who will focus on the dangers of techniques and numbers in general instead of stigmatizing the neuralgic role of capitalists and their very particular type of accounting.

[13] As Ogilvie shows in his "Homme jetable" (2012, 34) this company had the terrible slogan "navigare necesse est, vivere non necesse," that is to say that in the event of a navigation problem it is better to throw overboard crewmen than cargo!

[14] Sahlins (1972, 76) rightly says that "the household is to the tribal economy as...the corporation to modern capitalism." The philosophers before Marx, on the other hand, mainly dealt with the individual household and the domestic economy.

at the end of the Middle Ages, does not exist. His ideal is the extension of this type of small farm so that everyone can have a home, own a few acres of land and therefore enough to live freely, in peace, as a family. In such an ideal, bucolic setting, there is no risk of major conflicts of interest, even with nature: each small farmer knows how to manage his small property as a good father, taking into account the limits of the land use. It's basically going back to the days of ancient Greece. Locke, from this point of view, regresses compared to Machiavelli (1469-1527) who, for his part, saw the violent social conflicts fuelled by the capitalism of his time and who, like a good friend of the princes, had presented the revolt of the Ciompi as that of "bandits" animated by envy and violence (1571, 306-9). We can also note, still with regard to Locke, that his "successor" Hume (1711-1776), for his part, will be a little more verbose about the capitalists. As Hobson (1926,23) shows, this philosopher, in his Essays, describes the new mind of the modern capitalist well: "he has gains so often in his eye that he acquires by degrees a passion for it, and knows no such pleasure as that of seeing the daily increase of his fortune." Like what a philosopher, even at the time of the Enlightenment, can sometimes perceive, even very schematically, the originality of capitalism, which is not the case of Locke. We can understand the interest that Pelluchon (2015, 217-228) has in this philosopher who defends small farms and thus wants to solve the problem of hunger. But Locke tells us nothing about how to deal with capitalist enterprises, especially medium and large ones. This "moderate liberal" is silent on them although they are already numerous and powerful in his time: the question of the type of property and capitalist power obviously does not interest him. Similarly, later, Kant (1778), who defends the cause of reasonable reason in his "critique of practical reason," will completely miss a clinical examination of Prussian company law, in particular of its accounting aspects, even though it was enough for him to read this text to get an idea of the concrete reality of capitalism of his time and of the contradiction of its principles with his own. More generally, the Enlightenment, despite its brilliance, did not see the general laws of modern capitalism notably those related to the management of companies.

This fundamental law of capitalist companies will also be completely hidden afterwards by most economists, in particular by the neo-classical economists: they will put on an equal footing the famous three factors of production[15] that are capital (that is to say de facto financial capital), labor, and nature. Reading them one gets the impression of a totally egalitarian world where the mathematical and implacable play of the supply and demand curves of these three "capitals" determines the economic optimum, thus allowing, if nothing disturbs 'the normal' functioning of markets, fair remuneration for all factors of production. But whoever is willing to take the trouble to study the capitalist economy as it is actually practiced with its accounting system, and not on the basis of an economic theory idealized to satisfy the capitalists, sees that in fact the dice of this game are totally "loaded." This insofar as the accounting treatment of these three capitals is structurally unequal. More precisely, due to the fact that financial capital is the only one of the three to be systematically conserved on the liabilities side of the balance sheet while the other two, on the asset side, are simple means valued on markets (for materials and labor power) the concept of cost is totally biased in favor of the capitalists. As Kapp, one of the very few economists who accepted to take an interest in accounting concepts, saw very clearly as early as 1950, modern capitalism can be defined as an economic system which does not pay all of its production costs: like someone who consumes in a bar and slips away without paying the bill. Mandeville (1714), in his famous "Fable of the bees," asserted that the simple game of exchanges on the markets allowed everyone to win. As he dares to say "private vices manage the public good" and therefore individual egoism is a source of collective good. But he acts as if the capitalist world of his time did not exist: his fable is really a fable. Adam Smith (1776), both economist and philosopher, in his famous "Inquiry into the Wealth of Nations," saw "the invisible hand of the market" but he did not see the visible hand of the accountants who organize this market on the basis of a totally truncated cost concept. After him the myth of the "self-regulating market" will develop regularly with, in particular, with the writings of Hayek (in particular of 1941 and 1967). We then often speak of the laws and sometimes even of the divinity of the Market. But behind this "God" market, behind the scenes of companies, there are men (most often unfortunately) in flesh and blood who determine the structures which

---

[15] This term "factors of production" attached to the three capitals clearly shows that they are capitals to be used (resources) and not, like the accountants, at least with regard to financial capital, capital-debts.

condition its functioning. The famous objective ('scientific') game of supply and demand curves that are described is in fact subject to the subjectivity of the choice of modern capitalists: that of a unique type of capital to be conserved.

These observations seem important to us because if we refer to the law of the Market and, what is more, to its "invisible hand," it is very difficult, to use the words of Schmitt (1927), to identify the political actor behind these words. For our part, we have often seen these players at work, especially those who are at the origin of the current IFRS accounting system (see below) and we can certify that they have visible hands. As the study of current accounting still shows today, there are therefore many subjective choices of the capital to be kept which are the basis of the whole edifice of the capitalist economy. In this sense it is incorrect, as Weber (1920) will already do, to speak of "economic rationality" in general: we must speak of modern *capitalist* economic rationality, a very particular rationality. Let us underline that after Weber (1920), we will sometimes see even further in general abstraction that will no longer even mention the term rationality. Already, in 1948, Mounier, the father of personalism, spoke of economics without adding the qualifier of capitalist by asserting that "only despise economics those who have stopped harassing the neurosis of daily bread." In the same abstract vein, some will also substitute for the word capitalist the term "market": according to them we would not be in a capitalist economy but in a market economy or, more simply in markets. 16 . However, these markets are not abstractions: they are human constructions fully regulated by capitalist accountants and animated in particular by stock market players. Moreover, as Braudel (2008) shows very well, this term can refer to completely different meanings: the market of small shopkeepers has nothing to do with that of large modern capitalist firms. In this vein we will show that with the new accounting model that we are proposing we can have an "ecological" market economy which has nothing to do with the current capitalist market. The latter is based on an unequal

16 Polanyi, even, despite his insight, asserts that "the congenital weakness of 20th century society does not come from the fact that it was industrial, but from the fact that it was a market society" (in Flipo, 2014a, 234). This means absolutely nothing: what industry? What market?

treatment of capitals, whereas one can very well design a market which respects their equality of fate.

Our previous examples concern mostly old writers or philosophers, but today these traditional considerations on capitalism continue to flourish. Thus, for example, in his book on "Le capitalisme est-il moral?" (is capitalism moral?) (2004), the philosopher Comte-Sponville, whose economic and accounting knowledge seems superficial to say the least, still considers that the play of supply and demand curves on the market turns the capitalist economy into an "amoral" system: this institution therefore has nothing to do, according to him, with a question of ethics. As for accounting, for him, it is the reign of neutrality because this discipline is based on numbers: 2 + 2 = 4 !

Likewise, more recently, in the economic field, during the crises of 2008 and 2020 (that of the Corona virus), the good minds who demand (and obtain) massive subsidies for the big capitalist firms recite the antiphon according to which "the markets would risk losing confidence"[17] if these subsidies were not granted. We are thus in the presence of a whole series of terminological and conceptual variations which tend to obscure the reality of modern capitalism, a reality which can only be truly understood through an in-depth study of its accounting system. The omission of accounting is the rule among economists and philosophers, which can only delight capitalists. Fortunately, as we have seen, certain historians, such as Renouard (1949), very early on underlined that these practices of the founding businessmen of the modern capitalism are based on a fundamental selfishness, one of the forms of ethics based on consequentialism. Indeed, consequentialist ethics, like ethical selfishness, consider that any subject must choose acts which will produce the best consequences for him and only for him. This is indeed the case with the spirit of capitalism that Weber (1920) wanted to describe: all that matters in this terrible system imagined by these capitalists is the conservation of their financial capital, which will lead to the suffering of man-objects and the destruction of nature.

---

17 See in particular Pisani-Ferry's column on "We must succeed in European borrowing" (Le Monde, June 21-22, 2020 p.29).

In his interesting analysis of anthropocentrism and, more specifically, of human interests, the environmental philosopher Norton (1984) distinguishes between two forms of strong and weak anthropocentrism based on the difference between the felt and reflected preferences of human beings. The first would be devoid of value judgment (without critical thinking, based on impulses) and would lead to a "strong" anthropocentrism,[18] and therefore open to criticism by its excesses. The second, on the other hand, which modify the first, is only "adopted once a whole vision of the world has been rationally taken on board" and can then lead to a "weak," that is to say reasonable, anthropocentrism particularly respectful of nature. According to him, understanding in economic terms often amounts to adopting the felt preferences approach "because it abstains from any value judgment," unlike the second, which is more rational. But this thesis cannot be applied to our modern capitalists who founded classical accounting. Their hyper-sophisticated accounting model, which constitutes a structuring decision of the economy, not only of the mode of production but also of the mode of consumption, is not the simple result of an impulse but is the result of a well-considered act that confirms the dangerous object / subject split in the double entry system. Like what all the reflections of men do not lead to wisdom or reasonable reason.19. In any case, this pernicious, dangerous and evil accounting system is for us the major source of the current problems of humanity, both at the level of production and consumption. Unlike postmodern philosophers like Baudrillart (1970) or Debord (1967), we do not think that we can attribute to the "consumer society" or to that of the "spectacle," and, more generally, to conditioned individuals, the economic and social problems. This is all the more so since, as certain studies show, around 1% of the richest population in the world alone consumes as much as 50% of the total world population. We must first seek the sources of these problems in an aberrant type of accounting management led by an extremely powerful minority, supported by political forces for centuries. Its accounting system, which is dangerous for the planet, does not prevent, as we have seen, which may at first appear paradoxical, its leading to prudent management based on the

[18] Implicitly, in his text, dangerous for nature (for example irresponsible impulses of consumers).

[19] Which does not at all mean that Norton's overall reasoning is meaningless (see below).

"good use" of things, at least of some. But this initial prudence deteriorated in the period of the 1970s with the transition from classical modern capitalism to financial modern capitalism, which only made matters worse. We will now study this evolution of modern capitalism.

Chapter 4
From 'classical' modern capitalism to 'financial' modern capitalism

We will begin by studying the expansion of modern capitalism in the West and then we will show how this evolution of Western capitalism leads to a modern economic and accounting constitution that concerns practically all countries of the globe. We will then discuss the fact that this emergence of a global capitalist accounting constitution has not only been largely ignored by economists and even more so by philosophers, but also masked by various highly questionable interpretations of the evolution of the capitalist system. We will end this analysis by showing how the capitalist accounting ideology born in the West could also contaminate the so-called socialist theories and practices in the East.

The expansion of financial modern capitalism in the West

Rambaud (2018) has shown, in a fascinating article, that at the end of the 14th century the Franciscan monk Pacioli, author of a treatise on mathematics (1494), a small but famous part of which is devoted to accounting, had proposed a concept capital totally different from that of the classical accountants of his time. In summary, we can say that this was already a concept of capital as an asset like the one that economists were going to adopt, after Cantillon and Quesnay, and not the capital–debt concept of accounting practitioners such as Datini at the end of the Middle Ages. What is even more extraordinary, is that Pacioli proposed to value this capital-asset not in terms of costs but well on the basis of its price value, by discounting the future profits potentially generated by this capital. Pacioli, under these conditions, can be considered as the precursor of the economist Irving Fisher and of his famous book "The nature of capital" (1906): he is almost four centuries ahead of him! But the studies that we have carried out (see in particular Rambaud and Richard 2016 and Richard and Rambaud 2022c) show that the ideas of this "UFO" monk had little influence on accounting practices from the 15th to the 20th century, more precisely until the liberal revolution of Reagan and Thatcher in the 1980s-90s. Throughout this period, what dominates is the classical modern accounting that we have described previously, characterized by the following four elements:

1. Double-entry subject-object accounting.
2. Concept of capital-debt appearing on the liabilities side of the balance sheet.
3. Valuation in principle of unsold assets at their cost "value."
4. Frequent adoption of the accentuated principle of prudence (understood in the sense of taking into account potential losses and not potential profits).

We will not retrace here the different stages of the evolution of this type of classical modern accounting because they are characterized by changes that are after all of secondary importance[1]. To symbolize the significance of this type of classical accounting inherited from the Middle Ages and dominant until recently, we can notably cite the texts of the 4th and 7th European directives of the 1970s and 1980s which both still endorse all the principles that we have stated previously and make them mandatory in the European Community. As such, we can consider that the stock market type of accounting proposed by Pacioli and then taken up by Irving Fisher had practically no real influence, in any case, particularly in Europe and Asia, until the end of the 20th century. On the other hand, from the 2000s, under the influence of the United States which, from the 1970s, began to change from the old "classical" accounting practices, we observed at the international level a significant transformation of the accounting rules which took a connotation that can be qualified as "financial"·(Rambaud and Richard, 2015b and Richard and Rambaud 2022a). The decisive turning point towards this development was taken in 2001 when the European Union decided to give up applying the classic accounting standards of the 7th Directive to the groups of companies that are under its responsibility and to accept for these groups the proposed standards formulated by a

[1] See on this point, notably, Richard (2001, 2005a, 2012b et 2015a) and Richard, Bensadon et Rambaud (2018).

private body (initially named IASC in 1973, then IASB[2]). As we show elsewhere (Richard et al. 2018; Richard and Rambaud 2020; Richard and Rambaud, 2022a), this organism is in fact a kind of part inserted between the United States and the other countries of the world which allows the last to apply American accounting standards (or close to them) while making believe, to deceive their public opinion, that they are international standards. We can thus say that by adopting these new accounting rules Europa has tied itself (to put it mildly) to the American economic model contrary to the promise made to be stronger and thus more independent. The study of these IAS / IFRS[3] standards is made difficult by the fact that they themselves may differ from the conceptual framework on which they are based[4]. This conceptual framework, very strongly influenced by its American counterpart (developed around 1960-70), is dominated by a "Paciolian / Fisherian" financial conception which admits, if not privileges, the valuation of unsold assets in price value (and not in cost value) (Richard, 2015a; 2017). This theoretically leads to the abandonment of the classical principles of realization and prudence and of the principle of systematic depreciation of long-lived assets. In addition, the definition of the concepts of assets, liabilities as well as expenses and income is such that it means abandoning the classical concept of capital-debt (Nobes, 2012, 2014; Barker 2010; Richard et al. 2018). The philosophy behind this conceptual framework, strongly inspired by neoclassical economists, in particular the conceptions of Irving Fisher and the American school of agency theory, can be summarized in four points:

1. the conservation of capital of capitalists is no longer carried out at the level of the firms they finance but at the level of their personal assets;
2. the firm is no longer an entity with an accounting personality[5];

---

[2] International Accounting Standard Committee; International Accounting Standard Board.

[3] International Accounting Standards;International Financial Reporting Standards.

[4] Curiously, and no doubt to leave room for maneuver in the case of exceptional situations, the IASB has decided that the standards it issues may deviate from the precepts of the conceptual framework it has developed.

[5] This does not prevent it from having one in terms of company law, which allows capitalists to escape prosecution involving their personal assets. This ingenious

3. in conjunction with the two previous points, the concept of systematic depreciation is no longer relevant, which means that no substantive systematic retention in the company can take place to allow the conservation of the invested capital: the net operating cash flows must therefore in principle be fully distributed to the private capitalist who is responsible for reallocating them as she/he wishes;
4. the abandonment of the principles of realization and prudence allow the distribution of potential benefits.

Finally, with this conceptual framework, we are dealing with a system that shifts the management of financial capital to the level of the private capitalist. Seen from a strict accounting perspective, the firm itself is nothing more than an object (an asset) without personality. It is one more step towards even more power of the capitalists within the framework of what one can call a "financial modernity" even more modern than the classic capitalist modernity which had the merit of respecting a certain type of conservation of firms. This type of financial modernity is typically that which is designed and managed by the financial services of large firms: it is they who, in practice, are responsible for seeing if the stock market value of these types of companies increases regularly and who determine the investments for this purpose. They are pure agents of these "ultra-capitalists" who manage firms from home like stock exchange objects. Fortunately, for the moment, this final stage in the development of modern capitalism is far from being fully reached in accounting for several reasons. First and foremost, in most countries, traditional company law continues to impose rules for the conservation of financial capital at the firm level in accordance with the concept of capital-debt, and most often it is the same even in terms of accounting law with regard to the groups that are not covered by IFRS. Secondly, within the framework of IFRS and the groups concerned, the new pricing principles (based on values) currently concern, in practice, only financial assets and not other types of assets (materials, buildings, machines, etc.). Also, the abandonment of the principle of systematic depreciation only targets a few intangible assets, in particular

"pluralistic" legal system allows capitalists, with the backing of the law, to play on several fronts at the same time.

the famous goodwill: most tangible assets therefore remain subject to the traditional rules of prudent cost accounting. Finally, on a more theoretical level, we show in detail in other works (Richard 2015 a and b, Richard and Rambaud, 2022a) that the attempt carried out within the conceptual framework of IFRS to make capital a simple asset comes up against internal contradictions of this conceptual framework.

Thus in the practice of these standards themselves, that is to say of what is concretely applied by the capitalist groups, the capital remains a debt to be repaid appearing on the liabilities side of the balance sheet.

To conclude on this recent development of modern capitalist financial group accounting, we can therefore say that this type of "financial" accounting is currently in the middle of the ford: it has left the shore of classic modern accounting on certain points without yet reaching that of modern financial accounting as the "UFO" Luca Pacioli (1494) and his spiritual son Irving Fisher had advised. However, this development shows that we can get even worse than classical modern capitalism: an ultra-modern financial capitalism that is succeeding in (almost) commodifying everything, including its own businesses which are becoming pure objects. But, contrary to Polanyi's thesis (1944), even with this type of financial capitalism, there remains one thing that is not a commodity: it is the private capital of the capitalist that he now manages more and more out of the tribulations of businesses, quietly, warm, in slippers, at home, sipping a whiskey a sake or a vodka, often thousands of kilometers away from the companies concerned by his/her decisions and this with the help of the famous double entry accounting. Such is the development of the capitalist modernity, which was born in Europe at the end of the Middle Ages and which gradually gained the whole of the world economy[6]. The Earth is now under the control of the united people of the capitalists with the help of the socialist and liberal states: we have indeed shown that these states, whether they are governed by the first or the second, have supported the big

[6] Let us note, to come back to the question of the criteria of Modernity, that if the accounting philosophy of modern capitalism is still topical today, it is not quite the same for Cartesian mechanical physics: it was outdated by quantum physics. The accounting of capitalists is therefore much more future-proof than the physical sciences, at least for now.

capitalist firms to put in place, at their request, a true global economic constitution in the form of an international accounting law which must apply to all groups: the "IFRS law" (Richard and Rambaud, 2020; Richard and Rambaud 2022a). Indeed, the capitalists understood very early on, from the time of the republics of Florence, Genoa and Venice, it means well before Hobbes (1651),[7] that they absolutely had to wield the sword against those of their fellows accountants who would not want to respect their rules for reasons of selfish expediency. In this regard, we can say that the capitalists have been able to solve their problems of "free riders" (to use the expression of Olson, 1965): they have been remarkably successful in coordinating to guarantee their common good, their accounting system. And this thanks to clearly visible hands, those of the great political leaders.

Contrary to Marx's hopes they are the ones who achieved a kind of communism (of the capitalists) and not their employees. There is therefore now a worldwide law for the protection of financial capital and of it alone which can unfortunately very often pass, for those who do not know accountancy, as a true law of nature: it is well necessary that firms calculate a profit to measure their performance[8]. It is against this concrete world capitalist economic constitution and against the political forces which created it that it is appropriate in priority to fight and not against vague concepts like Technique, Progress (in particular of the productive forces[9]), Productivity, Productivism, Efficiency, Competitiveness, Homo economicus, System or Systems, Technico-Economic Order, Machinery, Industrialization,[10] Growth, or even, and above all, " Law of the Market." All these general, undefined terms mean absolutely nothing if they are not linked to concrete issues of conservation of such or such capital. What is at

[7] Hobbes quite rightly said that"covenants without the Sword, are but Words, and of no strength") (Leviathan, chap 17).

[8] Flipo (2014 a, 350) rightly underlines the ambiguity of the concept of law. Indeed, human laws like the accounting laws that establish capitalism are based on social inventions that have nothing to do with the laws of the natural sciences that result from scientific studies.

[9] The denunciation of the famous "progress of the productive forces" is unfortunately the cream pie of many critics of capitalism, unfortunately because this kind of vague criticism leads nowhere.

[10] In the same direction, it seems, Grange (2012, 64) although she evokes in other places of her book the problems caused by the advent of the "industrial age" (127).

issue in our case are precise economic systems put into practice. It means, currently, the modern capitalist system with its "Homo capitalisticus" at its head. We must therefore, for example, speak of the law of capitalist market, of capitalist progress, capitalist growth and capitalist productivity and not the Law of the Market, Growth, Progress and Productivity in general. We will show, further on, in particular, that we can perfectly speak of an ecological law of the market, of ecological productivity, ecological profitability and even of ecological growth[11] within the frame of a new anti-capitalist accounting model(see below). As it is the case with Stengers (2013, 43) our aim is to fight against the "grip" of capitalism, but with a focus on its accounting system.

It should be noted that the existence of this global capitalist accounting constitution supported by severe laws in all countries of the world, or nearly so,[12] shows that, contrary to the general vulgate, liberalism is in love with strict legislative measures when it goes to the interests and conservation of capitalist firms, the latter themselves wanting the intervention of states to bring recalcitrant companies to reason. In this area capitalism does not like flexibility and individual behavior at all. To ensure the good health of multinationals there has never been liberalism, laissez faire or anti-state accounting arguments, let alone free accounting trade. Philosophers like Tocqueville (1835-40), Nietzsche (1887), Deleuze and Guattari (1972), Foucault (1994), denounced all standards as contrary to individual freedoms, but the capitalists wanted such standards to ensure their freedom of action and their safety. They even wanted the creation of a huge bureaucracy of well-paid auditors to verify the application of these standards.

Thus legislative liberalism, self-regulation, it's good for the social and the ecological, areas in which the laws must be as "soft" as possible, if not totally non-existent, which would lead to "orgasm" capitalists in the latter case. There is therefore no liberalism at all in the field of accounting law, this law which constitutes the heart of modern capitalism. In this sense we

[11] Similarly, the productivity and growth of small African agricultural firms that respect the land have nothing to do with that of the single-product capitalist farms of the Beauce. To assimilate them has no meaning.

[12] The exception is North Korea. But its conversion to IFRS is expected.

can say, unlike the vulgate, that there has never been free enterprise in the modern capitalist world[13].

Moreover, contrary to what is often asserted, the absence of an international environmental law is not fundamentally due to the powerlessness of the liberal-socialist states but well to their desire not to have one[14]. The Westphalian model of the States, masters on their territories, is not dead, quite the contrary: these States simply consider that accounting law must be internationalized while they do not want international social or environmental rights. Contrary to what Pelluchon (2011, 102) asserts, it is not the old model of states "at war" which is responsible for the failures of international summits, but the outdated model of social-liberal capitalist states at war against ecologism. Liberalism, including political liberalism, is indeed a system which not only admits but promotes the modern capitalist accounting system and therefore capitalism on a world scale. Unlike the vulgate, there is therefore no essential difference between political liberalism and economic liberalism: both have the consequence, if not the essential vocation, of maintaining and supporting modern capitalism and its principles, in particular accounting principles.

These developments make it possible to say that Kant's well-known wish for cosmopolitan law has been granted by the capitalists. Genuine international accounting law was born out of an agreement between states. This under the leadership of the United States, it is true, but with the complacency of all liberal and socialist forces. Let us underline that this capitalist world economy is not only a market space. It is also as we have shown, a global space of unequal treatment of human beings with an arbitrary power of the capitalists in the firms. Pelluchon (2015, 320-1)

---

[13] A business manager who does not systematically depreciate 100% of his machines will be immediately sanctioned civilly and criminally. But he is not obliged to measure the depreciation of his employees nor of the nature.that it uses. Another fine proof of the unequal treatment of the different types of capital.

[14] We therefore cannot agree with Pelluchon (2015, 328) when she says that "the failure of international climate negotiations...is partly because they take place between states that continue to think that the world is divided into sovereign nations." The example of international accounting law established by practically all states, which is a fundamental right for capitalism, invalidates this assertion.

highlights, in an interesting way, the emergence of a "cosmopolitanization" of problems which would lead to a community of citizens on a planetary scale with equality of human beings. But, unfortunately, currently, it is rather the globalization of the power of the capitalists which is asserting itself, with its attendant inequalities. Note also that this accounting regulation by capitalism and its allies (notably the liberals) has nothing to do with the Fordist compromise and regulation of which the school of "Regulation" speaks [15]. This compromise, this regulation, are signs of weakness of capitalists in the very particular context of the post-World war two period, [16] while accounting regulation, which practically follows a growing trend over the centuries, is a sign of the continued power of capitalism. We can even say that, faced with the problem posed by Fordist regulation, capitalism responded by accentuating "its" accounting regulation.

But, some specialists in anti-capitalist experiments will say, one cannot put in the same bag of capitalist modernity all the economic experiments, in particular the (rare) attempts at self-management and the practice of the enterprise as a commons which have followed one another during of the 20th century. Moreover, on a purely theoretical level, one cannot put in the same basket the writings of neoclassical economists who supported capitalism and those of other thinkers who, like Marx, criticized capitalism. However, we will prove, later, that capitalist modernity has often even succeeded in "infecting" these spheres and that when it has not done so it could not be undermined for lack of a serious alternative to its model, in particular to its terrible accounting model. Thus capitalist modernism has so far won the battle and dominated the scene all over the planet. Marx gave the slogan for the proletarians to unite to overthrow capitalism. In fact, this union hardly ever took place on a lasting basis. On the other hand, the capitalists of all countries have constantly united to impose on themselves and on the planet, with the support of states, their tailor-made economic and accounting constitution. So far, they have largely won the

---

[15] See notably Bénassy, Boyer et Lipietz (1978).

[16] Context characterized, particularly in Europe, by the weakening of right-wing parties and capitalist leaders of large firms who had supported the Axis powers.

battle of the global social war[17]. We can now conclude on the nature and the scope of the accounting law which is the basis of this constitution.

Towards a modern economic and accounting world constitution

We have shown that in classic modern accounting capital is not an asset (a resource in the sense of economists) but a liability, an obligation, a debt of conservation. But an obligation of whom and towards whom? The answer invented by the founders of this system, from the Middle Ages, within the framework of their practice of the fictitious duplication of their personality is clear: it is a debt of the company, fictitious person, vis-à-vis the capitalist as a private person, the latter"lending" his money to his business. But this "theory," based on the fiction of the accounting personality of the company and its debt vis-à-vis the capitalist as a private person, if it was able to impose itself in practice in the lex mercatoria of early modern capitalists, has not been generally recognized by official law. This all the more so as the lawyers have practically never wanted or accepted to consider the sole proprietorship as a legal person, unlike certain companies (limited companies in particular). But then how can we explain, despite this situation, the presence of a financial capital on the liabilities side of the balance sheet in almost all companies in the world and even in all companies and firms that do not have legal personality (such as, in particular, general partnerships)? The answer is as follows: this registration is imposed, as it is the case for example in current French law, beyond any consideration of the legal personality or not of the firm, on all the capitalists who contribute a financial capital: they have to consider the latter as something to be strictly conserved. It is purely and simply an obligation inherent in their activities, in this case in the conduct of their business, in the same way that there are obliged to drive on the right when they take their car (or on the left, in the case of England, still original). With this legal conception there is therefore no longer any need, as Datini and his successors did, to imagine a fictitious personality of the company or of the

[17] And not, as Serres (2008, 137-139) says, that of the war which opposes everyone to the World...or our whole gender to the global environment." Unlike him, it is in fact, for us, the one that opposes human objects to the caste of capitalist subjects who have power in the economic and political spheres.

accounts themselves of this company to ensure the protection of financial capital. Let us consider this extraordinary legal conception: de facto, a capitalist international *corporate law* prevents what it sees as socially dangerous behavior: the wilful destruction of financial capital. It therefore requires the capitalists managing their business, for their own well-understood interest, to strictly conserve their financial capital, that is to say their money, an inert monetary object (case of "cash") or a claim on a State (case of scriptural money). In addition, this conservation of financial capital is, just as necessarily, effectively ensured, thanks to another international *accounting law,* which obliges the capitalist accountant to register the corresponding amount in the liabilities of the balance sheet. What is more, this conservation must be done within the framework of a principle of prudence which is akin to that of precaution, so decried by many capitalists with regard to environmental problems. Can we do better in terms of preservation of a capital?

Thus private law not only obliges a company to repair the damage caused by its fault but also to keep financial capital out of any fault context: “you will keep your financial capital” such is the law and the accounting prophets! And if you do not respect this law you will be penally sanctioned for the offense of distribution of fictitious profits and even, possibly for the offense of not respecting the principle of prudence. What a culture of security in favor of finance capital! What care for it on the part of the welfare states !

To our knowledge, it is rare to find a positive legal injunction to keep things and even less to elaborate the terms of its realisation. Yet this is what happens in capitalist law for financial capital. The capitalists have imposed the security of their financial capital: strict and narrow defense of the interests of this class of individuals. And this security is not in the context of a heuristic of fear but in that of their "reasonable" reason: to protect their interests and them alone. Indeed, there is no question that this type of strict compulsory conservation can concern human capital and natural capital. In general, moreover, as regards human capital, it is fashionable to say, when certain Keynesian measures are taken in its favor to ensure minimum conservation, that they are “benevolent” and "social" measures, the excess of which can only lead to serious economic problems and, moreover, that they will make citizens irresponsible recipients.

Let us add, to widen the field of the question, that these capitalists can also consider, as it is their right, that their objective is not so much to keep an undifferentiated mass of money as to keep its employment in the form of a physical object (like a machine) as they do in the context of certain so-called "replacement cost accounting",[18] oriented towards the conservation of "physical capital" (as opposed to monetary capital). In this case, the obligation to hold custody is also quite appropriate but concerns this physical capital within the framework, generally, of a very specialized activity. We then have a situation in which, for example, a machine, correctly depreciated, will be better protected than the human beings who operate it.

But let us now consider the situation of companies that have a legal personality. In this case things are different, for two main reasons. First, these are these companies which, as legal persons, are civilly responsible for the conservation of financial capital.[19] Second, insofar as these companies deal contractually with individual capital providers (or other companies), they have real capital-debts towards them which appear as liabilities on their balance sheet: we therefore find ourselves practically in the classical case invented by the capitalists at the end of the Middle Ages.

We can therefore observe that current accounting law has two means of operating the systematic conservation of financial capital. Either, at the price of the personification of companies, by registering a real debt towards individual capitalists (or companies). Or (practically in the case of sole proprietorships and partnerships) by imposing on the capitalists themselves a unilateral obligation to conserve their financial capital.

Whatever the process chosen, the lesson is clear: there is indeed an international accounting law which a priori ensures effective conservation

---

[18] One of the most famous examples of the practice of this type of accounting is that of "replacement cost" which was that of Philips for many years (see Richard 2005b).

[19] But it is their leaders who are criminally liable, particularly in the event of the distribution of fictitious dividends.

of simple inanimate objects such as capitalist money or capitalist machines. On the other hand, there is no equivalent of such a systematic conservation in companies with regard to human beings and even less to other living beings in nature.

Certainly, the great religions very early on established basic principles of conservation of human beings, in particular the general negative rule "you will not kill." Certainly, following them, the laws of the countries have ratified this fundamental rule of defense of individuals against criminal acts. But never these religions nor the laws of the States could, until now, go much further by ensuring a systematic *positive* conservation of the citizens thanks to the guarantee of normal conditions of life. Modern capitalism, for its part, has achieved the feat of getting virtually all the states of the world to vote for a general positive rule of unconditional and uncompromising conservation of its financial capital, that is to say of inert objects, a conservation moreover joined to power in the company. It won on all counts. This all the more easily as a good number of philosophers, sociologists, political scientists and economists have helped it, consciously or not, by deflecting the frontal opposition towards the capitalists and towards their terrible accounting law towards a futile struggle which targets intangible or even non-existent opponents, which is what we will show now.

The attempts to mask modern capitalist reality: Managerialism, industrialism and the administration of things[20]

At the beginning of the 19th century, in a context marked by what was called (wrongly as we saw with the case of the rise of industry in the Middle Ages -) the "industrial revolution", the development of capitalism raises more and more resistance from workers and questions from certain thinkers. To answer these questions and calm concerns, we see certain currents appearing which express the idea that in this new "industrial" era the power of financial capital providers would decline in favor of scientific and neutral managers of firms: we can speak in this regard of a current of "managerial industrialism." The words capitalist (or bourgeois) therefore

[20] This development owes much to Richard and Rambaud (2022abc)

will tend to disappear from the speeches of many thinkers. This conception appears, it seems, for the first time with the economist J.B. Say. In his "Treatise on Political Economy" (1803-1826) this author puts forward the idea that, in large companies, capitalists are mere lenders without decision-making power, remunerated on the basis of interests. For him, power in these large firms is now exercised by impartial managers whom he calls "entrepreneurs" (undertakers). This allows him in particular to show that, under the leadership of these managers, there could be a kind of harmonious balance in these firms with a fair remuneration of the three types of capitals invested in firms: interest paid to capitalists, wages paid to employees and rents received by landowners. This thesis of Say, which is completely contradictory with the characteristics of the capitalist accounting of his time, will inspire the thought of the sociologist Saint-Simon (1823). The latter in fact also considers that "industrialist" managers are neutral administrators who take care of both capitalists and workers. Saint-Simon adds to Say's ideas the thesis that these neutral managers should also govern the state and form a separate party: the "industrial party." As Peaucelle (2003) demonstrates, Saint-Simon himself would later influence Fayol in 1916, the one who will be named later the "French Taylor." He probably influenced Engels as well[21]. Indirectly, through Saint-Simon, Say will inspire the thinking of Auguste Comte (1830-42). This philosopher defends the thesis that humanity necessarily passes through three stages: the theological (Greek and Latin antiquity), metaphysical (Middle Ages) and scientific (19th century). This last stage, according to him, sees in particular the development of the science of administration, which he considers as one of the branches of science, just like the "hard" sciences, such as mathematics. Like Saint-Simon, Comte believes that industrialists must govern in the name of objective science[22]. As we have

---

[21] Engels (1880, 72)asserts that when the proletariat has seized power and transformed the means of production into state property, it will destroy the state in such a way that the governance of people will be transformed into an "administration of things" by production managers. He praises Saint Simon for showing the absorption of politics by economics (1880, 44).

[22] Grange (2012, 73-76) praises Comte's position because he wants "industrial patronage that leaves scientific research free, while admitting that the 'industrialist' (sic) can (and must) seek profit – its own as well as collective prosperity." We cannot agree with this opinion. It eliminates Comte's lack of criticism of the characteristics of capitalism of his time, under the cover of the notion of industrialism.

shown (Richard and Rambaud, 2020,2022b) this current will then influence Lenin's conceptions. Its ideas will be renewed in the 20th century (without being able to identify a clear filiation) by Berle and Means (1932),the famous authors of a book which tends to show that in the large American firms of the time the capitalists no longer have power (see below). Subsequently, after the Second World War, a large number of philosophers and political scientists, such as, for example, Galbraith (1967, the New Industrial State) and, more recently, Musso (2020) will take up this thesis of the major role of industry, technology and industrialism in the world, and the "disappearance" of capitalists. This, either to praise this victory of industrial techniques,[23] or, on the contrary, more and more often, to criticize it. In the latter case, it is the powerful German philosophical school which appears at the beginning of the 20th century with, in particular, Schmitt, Husserl, Heidegger, Adorno, Horkheimer, Habermas,[24] Jonas[25] and Illich which will play a driving role in the stigmatization of the role of techniques or technologies, or in a larger sense, engineering[26]) in the crisis of modern civilization, all to the detriment of an analysis of the power of the capitalists on the evolution of these techniques. Schmitt is a very important author of this current. In his book on Political Theology (1922, 73) he considers that "there should be only technical and economic problems... political problems are destined to disappear." In 1927 he published his "Concept of the political" in which he defended the idea that the fundamental distinctions between orders are "in the moral order the good and the bad, in the aesthetic order the beautiful and the ugly, in the economic the profitable and the unprofitable "(1927,63). He then asks himself if it is possible to find a criterion which allows to characterize politics and he answers that it is "the discrimination of the friend and the enemy," an enemy being always a group of individuals, and not a personal rival "(idem, 67). His thesis is that "there are no enemies in the economic order,

---

[23] Among the defenders of this thesis we find Mounier, the father of personalism. As Flipo shows, citation in support, (2014b, 20) for this philosopher, the criticism of the technique "is an infantile reaction of incompetent and panicked travelers" (according to The little fear of the 20th century, 1948).

[24] Notably his works of 1968, 1975 et 1987 (Bibliography).

[25] Jonas (1979) speaks of the "empire of techniques" to which he wants to oppose a heuristic of fear.

[26] This term engineering encompasses, in a broad sense, accounting and, in general, all kinds of calculations.

only competitors" (idem, 66). He sees the development of the European Spirit in five stages: theological (16th century), metaphysical (17th century), humanitarian (18th century, economic (19th century) and technical (20th century) (idem 133-137). We can consider that he takes up the ideas of Comte and Saint Simon except that he adds the last stage of the technique, which is an important new element. Schmitt considers as Comte (which he cites on page 142), that in the economic stage "the state... gives up distinguishing and correctly regulating economic facts" (1927, 141). According to him it becomes "a neutral and agnostic state" (142). But he thinks that this neutrality of the state is even more accentuated in the 20th century with the era of techniques. He concludes that: "the process of progressive neutralization of the various aspects of cultural life is coming to an end because it has reached the stage of techniques" (idem, 150). All of this shows that he never had to read a book of corporate law or a book of corporate accounting of his time, while Germany was in the midst of "accounting effervescence" with the development of an extraordinary standardization of balance sheet models, in particular with the help of charts of accounts whose use was made compulsory by the State (Richard, 1995). It is probable that he influenced the American Mumford, considered as "a tutelary author of the thought of degrowth" (Sinaï, 2013,24[27]), who published in 1934 an influential book: "Technics and civilization."But he will also be followed in his own country. Heidegger, already, will adopt his theses. In his famous work"Holzwege" (Off the beaten track in English, Chemins qui ne mènent nulle part in French edition 1962) this philosopher declares (our own translation): "the fact that man becomes a subject of technique[28] and the world an object, is only a consequence of the essence of technique which is gaining room and not vice versa." Heidegger visibly blames the techniques that lead the world and not the capitalists. He

[27] It is symptomatic that this book on the theme of "thinking about degrowth" contains, unless I am mistaken, only twice a very brief allusion to capitalism (pages 29 and 54): the focus, like that of Mumford (quoted on page 25) is obviously on technology and industrial society. Moreover, logically, the origin of ecological problems does not go back to the creation of the modern capitalism system but to the beginning of the industrial era between 1750 and 1850 in Europe with access to coal and the New World (30-31).

[28] A remark: the fact of translating "technique" by technology or government of numbers (in a more modern approach) does not change the problem: in any case the capitalist model is not in question.

advises human beings to promote an ethic that allows them to put their Dasein (Being there) up to their Sein (Being): this by getting out of the grip of the instrumental civilization dominated by techniques. But how to attack machines or computers except to return to the level of Luddites? In the end, all he offers as a solution to get out of this "technical danger" is to call on a saving God (Heidegger, 1977).

Even his dissident disciple Günther Anders (2002) sees the supreme danger in a (third) technical revolution with the appearance of nanomachines. He too, instead of denouncing the promoters of these technologies and regulating their activities, attacks the uneducated man of his time, stupefied by technology and unable to imagine the ends of his activity[29]: he is a man who thinks only of consuming in order to consume and enrich himself in order to enrich himself. As if the struggles of German workers for participation in the management of their companies and even their countries had never existed. And as if the power of the big capitalists who were going to come to an agreement with Hitler and finance his activities were a joke. This theory of the power of technique with an extension to the problem of numbers (the computational technique) was then taken up and developed in the writings of Adorno and Horkheimer[30] in 1944, then, resumed later, by Jonas (1979)[31] and Habermas[32]. It will also leave Germany to influence in particular the conceptions of Bernanos (1946) who wanted to fight the robots. But it still remains largely anchored in the homeland of Kant and Hegel, notably with Illich [33] (Simmonet, 1979,37). This philosopher, who moreover has very interesting ideas on ecology, is also marked by this "technical disease": he considers that "the relation of man to the tool has become a relation of the tool to the man" and that this comes

---

[29] He gives a special name to this incapacity: "discrepancy."

[30] According to them, the number would become the dangerous "canon" of the Enlightenment (La Dialectique de la raison, Paris, Gallimard, 1974, p. 25). They even think we should "kill Bacon" and "calculating reason" (p. 57).

[31] This author, in his famous "Principle of responsibility" makes technology and science responsible for the rupture between man and nature.

[32] Jürgen Habermas, *op. Cit.*

[33] Note his works of 1971, 1973,1975 et 1977 (Bibliography).

from the fact that man, in general, no longer masters his own techniques, a thesis that will influence many environmentalists[34].

This emphasis on the dominant role of techniques and the general responsibilities of all men is very problematic for us. As if, for example, the reduction in the lifespan of products sold by capitalist firms came from a demand from customers eager to see their goods obsolete as quickly as possible. As if the choice of ICT(Information and communication technologies) to the detriment of paper had germinated in the brains of associations of consumers invited to participate in the management of multinational firms. As if there had been no regulation of economic activity by the capitalists with the help of socialists and liberals or, in the fascist era, with Hitler power. One can hesitate between two opinions on these theses defended, mainly (but not exclusively) by these luminaries of German philosophy: either a blindness of people who do not have their feet on the ground, or, on the contrary, an acute awareness of " social risks "of their time which threaten in particular the big German capitalist firms, which would lead them to invoke the responsibility of technology to divert attention from the responsibilities of the principal actors of capitalism. Perhaps the truth lies in a mixture of the two elements[35]. Even Morin (1980; cf Flipo, 2014a, 255),in France, was won over by these ideas. He sums up the ideological conflict with that which opposes "Marxist –Stalinist" ideology to "sociological ideology," the latter seeing a society "founded on the solid foundations of industry developing ad infinitum": capitalism has

---

[34]Simmonet (1979), for example, who nevertheless mentions the influence of capitalist society (32) and "values of profitability" (54), speaks, with reference to Illich, of the "tyranny of tools" (37). She also speaks of "the [denatured] man of industrial society" (49) who is "chained by money" (53). However, she cites the work of Paul Goodman, an inspiration for Illich, who shows that the effect of the technique depends on the conditions of its use (99).

[35] Although she sometimes seems sensitive to these industrialist theses, Grange (2012.83) rightly emphasizes that "this philosophy of technology is foreign to the concrete world and the men who work, the displaced populations...the cultures in danger are forgotten. She adds, about Heidegger, that the threats he identifies are less those concerning men and cultures than those aimed at poets: "a technical/art opposition which seems on this point too academic."

disappeared in this opposition or is confused with an industrial society. He will be followed by a good number of French or French philosophers[36]

On the sociological side, as shown by Flipo (2014a, 288 and 300), authors such as Schmidt (1962-1994), Aron(1966) and Louis Dumont(1967) will also speak of "industrial civilization" and the independence of technology from social organization. But there is another theme, also of German origin, which avoids talking about capitalism. It is that of the "rationalization" of the world. It comes from the sociologist Weber (1920), who confused capitalist accounting rationality with simple economic rationality (Rambaud and Richard, 2022a). In France, Gauchet will also take up this theme by attributing the disenchantment to this rationalization that goes everywhere and not to its specific implementation by capitalism (Flipo, 289)[37]. The same is true of Mumford (1934-1950,cited by Flipo, 2014a, 290). These converging ideas, resulting from a large number of German philosophers and sociologists, will be widely disseminated, including in the sphere of environmental ethics and its critiques. As regards the promoters of environmental ethics, reading a work like that of Afeissa (2007, 96) shows that the term capitalism is hardly ever pronounced in the general charge of these authors against the destructive actions of men on nature. On the other hand the problematic role of sciences and technociences is widely emphasized. As for the opponents of environmental ethics, such as, in particular, Ferry (1992) and Gauchet (1990b), if they make technologies play a leading role in ensuring the conservation of nature, they nevertheless have one thing in common with environmental ethicists not to question capitalism (Flipo 2014a, 167). According to Flipo (167) one can find in ecologists like Bourg a kind of middle way: to put certain techniques on trial, to propose other more

[36] A striking example is the case of Dalsuet (2010,92-117) who, influenced by Heidegger's theses, believes that the material power ensured by the technique has induced a sense of Prometean confidence in it from the 17th century and that this technique ended up getting globally out of control or not controllable.

[37] Flipo (2014a, 289) rightly points out that "this rationalization is not one because it disrupts ecosystems and oppresses human beings." But it should be specified that it is a question of capitalist rationalization.

ecological techniques (such as industrial ecology or functional economy), all this without ever questioning the capitalist system.

Such is the impressive army of intellectuals who generally defend the thesis of the domination of technology over men and nature. We have, however, provided substantial elements on the very problematic nature of this thesis, often coupled with the idea of the disappearance of the power of the capitalists or, what amounts to the same thing, their "overcoming" by their own technical system: this like the learned apprentice who no longer manages to master his creation (Richard 2015a, Richard and Rambaud, 2022a). In this work, we persist in questioning the thesis of the primary responsibility of science and technology and we will come back to this fundamental point later.

But there is something more serious than this error of target emanating from critics of industrialism and technology. There is the position of those who consciously use the managerialist-industrialist thesis to better preserve capitalism under the guise of an objectification of their behavior. Their action not only aims to deny the role of capitalists in the world since the Middle Ages (no question in particular of the existence of a capitalist stage, in the famous "law" of the three States) but also leads to raise administrative science to the rank of an exact science: like the natural sciences, make it the equivalent of a science that would always tell the truth. However, with regard to the first type of science, we believe that any administrative science, whether it concerns the administration of companies or countries, cannot be exact or neutral insofar as it is always based on an ethical choice: starting with that of determining the type of capital that will be conserved or not. It is therefore not such sciences that can tell the truth. This is what we believe we have demonstrated with the example of modern capitalism and which we will further confirm with those of equally modern socialism (see below). As for the second type of science, the so-called "natural" sciences, while it is fair to say that they can tell the truth, that does not mean that they say it systematically. Of course, a first reason is that the scientists are wrong in their reasoning: errare humanum est. But this does not concern us very much: it is likely that one day or another this type of error will be demonstrated and corrected by these scientists. This is the second reason that interests us: that of a natural science at the service of administrative "sciences," in particular those which serve capitalism or socialism. In Serres's (1990) fresco of the development of the natural sciences, it only a question of scientists unfairly condemned by social laws. This philosopher shows the injustices on the part of lawyers of which many courageous scientists are victims who simply wanted to speak the truth. This starting with Anaxagoras, and continuing with Galileo and his successors.

It is obviously not a question of denying these facts which are not to the glory of the social powers which reigned in those times. But Serres forgets to say that other scientists will "knowingly" falsify the truth, especially those who will work for socialism (real or not) or capitalism. The examples of these scientists abound with glaring cases, even in the 20th and 21st centuries, such as the "exemplary" ones of the Soviet "scientist" Lyssenko and those in the service of the American firm Monsanto (on the question of the harmfulness of certain weedkillers). The ecological movement must obviously rely on scientists who struggle to make the reality known of the situation of ecosystems, in particular the threats to their resilience. This does not mean, as Ferry (1992) argues, that hard sciences will eliminate political choices and that all scientists are "saints." Serres, meanwhile, also forgets to congratulate the sociologists and jurists who have braved these powers and succeeded in making them bend like what, unlike his words, things are not so simple. All of this is an incentive to find ways to thwart the financial powers that are capable of subjugating scientists to their interests. We believe that this will not only go through beautiful declarations like those of the philosopher Comte who wants "independent scientific research" or "scientific administration." Above all, we must denounce and thwart the power of the capitalists, which is at the origin of these situations of dependence of scientists. We must call a spade a spade and not invoke in vague terms "industrial power" or 'the power of techniques." These industries and techniques do not spring from Jupiter's thigh, nor do the supply and demand curves of simple anonymous market action. Behind the industry and the techniques employed there are plump men who exercise power in large firms, within the framework of laws made by other men: the capitalist system to name it (in this sense Lenoir in Flipo, 2014a, 291)

The same observation must be made against the conceptions of Beaudrillart (1970), who, basing himself on Bataille and Veblen (Flipo, 2014a, 201-2), considers that exchange value dominates manufacturing collective of uses: he does not see that this exchange value is conditioned by the concept of capital inscribed in the accounting codes of capitalists. It is symptomatic that this current of ideas, as shown by Flipo (2014a, 208, 291), is inspired by American authors like Galbraith (1967, Packard (1957), Riesman et alii (1950), Reich (1933) and Goldsmith (1992). All these authors pronounce the thesis of the domination of managers and engineers in firms. In this conception, which strangely resembles that of Say, the role of capitalists and, in particular, their choice of an egoist type of accounting disappears completely. Likewise, concerning Illich and Moscovici, [38] the latter influenced by the former, it is more the tyranny of technical society that motivates their research than the concrete economic cogs of capitalist enterprises. The same goes for Ellul (1988) who has a particular focus on information technologies (Flipo, 2014a, 253). Sartre and even Lipietz will also be partially influenced by these erroneous theses which do not directly target the capitalist production system but its consequences. The author of "Being and Nothingness" proposes to flee existential anxiety in joint action (Mitsein), especially in joint work. In his "Critique of Dialectical Reason" he sees above all in advertising the misdeeds of capitalism (Flipo, 2014a, 207-9). As for Lipietz (1996, 120),[39] in his "Société en sablier," he sees the solution to the problems caused by capitalism rather in a strategy of citizens to gain free time, at the very cost of a reduction in their wages, in order to develop independent activities that are more ecological[40]. All these escape solutions seem harmful to us, although they are, all in all, understandable in the face of the power of the capitalist model.

But there is much worse in the philosophical realm with postmodern positions like those of Derrida, Deleuze and Gattari. These last two philosophers (1972) believe that capitalism is a very flexible system which runs counter to the Codes (which they deem uneconomic). Their thesis is

---

[38] See Flipo (2014a, 253).

[39] After his green revolution of 1986 and his call for "the conditions for an alternative movement in France" (Intervention at the AERIP days.Marx's institutional and political issues, January 31 and February 1, 1986.)

[40] See also his "Green Deal" of 2012.

that other economic systems, like that of the Soviet Union and its satellites, failed because they were coded. This thesis is false. It is clear that they have no idea how capitalism actually works, especially its system of accounting laws and drastic codes: they indulge in pure philosophical speculation about it. What is more, they go so far as to encourage this iniquitous model: they believe that the best solution is to ensure that it leads its development to completion[41]. In this respect we agree with the positions of Meera Nanda (2003, 160-5). She taxes precisely this current of reactionary because it preaches that nothing allows to distinguish the truth from the fiction and is located in the line of German philosophers like Spengler, Heidegger and Jünger, an intellectual elite which gave up enlightening the people.

Fortunately, there are those who resist this current which denies the practice and the defects of capitalism. Among them is Gorz who speaks of the misdeeds of "industrial capitalism" (1990, 76) and who clearly affirms the neutrality of techniques while asking that their use be under constraint of social actors within the framework of a society oriented towards self-management(1990, 44,49-54)[42]. Likewise, for example, the philosophers Grange and Stengers lead a clear and courageous fight against capitalism.

The conclusion to be drawn from this development is that rather to refer to the confused and dangerous ideas of industrialism, or even of "reasonable" industrialism, and thus to philosophical considerations which disregard the foundations of capitalism, it is better to return to the bottom of the problem and be interested in the drastic reform of the heart of modern capitalism: its type of management and, in particular, its accounting system. This system, in fact, as we have seen, is not a simple technique but a veritable ideological weapon in the service of particular interests. Finally, the problem of techniques and sciences is not that they are autonomous, a thesis notably supported by Ellul, but on the contrary that they are used for unacceptable ends, in particular within the framework of capitalist management. This also applies to certain so-called "socialist" practices.

---

[41] Flipo (2014a, 300-302) is also very severe with them: he considers, on the subject of ecological problems, that "their remarks always remain extremely vague." About Deridda he affirms that he "deconstructed everything, except the growth."

[42] See also his other works cited in the bibliography.

The influence of modern capitalist ideology on 'socialist' thought and practice

The ability of the modern capitalist system to impose its accounting model as the basis of any economic system is impressive. It is certainly undeniable that certain economists have made a severe criticism of this system. Marx, in particular, had the merit of showing that it is based on the exploitation of man by man. Moreover, although other economists, like Cournot(1838)[43] anticipated him on this point, he was even, to a certain extent aware that this economic system was destructive of nature. We have however already indicated that if, as Foster (2000, 2002) shows, certain writings on his part can apparently testify to this fact, his ecological approach remains very ambiguous and connoted by an economic approach in line with the school of forest economists (see after for more details). Moreover and above all, as we have shown (Richard and Rambaud 2022ab), beyond his justified criticisms of the capitalist system, with regard to its "reconstruction" he confined himself, at best,[44] to formulating general principles aimed at promoting the system of workers cooperatives. He was not able to come up with a new concrete economic model and, in particular, a new management model adapted for these cooperatives. Likewise, Engels, despite his knowledge of accountancy, did not propose anything specific on this subject to drastically and concretely change the capitalist system. Even in one of his last writings on Dühring (1880) he also does not deal with the

[43] Vivien (2005, 52), based on Vatin (1998), stresses that Cournot (1838) is worried about a capitalist economy that consumes fossil resources at a breakneck pace and does not ensure the reproduction of renewable resources. Cournot even goes so far as to assert in his book that "the civilized man laughs at the savage who cuts down the tree to have the fruit, but in this respect the civilized man still holds much of the savage." He is particularly aware that the "wild" cuts of wood to ensure crops will have the consequence that "the impoverished soil will become a moor, where the rains will gully it, strip it bare and transform into an arid soil this wooded mountain which maintained..fertilizing rains and protected it against the devastation of torrential rains."

[44] We will not mention here his utopian ideas professed in the "German Ideology," of a totally unspecialized work: "to do this today, that tomorrow, hunt in the morning, fish in the afternoon, do breeding... without becoming a hunter, fisherman or herdsman": they are unfortunately of little use to us in our current world. It would have been more important to design a new ecological and social management of companies, which he never concretely proposed.

description of an economy based on production cooperatives. He only proposes that the proletariat transform the means of production into state property (1880,71). Wrongly, he believes that the capitalist system will lead to a progressive socialization of the means of production by the state, preceded by that of the socialization of these means of production at the level of the limited stock holder companies (SHCs) [45] (1880,69). This view would then inspire Lenin and his conception of a kind of state capitalism under, supposedly, workers' control. The main focus of these fathers of real socialism is therefore always on questions of property and not on questions of management, in particular of accounting management. As a result, they have been unable to imagine an alternative to modern capitalism but have led their successors to continue to want to eradicate private ownership of the means of production and company shares.

Even more problematic these successors have been reduced to drawing inspiration from the management tools of modern capitalism notably its accounting system. Let us underline in this respect that Marx, in spite of his reluctance to take account of the real concepts of capitalist accounting, notably that of capital-debt, *was perfectly aware of the utmost importance of accounting* for rebuilding a socialist or a communist society after the 'obligatory' collapse of the capitalist system. This may be evidenced by this sentence of the author of Capital that almost all the accounting textbooks of the former USSR will repeat to satiety: "accounting is fundamental for the capitalist economy; it is even more important for the socialist economy"(Richard 2000, page 18 based on Complete Works of Marx in Russian language: Moscow, tome 24, page153)[46]. Echoing these statements

---

[45] As Berle and Means (1932) will do later, he estimates, naively, that the capitalists, in this type of companies, will lose power because the SHC is no longer the owner of the means of production and this, too, due to the proliferation of a large number of small stakeholders: as a result, the State will only have to take advantage of the opportunity to "pick up the stakes." History has shown that it was not so.

[46] The complete and correct sentence is the following: "Accounting as a means of control and ideal synthesis of the process (of reproduction) becomes all the more necessary as the process takes place on a more social scale and loses its purely individual character; thus the keeping of accounts is more necessary under the regime of capitalist production than it is under that of the fragmented production of artisans and peasants and it is much more necessary under the regime of communal production than it is under the regime of capitalist production." (Marx,Capital,volume 2 translated from Marx Engels Werke (1973), Band 24, page 137.

of Marx Lenin himself will say: "socialism is above all accounting" (socialism eto predje bcevo ychet) (Richard, 1980, based on Makarov, 1966). We can therefore only congratulate Marx on to have precisely perceived the crucial importance of this discipline for the foundation of economic systems, a quality that his followers, notably economists, generally will not have thereafter. Many of them, no doubt inspired by the German philosophical school and its hatred of "government by numbers," will profess a clear hostility towards this discipline symbol of a market and capitalist economy.[47] But this will not be the case with the founders of what will be called "real socialism."

In the case of the soviet economy, it is fascinating to note that its leaders, whether Lenin or Stalin and their followers, could not come out of the clutches of a particular form of modern capitalist accounting. As we have demonstrated (Richard, 1980, based on Makarov, 1966) the accounting system of companies in the former USSR, after the NEP (New economic Policy), was designed on the basis of double-entry accounting directly inspired by that one created by capitalists at the end of the Middle Ages. It was on this basis that some modifications were introduced to reflect the type of Soviet power. The double entry type of accounting remained. There was also a balance sheet and a profit and loss account, with expenses and revenues. The balance sheet showed only one type of capital to conserve among the liabilities. It was no longer the financial capital of private capitalists but the financial capital of the "socialist" state: thus a public subject replaced a private one. The profit and loss account showed among the expenses, as in the case of private capitalists, the expenses of wages on the part of the employees which diminished the profit of the state, that is to say, in fact, that of the class of soviet bureaucrats. Thus the workers remain simple salaried people. As far as nature is concerned, it was treated as a simple resource, a mere means of action, which led to its destruction, like in the West, if not worse. Indeed, Barbault (2006, 149) has shown, for example, that the drying up of the Aral Sea was "one of the greatest ecological tragedies on the planet... and" an economic and human tragedy... which affected 2 million people." Although the USSR's accounting system was presented as Marxist

---

[47] The reader will be able to easily verify that up today the proposals of Marxist literature *in economics* on *ecological business* accounting are almost inexistent.

and new by Makarov (1966, 3 and 4), the father of Soviet accountants, it had in fact "aped" that of modern private capitalism.

As certain critical commentators have pointed out, such as Rühle (1932), Bettelheim (1974), Cliff (1955), it was an accountancy adapted to a "state capitalism." Indeed the concept of profit reflected the added value available for the state bureaucrats after payment of employee salaries. Compared to that of private capitalist companies in the West, this type of profit, if we define it additively, corresponded to the sum of the interests paid to the state bank (Gosbank),plus the taxes paid to the state and the profit of the Soviet firm. It was therefore a transposition of modern capitalist accounting invented at the end of the Middle Ages but with the Soviet bureaucracy as its subject. We can consider that it was the effective realization of the dream of Berle and Means who believed in 1932 that the American economy was heading towards a "managerialist" type society in which the shareholders of SHs would have lost power in favor of a caste of managers. But, in fact, it was in the USSR and its satellite countries that this transformation really first took place. All of this is in a way consistent with the assertions of Lenin who hoped to increase the productivity of Soviet companies through the accounting system of large capitalist Western firms (Makarov, 1966, 5).

Maoist China would subsequently follow the same direction. Makarov's book, once translated into Chinese, would inspire some accounting books such as that of Zhao, Lou, Ge, Wu, (1979 [1962]). Hence, practically, the same system of accounting, borrowed from private capitalists, in the two great "socialist" countries, despite some ideological differences. To keep up appearances the Soviet Communist and Maoist accountants had carefully avoided using the term capital (Kapital in Russian and Zi Ben (资本 in Chinese). To achieve a (formal) distinction with the Western accounting system they came up with the idea of using the term statutory fund (Ustavni Fond in Russian and ZI Jin (资金, in Chinese). But all this did not change the (modern) capitalist nature of their accounting systems[48]. It is thus hardly surprising that after the collapse of the Soviet Union and the disappearance of Mao these two communist countries were able to adopt

[48] The equation Assets = Liabilities was classically interpreted in China as "use of funds = source of funds" (资金运用=资金来源, zi jin yun yong = zi jin lai yuan)

without great difficulty the IFRS (American accounting standards in fact) and the economy of Western capitalist market.

The only experience that could have caused certain difficulties for the capitalist system was that of Self-Management, in Tito's time in Yugoslavia (Samary, 2017). During the years 1960-70 the economist Kardelj (1975), assisted by innovative accountants, had devised an original type of accounting adapted to the self-management ideology (Richard 1983, based on Jezdimirovic 1974). It remained, however, based on a double entry monetary accounting of the classic type adapted to a market economy. Its most original aspect, by comparison with the Soviet case, was that the employees of these firms, theoretically if not practically, ceased to be mere employees and became self-managers. In particular, they had obtained the right to decide on their own the allocation of a new type of profit. This new profit, which appeared in the balance of the new income statement, was conventionally based on a difference between revenues and expenses. But what changed everything was that the notion of expense was reviewed and corrected. Unlike the case of the USSR and Communist China and, more generally, the capitalist systems of the East or the West, the pay of the workers was no longer considered as an expense but as a distribution of profits, themselves redefined. Indeed the self-managed workers were supposed to be the masters of the management of these new firms[49]. Kardelj and his accountants had somehow reversed the situation: the workers self-managers apparently became the masters (the subjects) who received a profit (the bottom line of the new profit and loss statement) while the financiers, often banks, apparently became the "slaves" whose interest expenses weighed on the profits of the new masters.

But, in contradiction with this revolutionary approach, the new "self-managed human capital" did not appear on the liabilities side of the balance sheet as having to be strictly preserved while the financing,

[49] Concretely, the profit, in the case of this self management was, schematically, the difference between the revenues (sales) and the expenses, the latter including only the materials and services consumed, the depreciation of the instruments of production, and the taxes and financial charges paid to the banks: the remuneration of the self-managers was therefore no longer considered as expenses but as levies on the profits thus redefined.

generally that of the State, continued to appear there as a capital-debt. Furthermore, this contradictory accounting remained modern insofar as nature also did not appear as a capital to be kept on the liabilities side of the balance sheet: it remained treated as a simple resource subject to human activity, even if it was within the frame of self-management.

Another big problems was the financing of these companies. As Tito and Kardelj, influenced on this point by the theses of Marx and Engels on the harmful nature of private property, had excluded any participation of citizens in the financing of their firms, the financing of these firms continued to be largely provided by banks placed under the central and bureaucratic control of the communist state.

This experiment, given these shortcomings, and other geographical problems (isolated experience in one country, political problems, conflicts between several nations "brought together" by Tito) also failed. After it the West's capitalist accounting management system was given a free rein.

It is true that, nowadays, the very old and very diverse experiences of the cooperative economy, initiated by avant-garde like Proudhon, and taken up more recently by the movement of the commons dear to Ostrom (1990) and the social and solidarity economy (SSE) could have given ideas for getting out of the orbit of this type of capitalist accounting management. In any case, they have notably influenced certain sociologists and economists such as Latouche, O'Connor and Lipietz (Flipo, 2014a, 197). These authors have argued that these types of marginal economies could expand and become the rule and thus re-embed the economy into society as Polanyi wished. But as Laville (2010), one of the specialists in the question, recognizes, these experiences have never been able to constitute a threat to modern capitalism and, moreover, as underlined by Flipo (idem 197-8), they are practically not concerned with ecology, as indeed the writings of Polanyi himself.

In any case, it is very difficult to impose oneself by gradual infiltration in this capitalist world marked by social and environmental dumping: this dumping leads a very large part of modest wage earners to prefer products that destroy the environment at low prices. All the more so as the capitalists oppose a united front against these disparate movements. In particular, as we have seen, they succeeded in forcing all members of their community to adopt a single management method, essentially based on standardized accounting on a global scale and made compulsory by strict laws, accompanied by severe penalties in the event of non-compliance. It is very difficult to oppose this accounting situation which constitutes a real-world economic constitution. The power of the "accounting weapon" of this capitalism is such that it even manages to impose it on companies that refer to models of the SSE and the commons. To our knowledge, there is no specific accounting model for these movements: they are obliged to comply, or comply voluntarily, with capitalist accounting rules, in particular those which govern the presentation of balance sheet and income statement models.[50]

The preceding developments therefore seem to show that despite certain differences of a secondary order, the modern accounting system invented in northern Italy at the end of the Middle Ages ended up spreading the whole planet, mainly under the direct influence or indirect from the United States. It is through this that, in practice, capitalist modernity has imposed itself almost everywhere in the world under the leadership of large international organizations, and this not through growth, which can be very variable according to geographic areas and countries. "Traditional" societies that do not use capitalist double-entry accounting are on the way out. The world is therefore practically unified in modernity under the aegis of capitalist accounting.

Catherine and Raphael Larrère affirm that the protection of nature is a "modern concern" insofar as nature is to be protected only when human action reaches a certain amplitude (Flipo, 2014b, 73)but the extraordinary extension of modern capitalist accounting, which protects only financial capital, is contradictory with this "concern," which in our eyes is only a simple virtuality, if not a deception (see below).

To conclude on this point, we can return to the definition of liberalism, socialism and Soviet Marxism actually practiced. All three are systems that *accept the modern double-entry capitalist accounting model* that was invented in

[50] Ostrom (1990) has shown very well the need for clear rules of governance for the conservation of corporate resources in common, but she has never proposed a real economic (and even less accounting) model for this purpose.

the Middle Ages and its consequences (systematic protection of only financial capital and power to the capitalists who advance the financial funds). While soviet Marxism prefers public property and generalized state laws, liberalism "likes" private ownership of the means of production and selective laws: as soft as possible or non-existent with regard to protection of human and natural capitals and the hardest possible to safeguard the interests of the capitalists, in particular their accounting system[51]. As for socialism, it generally admits (depending on the movements) both private property and public property and differs from liberalism only by a tendency (more or less accentuated according to its followers) to make a certain redistribution of wealth by means of taxes on the rich and or, more broadly, Keynesian policies. In no case does it call into question the foundations of the capitalist system, in particular its accounting model.

In conclusion on this chapter we can affirm that the drama of the theorists of all the attempts to overthrow the capitalist system has been to be unable to understand the reality of its economic system and in particular its accounting model: as we show in detail in another book (Rambaud and Richard, 2022a) very few economists,[52] sociologists or political scientists[53] and even fewer philosophers[54] have really taken an interest in the basis of

[51] We cannot therefore agree with the theses of Audard (2009) who bases his definition of liberalism on non-intervention in the private sphere, the invisible hand of the markets and self-regulation through the play of supply curves and request. In fact, the example of accounting law shows that there is no spontaneous order in this matter. Not even for the market, which is also a state construction (Richard and Rambaud, 2022a).

[52] The major old exceptions are Kapp (1950), Perroux (1982, 1991), El Serafy (1991) and Passet (1979) who understood the role that the accounting concept of depreciation could play in an ecological economy. But even these remarkable authors failed to see the specific nature of the concept of capital in accounting. More recently, the articles or books of Aglietta (2019), Berger (2017; 2022a), Grandjean (2018), Jorion (2020),), and the reflections of Favereau and Beaudoin, within the framework of the circle of Bernardins, have had the great merit of integrating the theme of ecological accounting in the economic field.

[53] Among them Sombart and Weber had the merit of being interested in the double entry accounting but could not understand its essence. Nowadays Daniel Bachet (2019) is one of the very few sociologists to integrate the "accounting weapon" into his research on corporate reform. For his part, the political scientist Jourdain (2019) also reserves a major role for the question of corporate accounting.

[54] One of these very rare exceptions is the work of Bommier and Renouard (2018) on the formation of a new type of enterprise based on the theory of commons.

modern liberal capitalist economy: its accounting law. With regard to economists, one of the possible reasons is that the young economic science which was born only in the 18th century absolutely had to distinguish itself from the old accounting technique in order to be able to appear as a new, autonomous and truly "scientific" discipline. As far as philosophers are concerned, the domination of Greek philosophy and its focus on the search for individual happiness hardly encouraged any interest in the turpitudes of the chrematistic practice denounced by Aristotle. Under these conditions the attention of critics of the capitalist system has unfortunately mostly focused on economic theories unrelated to the reality of the practice of the capitalist system. This to the great relief of the capitalists, very comfortable with this situation. These considerations lead us to the next chapter.

Chapter 5
Diversity of points of view on the reality of capitalism and the notion of modernity

We will address two main questions here. The first is that of the different views that economic disciplines have on the reality of capitalism and their impact on the conception of the firm; the second is that of the link between modernity and types of property: is the type of property a constituent element of the definition of modernity?

The different views of economics on capitalism and their impact on the conception of the firm

Before dealing with this question it is important to know what is meant by economic discipline, in particular its relation to accounting. For us, accounting is a branch of economics and constitutes a foundation on which, in particular, economic theories should be based. However, more often than not, with rare exceptions, which include Proudhon (1846), Sombart (1902), Weber (1920)and, more recently, Hodgson (2015), the accounting discipline inherited from the Italian founders is not considered a branch of economics. Its fundamental instruments, including that of the double entry, as well as its specific concepts of capital-debt and profit which derive from it, are not considered worthy of attention by almost all economists. As a result, it can be said that modern economic science which deals almost exclusively with capitalism, due to the disappearance of the Yugoslav experience and the weakness of the social and solidarity economy (taken in the broad sense), is made up of two completely separate branches: that of accountants practicing modern capitalism and that of economists, mainly, nowadays, neoclassical economists who dominate the scene. Certainly Proudhon, this economist with often provocative formulas, affirmed in his book Philosophy of Misery (1846) that "the accountant is the real economist from whom a host of false literati stole his title" but this diatribe against his fellow economists has not prevented the astonishing cleavage between "economists - accountants" and economists "quite simply" (or Economists) to continue over the centuries.

There is, however, a de facto commonality between capitalist accountants and economists of the neo-classical mainstream. It is their admission, most often tacit, of the current system based on the ideology of modernity: concretely, in the company, at least the big company, the distinction between the subjects, that is to say the capitalists and their allies (the big managers),and the objects of which nature and simple salaried humans are part. For the rest they differ fundamentally on the concept of capital and the purpose of valuing assets. For classic accountants, capital is a debt owed to the capitalist in respect of his stakes and the "value" of the company is based on the sum of this capital and the profits really made: the idea of valuing unsold assets at their potential selling price is totally foreign to this type of accounting economics, at least in its classical version.

On the contrary, for neoclassical economists, capital is a resource (an asset in accounting terms) valued on the basis of its potential selling price in a market, with the aim of measuring wealth and, more broadly, the utilities derived from economic activity. These points of disagreement will lead to different conceptions and definitions of the company.

In most analyses of modernity, in particular in those of the greatest number of economists, of neoclassical tendency, these are most often broad definitions of modern business that are adopted. Thus Koza and Thoenig (2003),in accordance with this type of economic theory, assert that firms serve to maximize the utility of the preferences of individuals and groups who join and serve these organizations. Likewise Mäki (1985) emphasizes that traditional neoclassical microeconomics describes firms as rational and completely informed and as profit maximizers without internal structure, connected to each other by the external links of the price mechanism within the framework of a perfect competition. According to that neo-classical description, firms have only one goal, namely, to get maximum profits. However they do not try to reach this goal by means of strategic manoeuvres but just by reacting passively to external stimuli which consist in price information. Thus with this vision the modern capitalist enterprise becomes a form without substance determined rationally and passively which obtains and provides objective representations under the control of the subjects, the managers of the enterprise. We can link this conception to that, more modern but hardly different, of Jensen and Meckling (1976) who see in the company a simple nexus of contracts between actors (capitalists, managers, workers) who all freely accept that the company maximizes shareholder value in the context of supply and demand markets. This neoclassical view of the firm is currently the dominant vision in economics despite courageous attempts by certain economists to oppose it, such as those of Favereau (2014) and Favereau and Beaudoin (2015), authors who see the firm as a political institution.

We can also oppose to it that of the practice of classical modern accounting inherited from Italian founders. Indeed, the study of the reality, including the recent one, of this fundamental discipline of capitalism makes it possible to show that, far from the a priori of the neoclassical theory which considers the firm as a nexus of contracts, orthodox accounting, for its part, is conceptualized and materialized to ensure a practical functioning of capitalist companies which guarantees to their subjects, that is to say to the owners of individual companies or to the partners providing financial capital to a company, the optimal development of their capital-power.

This practice is organized around *several central accounting principles* establishing a set of internationally recognized rules, concepts, conventions or assumptions. These principles are notably enumerated today by the International Accounting Standard Board (IASB).

The first of these is based on the concept of fair presentation: financial statements are supposed to give a true picture of the results and the financial position of the company. This concept of fairness, which is not strictly speaking a principle, expresses the idea that (capitalist) accounting is a means of faithful representation of the objective reality of the orthodox modern capitalist enterprise. In order to achieve this objective, several other principles are mobilized. In particular, the quality of information must be able to be controlled in order to be useful to decision-makers. Concretely, the conceptual framework proposed by the Board of the IASB corresponds to the most advanced application of the spirit of orthodox accounting. It highlights several central characteristics defining the quality of this financial information.

Faithful representation is defined by the following assertions. Financial statements are meant to represent economic phenomena in terms of words and numbers. To be useful, financial information must not only represent adequate phenomena, but it must also accurately represent the phenomena it is intended to represent. To be a perfect faithful representation, a depiction would have three characteristics according to this view. It would be complete, neutral and free of error. Of course, perfection is seldom, if ever achievable and the Board's objective is to "maximize these qualities to the extent possible "(IASB 2010). The same source indicates that a neutral representation must be "without bias in the selection or presentation of financial information," with the precision that " free from error means that there are no errors or omissions in the description of the phenomenon, and the process used to produce the reported information has been selected and applied with no error."With these two notions of fidelity of representation and accuracy of sound reporting we find the two principles of objectivity which we spoke about previously concerning the description and the transmission of information among the moderns: a fiction of a faithful representation of objective reality and a possibility of its transmission without bias. There is also a claim for completeness: "A complete depiction includes all information necessary to understand the phenomenon being depicted, including all necessary descriptions and explanations" (IASB, 2010). All this to serve as a basis for the decisions of the users of this information: "relevant financial information is capable of making a difference in the decisions made by users" (ibid). Reality thus becomes a means at the service of the users, that is to say of the capitalist subjects. It is only entered in the orthodox financial reporting if it is relevant for this type of subjects-users as "predictive value. We can therefore say with Deegan (2013) that "if accountants do not measure something it effectively does not exist." As Deegan (ibid), leaning on Yankelevich (1972), stigmatizes: "the first step is to measure whatever can be easily measured. This is OK as far as it goes. The second step is to disregard that which can't be easily measured or give it an arbitrary quantitative value. This is artificial. And the third step is to presume that what can't be measured easily really isn't important. This is blindness. The fourth step is to say that what can't be easily measured really doesn't exist. This is suicide " (138-9). Thus, capitalist accounting clearly appears as a medium devoted to the finalities of dominant subjects: practically the shareholders of large corporations (Hendricksen 1970, Richard 2015a). The reality of the enterprise is defined by and for these subject-capitalists within the framework of a technology implemented by the Italian founders. We are very far in this framework of reasoning based on the power of the capitalists and their shaping of the reality of the passive and incorporeal conception of the firm dear to neoclassical economists. So while the accounting vision of the firm leads to the conclusion that this type of firm is intrinsically and concretely modern (with its subject / object cleavage) it is quite different with neoclassical economists, who, despite their scientific claims, do not give any corporeality to the capitalist firm[1]. Faced with this denial of reality, one can hesitate in their regard between two positions. Or to consider, in a "nice" way, that they are amateurs of abstract theories who have isolated themselves in the world of their ideas for the pleasure of pure intellectual research. Or, in a more "accusatory" way, to consider that in fact they are agents of capitalism who knowingly disguise the reality of this system the better to make it endure. The philosopher Stengers (2013,39), whose pugnacity we appreciate in her struggle against capitalism, decided clearly: for her "economists and other candidates for the production of global responses based on" science" only exist(..)"as a power to harm. Their authority only exists to the extent that the world, our world, remains what it is - that is, doomed to barbarism." But, to escape this barbarism, must we oppose socialism and capitalism?

Capitalism, socialism, property and modernity: What real links?

The question of the definition of terms is always complex. So it is with the terms that are the subject of this study. The problem posed by the concept of modernity is, it seems, the least difficult. As we have seen a large number of scholars from different disciplines, including those in economics, agree

---

[1] Although our subject here does not concern this current, we must pay tribute to the work of the school of "Conventions," in particular those carried out by O.Favereau and R. Beaudoin (2015) within the framework of the Bernardins, who,against the neo-classical view, consider the firm as a political and social institution.

that the subject-object divide is an essential part of the definition of modernity. But the same is not true of the other terms, at least from our perspective. [2] Regarding capitalism, economists, followed by most dictionaries, define it fundamentally as an economic system based on private ownership of the means of production and the market, with the objective of seeking profit. Socialism, on the contrary, would be an economic system based on collective ownership of the means of production, the absence of a market (replaced by planning) and the search for a more general interest. The major consequence generally drawn from these types of definitions of capitalism and socialism is this: modernity, which is based on the subject-object divide, can relate to capitalism as well as to real socialism. Indeed, both can very well lead to the destruction of nature whatever the type of ownership of the means of production used, whatever the absence or presence of markets or not and, even, whatever the type of management aimed at seeking profit or not. This is equivalent to saying, in this perspective, that the type of property, market, and management are not defining criteria of modernity, whereas they are for the definition of capitalism and socialism.

Our position on this issue is both similar and different.

It is similar insofar as we admit that modernity can characterize the "capitalist" as well as the "socialist" mode of production as understood by the defenders of this vision of things. But this common position hides an important difference. Indeed, for us, the type of property (private, public, common, etc.) is not a criterion for defining capitalism in the sense in which we understand it: a mode of capitalist management in the broad sense encompassing both private capitalism and state capitalist, both characterized by the use of the double entry accounting with its focus on the protection of financial capital alone. Certainly, modern classical double-entry accounting developed mainly from the 14th century until the 19th century within the framework of private companies where the subjects were the private capitalists and the objects the employees and nature. But, as we have shown, it is however wrong to believe that it cannot concern other types of business. Indeed its fundamental characteristic, the subject /

[2] See for more details Richard et Rambaud (2022a).

object dualism, can be applied to all kinds of modern businesses in which nature is treated as a simple resource. As such, the standard of using modern double-entry accounting goes beyond the division of property types. It was applied, as we have seen, within the framework of state capitalism of the Soviet type, based on public ownership of the means of production: in this type of accounting, close to private capitalist accounting, workers remained wage-employees and nature a simple resource. It may also have concerned forms of social ownership such as the companies of the former Yugoslavia in Tito's time: if workers became, at least in theory, self-managing partners, nature remained a simple resource. More recently, companies of the kind that Elinor Ostrom promoted could very well be managed within the framework of this modern accounting if the subject / object dichotomy is maintained with regard to nature[3].The conclusion to be drawn is that there are therefore different forms of ownership that can serve as the basis for modern businesses. Clearly, for us, the type of property, contrary to what one might a priori believe, is neither a fundamental element of the definition of modernity, nor of those of "capitalism" and "socialism" (see for further details Rambaud and Richard, 2022a).

Conclusion of the first part

Our historical study of the development of modernity has led us to favor the explanation of its origin in the emergence of modern capitalism at the end of the Middle Ages, a system marked by the invention of a new type of management, based on modern accounting. This accounting system has gradually taken over the whole planet. It is nowadays applied everywhere in the world in practically all the companies as well in the South as in the North, in the West as in the East whatever the political differences which separate the various countries of the globe. Whether these countries claim to be politically liberal, neoliberal, socialist or communist, they have all "dipped into the modern accounting bath." We draw three fundamental conclusions from this extraordinary situation.

[3] All of this therefore already poses a problem of definition: can we speak of capitalism and/or modernity in the case, for example, of common ownership of the means of production by the workers of a Scop? We will come back to this question later.

Firstly, it is wrong to accuse Europe and more generally the West of being solely responsible for this situation. Admittedly, the double capitalist party was indeed born in Western Europe, but it was dubbed all over the world in the years 1970-2000 with the IFRS standards in a global context where colonialism has practically disappeared.

Secondly, on the other hand, what must be fundamentally accused is the lack of will of many economists and philosophers (-but fortunately there are exceptions-) to understand the reality of the accounting practice of capitalism and the ideological, political and even philosophical questions that are linked to this practice. Thirdly, we must also insist on the problematic role of Marxist thought in this affair: not only did Marx and his followers fail to understand the concept of capital-debt of accounting practitioners and were unable to propose an alternative model to capitalism but they have at the same time (by focusing on a concept of capital-asset) put the accent on problems of the type of property which have nothing to do with the question of capitalism.

Indeed, as we have shown in our writings, any type of property can be well or badly managed depending on the choice of capital to be kept and the methods of conservation of this capital. This crucial error of Marxists and their followers is one of the fundamental reasons why capitalists have been able to prosper so easily by playing on the fear of peasants, artisans and small entrepreneurs of having their productive assets confiscated. Once these three conclusions have been drawn, we still have one question to settle concerning the appearance of modern capitalism in the West: why has this type of management not appeared before? This is what we will answer in the next part.

Part Two
Why Were Civilizations Before the End of the Middle Ages Not Modern?

Four main questions will be debated. The first is that of the existence or not of a concept of capital similar to that of modern accountants in connection with the practice of lending at interest in antiquity. The second deals with the influence of the Greek philosophers on the relationship of people to nature. The third deals with the possible existence or not of modern type of business management in ancient Rome. The fourth is concerned with the development of a new conception of capital and of interest which appeared around the middle of the Middle Ages: this will provide a clue to explain, at least partially, the emergence of modern capitalism.

Chapter 6
A brief history of the question of interest and capital in antiquity[1]

One question could invalidate our thesis of the specificity of modern capitalism which developed at the end of the Middle Ages with its particular concept of capital-debt. This is the practice of lending at interest. This practice is not only much older than that of the double entry but it is also accompanied by expressions such as interest is the "fruit" or the "small" of a capital which seem in perfect osmosis with modern financial capitalism we talked about. On the other hand, it is obvious that if someone lends his money capital at interest, it is because he wants above all to be reimbursed for it. Isn't this already the same type of capitalism as that of the founders of modern capitalism? This leads us to carry out a historical study of this fundamental question. The notions of capital and interest are indeed very old but also, major point, multiple. Very old because they date back to the Sumerians. Multiple, because they arise in very different contexts. This is clearly shown by an author like Hudson (2000) whose main theses we will first present, those which relate to the relativity of the concepts of interest and capital and to the dissociation of the commercial / financial spheres and agricultural one.

Relativity of the concepts of interest and capital in antiquity

Hudson starts from the problem of the etymological links between the words interests and "small" in various ancient languages, on the period going from the Mesopotamian civilizations[2] (beginning with the Sumerian period, followed by the Babylonian and Assyrian periods) to Ancient Greece, to end with the Ancient Rome, which leads to the gates of the

[1] This chapter owes a lot to Alexandre Rambaud (2015).

[2] These civilizations are particularly interesting because they saw the birth of the first accounting systems (Hudson, 2004b), with regard to the "Sumerian" periods, and the first forms of entrepreneurship in Assyria and in the Kingdom of Babylon, from 2nd millennium BC to 5th century BC (Hudson, 2010; Wunsch, 2010).

Middle Ages. His central thesis is that the existence of the terms "Mash" in Sumerian, "Tokos" in Greek, and "Foenus" in Latin does not derive at all from a metaphor of the reproduction of money (as in the case of modern financial capitalism), but from an analogy with a division of time: the metaphor of 'birth', of 'child' for self-interest actually refers to baby-fractions of time and not, literally, babies (especially of animals). Specifically, this author indicates "that a comparison of Sumerian, Greek and Roman interest rates and their terminology shows a structure that is not evident when one takes these economies in isolation. In each region the usual rate reflected the local system of numerical fractions, and especially the unit fraction: 1/60 per month in Mesopotamia's sexagesimal system, 1/10 in Greece's decimal system, and 1/12 in Rome's duodecimal system "(Hudson, 2000).Hudson goes on:" although the words for interest in Sumerian, Greek and Latin all have an association with 'birth' or 'newborn', what is meant seems to be the periodic accrual or birth of a unit fraction, not literally of young cattle or crops. It was the local numeric system's basic unit-fraction, that is, the smallest unit of the sexagesimal, decimal or duodecimal system: a 60th, 10th and 12th respectively"(Hudson, 2000). Hudson therefore aims to explain that the interest does not correspond, during Antiquity, to a return to a principal supposed to be productive and capable of reproducing itself (contemporary modern vision), but that it is only an addition, a supplement to money loaned, based on administered rules[3] (and not purely economic ones), arising from fractions of time. He links this vision to cosmology, in particular Sumerian, which conceptualized time according to loops, with regular rebirths (cyclical time), which also gave rise to rites of erasure of certain debts (clean slates) at each rebirth (Hudson, 2000). The link between representation of time and interest is, moreover, an element to which we will come back. Hudson further argues that "a mundane corollary of this cosmology was that, to the extent that payment of debts and the accrual of interest became important social phenomena, their timing was set by calendrical renewal moments. In the case of commercial debts this was the transition from one month to the next. In the case of crop debts, payment was made annually at the appropriate new year. In this way Sumerian debts were associated with the

[3] Most of the interests were collected by the Temples and Palaces in Mesopotamia,the two main types of public institutions of the time (Hudson, 2004a; Wunsch, 2010).

traditional birth metaphor for the periodic renewal of time. The monthly payment of a shekel - 1/60th of a mina - appeared as a newborn unit augmenting each month "(Hudson, 2000).There was thus an association between newborns (the little ones) and small fractions of time which 'reproduce' cyclically, punctuating the structure of interest.

The reproductive character is therefore that of time and not that of money, which is the exact opposite of the modern relation to the world, dominated by linear time, associated with continuous progress (Ariffin, 2012), as well as productive money in the case of financial capitalism (see below). From this perspective,[4] Hudson moreover draws a fairly convincing explanation for the stability of interest rates, stability[5] summed up as follows: " The rate of 1/60th per month-one shekel per mina- seems to have remained stable within Mesopotamia for over a thousand years, starting with the laws of the Third Dynasty of Ur, shortly before 2000 BC, and extending through the laws of Eshnunna and Hammurabi to Neo Babylonian times. Also stable for many centuries was the Roman rate of 1/12th, that is, an uncia (ounce) of copper per year on every pound, except when public law (widely flouted, to be sure) cut it in half in the 4th century BC. Greek bankers typically paid a decimalized 1/10th (dekate) on deposits "(Hudson, 2000). Thus, "the apparent chronological decline in these interest rates was an accidental by product of the numerical fraction system in each region, rather than reflecting economic rates of return or the debtor's shrinking ability to pay " (Hudson, 2000). Stability, followed by the fall in interest rates, was thus not an economic phenomenon during antiquity, but rather the consequence of institutional changes in relation to the division of time. In fact, the analogy "capital: interest" / "cattle: small" taken seriously has a negative connotation generally in the Ancient world. As Hudson (2002) points out," from Babylonian times through classical antiquity, usury was denounced as an exploitation of needy borrowers by the well-to-do, a

[4] See also Nitzan & Bichler (2009).

[5] We can also point out that, in connection with this state of economic stability, the "initial objective [of accounting in the Mesopotamian civilizations] was to provide stable value equivalences, and not to open the way to price flexibility in response to changes in supply and demand. Such fluctuations were seen as disorderly, especially in barley-based transactions and other crops at the interface of the land-based family economy" (Hudson, 2004b).

violation of the traditional ethic of mutual aid. In nearly all communities studied by anthropologists, personal gain seeking is discouraged, in favor of socializing individuals to support group solidarity so as to survive in a hostile world." In this context, we find Plato's famous words in The Republic[6] and obviously Aristotle's thesis on the sterility of money, a central thesis during the Middle Ages: "we are above all right to hate the usury, because it is a mode of acquisition born from money itself, and not giving it the destination for which it was created. Money should only be used for exchange; and the interest that one draws from it multiplies it itself, as the name given to it by the Greek language [Tokos] sufficiently indicates. The fathers here are absolutely like the children. Interest is money from money, and it is of all acquisitions the one that is most contrary to nature "(Aristotle, La Politique, 1258b - 1259a). We can clearly see here the problem that the reproduction of money poses for this author. This moral condemnation does not mean, however, including in the ancient Greek world, that the interest, the reproduction of money, were absent. Migeotte (2007) indeed emphasizes that "most men engaged in business were certainly unaware that their activity aroused the concern and the blame of certain philosophers [...] It is especially with the small shopkeepers of the agora that one reproached the spirit of profit and dishonesty." The individuals concerned by this type of practice were in fact mainly non-citizens (Finley, 2007; Migeotte, 2007), such as slaves or metics (foreigners domiciled in a city other than the one from which they come). Here we find a fairly constant fact during Antiquity: the practice of self-interest is a practice linked to "differentiation." Hudson (2002) shows that "he essence of usury is otherhood, not the brotherhood of mutual aid. [...] Throughout antiquity interest was charged most readily to outsiders or by patrons to clients –by the temples and palaces in Mesopotamia [...]." If certain Greeks, especially Athenians, could charge interest, but, within specific limits, on small loans in particular, as in the case of big adventure loans for maritime companies, they had as their first goal "to maintain their

[6] However, the usurers go headlong, without appearing to see their victims; they hurt with their money whoever gives them a hold among the other citizens, and, while multiplying the interests of their capital, they cause the race of the hornet and the beggar to swarm in the city" (Plato, The Republic, 555th – 556). The expression translated by "the interests of their capital" is in the original text the following: "πατϱὸς ἐκγόνους," which literally means the descendants of the fathers.

social rank, not simply to enrich themselves" [...]; "this is why, [...] they have been able to diversify their heritage, by doing business, without being in business" (Migeotte, 2007). Thus, in Athens, where, unlike the rest of Greece, the fact of having an occupation, notably political, does not prevent participation in economic affairs, the Athenian man is not chiefly motivated by profit but by power(Vidal-Naquet, 1990). In fact, Finley (2007) notes that "Eranoi [friendship loans], ransoms, prestige expenses" [...]" constitute the bulk of loans." As previously indicated, a few performing loans exist, but of low importance. Thus when a large sum was borrowed with real estate guarantees, "the loan was never intended to finance a productive activity" (Finley, 2007). This author explains that "there was no shortage of wealthy people, but not of those interested in production (other than agriculture). As soon as we turn to industry and commerce, the picture is the same everywhere, and always negative."In studies of ancient economics, "we see the desperate search of 'modernizing' historians to find something that they can unashamedly compare with Toulouse or Lübeck in the 15th century" (Finley, 2007). This fundamental differentiation of activities leads us to its in-depth study.

The dissociation of the commercial, financial, and agricultural spheres

A characteristic feature of ancient societies is indeed that there is a clear separation between commercial and agricultural spheres (Finley, 2007; Hudson, 2000, 2004a; Ingold,1980). So, for example, Hudson (2004a) explains, that in Mesopotamia, there are no traces anywhere of interest being paid in the form of offspring of livestock. He also mentions that interest in these agricultural civilizations" emerges only in the commercial sphere "and that the practice of increased interest seems to have been first invented in the commercial sphere of Sumer" (Hudson, 2000). In addition, "interest in Mesopotamia is linked to debts in silver money and not physical ones (especially not in terms of livestock). From then on, the first loans in Mesopotamia, mainly by Palaces and Temples, to promote the purchase of land, workshops, boats, etc, were in the exclusive form of money" (Hudson, 2004a). Generally speaking, in pre-Modern civilizations, physical debts were of a completely different type: they were unsecured, only unproductive but they generated a very strong dependency between the debtor and the lender (Hudson, 2004a). For example, as Hudson stresses, " anthropologists studying tribal economies have found that when cattle or land are part of the loan process, it is as antichretic collateral (that is, a pledge) that produces a stream of services or usufruct for the creditor. The essence of usury is that the usufruct is not produced by the borrowed capital itself. The normal practice in herding economies is for debtors to pledge their cattle to their creditors, not to receive cattle and prosper by generating a usufruct. The only instances of productive lending (defined as that which provides borrowers with the means to repay their obligations) are commercial advances to merchants "(Hudson, 2000). Thus, in the Ancient Greek world, with regard to physical loans in land, Finley indicates that "Land was not a commodity. Greek did not have a word for 'real estate' [...] There is not a single Athenian text to illustrate the modern practice of mortgaging property in order to obtain funds for building or for improvements to the property "(Finley, 2007). Land is therefore not conceived as a good for yield or a pure productive means, capable of increasing in terms of production (Finley, 2007). The studies of this researcher therefore invalidate a thesis by Arendt, supported in his famous speech on the crisis of culture (1954) and taken up by Pelluchon (2011 256-7). According to Arendt (1954-1999), unlike the Romans who were a farming people who took care of the land,[7] the Greeks would have been destroyers of the land [8] because of their civilization based on "the predominance of the arts of manufacture." This simplistic thesis of the philosopher, which consists in opposing agriculture to industry in antiquity, does not stand up to the objective study of the facts by historians. Finley, moreover, to clearly distinguish the modern perspective of capitalist traders from that existing in Ancient Greece, explains: "when Notthingham in the eighteenth century declared that the principal right of the mortgagee was a right to money, and his right to land is only a guarantee for money, the idea of collateral had finally triumphed in England. Behind this transformation emerges a conception of property according to which

---

[7] In Latin colere, the verb that gave rise to the word agri culture, means not only to cultivate but also to take care.

[8] Arendt refers in particular to a quotation from Sophocles in Antigone according to which plowing among the Greeks is "a bold, violent enterprise, in which...the inexhaustible and indefatigable earth is disturbed and violated." But this expression is ambiguous and can mean compassion for the earth as well as an incitement to violate it.

anything can be immediately transformed into money. Rather, the post-Nottinghamian English creditor [...] saw so many pounds hiding in the form of land [...] while his Athenian counterpart saw only land, and nothing else "(Finley, 2007). We would therefore have on the one hand a commercial / financial world, manipulating and lending money, and where interest emerges and is practiced - largely administered by institutional and cosmological rules -, without it being endorsed as a reproduction of money, and without the loans necessarily being productive, and on the other hand, an agricultural, physical, land world, caught in other rules, and other issues.

Armed with these elements, we can return at this stage to the "capital: money" / "livestock: small" debate. In response in particular to the posture of Paine on the assimilation of animals to capital in certain pre-Modern societies (Paine, 1971), the anthropologist Ingold (1980) confirms that "the natural reproduction of animal property and the social reproduction of capital" in pastoral societies (especially during Antiquity) is a (modern) myth [...]: "the fact that western society has found it convenient to base its categories for the social reproduction of economic goods on those for the natural reproduction of animate beings must not lead us to take what is no more than an analogy for an identity between these two processes." Here too, the cosmological problem of the representation of the world has often been overlooked. Ingold (2013), an anthropologist and specialist in ecological issues, provides an analysis crossing human and non-human questions, caught in ontological issues. He thus criticizes, for example, the Marxist vision (just like the Capitalist vision): "in Capital [the book], domestic animals are classified alongside primitive tools as instruments of labor. This, however, is to relegate animals to the status of mindless machines. In truth, the domestic animal is no more the physical conductor of its master's activity than is the slave: both constitute labor itself rather than its instruments, and are therefore bound by social relations of production. In other words, taming is not a technological phenomenon." Thus in pastoral societies (especially in Antiquity), the animal is not conceptualized as a pure object in the service of human subjects, as a pure technical means and, in fact, 'productive capital'. The relationship between man and domestic animal is based on a special reciprocal bond that permanently co-defines 'work', in a kind of 'partnership'. As Lewis &

Llewellyn-Jones (2018) stress"traditional top-down views of domestication present working animals simply as the tools of humans, but examples of animal agency are not difficult to find in antiquity. The plow ox and the pack ass defy their owners' wishes and refuse to carry out their tasks. At first sight this seems no more than a problem for the plowman or pedlar, but the stories in fact reveal some deeper truths. The tale of the unwilling ox demonstrates that agricultural work was a partnership: a farmer and an ox need to work together for a successful outcome. [...] just as with the ox, the pedlar does not turn to force to deal his donkey, but engages with it as an intelligent creature." We understand, therefore, that the physical world, whether agricultural, animal, land, etc is really outside of productivity issues per se. We find here the idea that modern capital does indeed historically come from a purely monetary underlying, and not expressed in terms of goods, and that this type of capital is reserved for very specific activities, essentially commercial ones. The ancient world is therefore very different from the one that began with modern capitalism in the early Middle Ages. But did the ancient Greek philosophers also play a role in this ancient conception, in particular in the relationship of their fellow citizens to nature?

Chapter 7
The influence of the Greek philosophers on the relationship of the ancients to nature

We will deal successively with the context in which these philosophers intervene and then with their behavior and their moral precepts.

The context

In most works on the philosophy of nature and even, sometimes, in some books on economics, reference is made to the Greek philosophers and in particular to their attitude towards nature. Nowadays, some philosophers go so far as to assert that certain very recent currents in ecological economics are directly inspired by the position of these ancient authors who would have had a position favorable to the harmonious integration of man in nature. On the contrary, others believe that already in Aristotle (Politics I, 8,1256b, 11-12; Physics, II, 8-9) "man is clearly presented to us as being the end of nature within a hierarchical universe where each level or each degree appears as the means of a higher degree, the whole being ordered in a final way to man and to man alone" (Afeissa, 2007,95[1]). It therefore seems interesting and useful to us to begin this section with a panorama of Greek thought in this area. The problem is that these Greek philosophers and their Latin followers did not all have, far from it, the same conception of the relation of men to nature. To try to see clearly in this complex question, we will propose an analysis of their main conceptions by distinguishing several levels and criteria. One of the nodal points, it seems, according to the most widespread opinion of scholars,[2] is their attitude towards the polytheistic religions of their time. In this regard, we can distinguish those who are theists or, on the contrary, atheists.

---

[1] This author cites Aristotle as the beginning of a filiation that goes from Thomas Aquinas to Kant via Bacon and Descartes (95-6).

[2] We refer in particular for the following, while possibly differing in their opinions on certain points, to Callicott (1992), Schrödinger (1992), Hadot (1995), Onfray (2006), Larrère and Larrère (2009) and Maris (2010).

In the *first group of those who admit the existence of gods* we can classify a clear majority of very diverse philosophical obediences including, in particular, Pythagoras, Plato, Aristotle, Epicurus, Leucippus of Miletus. Plato, notably, in Timaeus, marvels at how the Demiurge first created the gods and then three mortal races so that the sky will be "perfect enough." Maris (2010, 15-19) underlines in this regard that this perfection "manifests itself in the diversity of species and individuals that it contains" and that it leads to the thesis of the fixity and eternity of species within the framework of a strict hierarchy. She adds that Aristotle will follow Plato on this idea of plenitude thanks to this multiplicity of living beings and, under his influence, will inspire Judeo-Christian thought, notably Thomas Aquinas. However, we should already note that their conception of these gods is not necessarily the same. While the Epicureans, with their leader Epicurus and his inspirer Leucippus of Miletus, consider these gods as "gentle" gods and, practically, without power over men or the course of the world or interest in these questions, on the contrary, for others like Plato, these gods not only forged the world with a finality but intervene to criticize humans when they do not act in the right direction. These different attitudes can be compared to the very conceptions of the action of these philosophers by contrasting the "authoritarian" conceptions of Plato with those much more "liberal" of the social life of the Epicureans (see below).

The second group, that of atheists, brings together mainly, in addition to their founder, Democritus of Abdera,[3] Diogenes the cynic, Lucretius the Latin

[3] Democritus could have been influenced by authors older than him. Indeed, from the 6th century AC a Greek science emerged with Miletus, Thales, Anaximander and Anaximenes. These authors, who are often called pre-Socratic, have recourse to the notion of rational causes. Nature is then considered as a whole and is distinguished from supernature. In their writings there are no supernatural causes, "no Zeus who launches lightning" as Larrère and Larrère (2009) say. Moreover, their investigations of nature are not part of a cyclical time closed in on itself like Middle Eastern mythologies, but in a linear and necessary structure.This is the case with the Theogony of Hesiod: an anthropogony where the city is part of nature which is the only reality: this author is described by Naddaf (1992) as an evolutionist. Phusis then refers to what is born, which develops in a process of formation of the world and the result of this process. So a natural philosophy that asks the three fundamental questions of science: what is the world made of? Are things changing and how? What are the main forces at work? The Milesians (like Thales) are interested inthe first and reply that the world is made of liquid, Anaximander sees in it an apeiron and Anaximenes the air. All these

Epicurean and certain sophists such as Antiphon. All these philosophers give a priori a central place to man in the course of their affairs and, in particular, in their relations with nature. Moreover, these philosophers are not required to consider that nature is perfect and fixed: it can evolve. Thus Lucretius, from the first century BC, in his famous De Rerum Natura, maintains that ill-adapted species can disappear.

Another of the immediate consequences of this opposition between these two categories is that, generally, theists are dualists who believe in a partition of human reality between a material body and an immaterial soul (which survives after death) while atheists reject it: they are monists who consider the soul as inseparable from the body and thus will die with it. It is clear that these antagonistic positions will have very important repercussions on their concept of life and of action. This partition makes it possible to divide the philosophers concerned into "materialists" like Democritus of Abdera (their leader) and "spiritualists" like Plato: for the first all in nature comes down to material particles in a vacuum[4] while for the second the soul, immaterial, has a special fate, which obviously does not mean that it rejects all materiality of atoms.

Another consequence to be drawn from this partition, which will oppose these philosophers even more, relates to the question of the purpose of the world. For theists the creation of the world by the gods presupposes a creator who pursues an end and who therefore gives meaning to this world, while for atheists the world does not have one: it is in a way infinite[5]. This obviously does not mean that the latter deny all movement to this world but that they reject any objective given to it by a force external to it. With regard to this movement of the world we can more precisely, distinguish

---

elements produce three states in a continuous process without external intervention. Therefore a developmentaccording to an immanent principle, like the living. Anaximander also sees an organism but considers the being to be imperishable.

[4] According to Larrère and Larrère (2009) Democritus is opposed on this point to pre-Socratics like Parmenides and Heraclitus who see a perpetual change of substances. Heraclitus indeed abandons the question of the primordial substance (the arché) of the Milesians to focus on questions of structure and changing order. For him nothing is born or dies: everything is transformed.

[5] According to Larrère and Larrère (2009) this thesis of the atomists, following Democritus, will continue with Anaxagoras and, in the classical period, will influence the thought of the sophists.

three main schools. The first school, that of the finalist theists of the Plato type, sees a general movement towards the reunion of men with the Gods, shown as a model. In contrast, pure materialists like Democritus and practically Leucippus of Miletus[6] see only a chaotic movement of endless collisions of atoms in a vacuum. But between these two extreme positions appears an intermediate position, that defended by Epicurus and his successors, like Philodemus of Gadara and, later, Lucretia and Diogenes of Oenanda. It consists in thinking that the mechanics of the movement of atoms is not strictly chaotic but can be influenced by complex causes including those relating to the conscious action of humans: this is the famous factor of "clinamen." So if all the Greek philosophers agree on the movement of the world, they differ on the causes and consequences of this movement. This, according to them, is the conceptual framework in which men's action takes place. It is now necessary to see how they adapt their behavior and their moral precepts according to this context

Behaviors and moral precepts

We can consider three main types of behavior that favor three types of ethics: ethics of asceticism, hedonism or ethics of good, which however all have the common point of being based on individual research, or on a small-scale committees, of a form of happiness.

The Stoics (notably with Zeno), of a rather pessimistic or fatalistic nature, have a very particular focus on the forecasting of misfortunes, especially death. Without being theists, they regard the evils which occur to men as a fatality which it is useless to resist and want to prepare themselves as best as possible. They admit that anything can exist in nature, be it unfortunate events (natural disasters) or dangerous beings for humans (ferocious beasts), just like in the Heraclitean model with an eternal cycle. Their first goal is to harden oneself to endure these unhappy or dangerous situations, which can lead them to a form of asceticism by refusing the pleasures of life. Thus take care of yourself (prosiché) in the sense of hardening to keep as long as possible.

---

[6] Leucippus is theist but considers the action of the Gods as negligible.

The Epicureans, whether atheists, like Democritus of Abdera, or theists like Epicurus himself (but theists considering the role of the Gods to be negligible), favor a more hedonistic perspective. Their main criterion of conduct is also that of the inexorability of death and disease, but unlike the Stoics, this leads them to make the most of life, which is short. The pleasures of life are therefore not refused and even sought after, provided however that they do not turn, because of their excess, into suffering or loss of independence. After Democritus of Abdera, the initiator, Epicurus is the one who is the closest to the asceticism of the Stoics: his goal is first of all not to suffer and to end in ataraxia, this thanks to a kind of arithmetic of desires by seeking only those which are natural and necessary. In practice, as with the Stoics, it is first a question of ensuring the physical preservation of the body. But his successors do not agree with this austere pleasure. Thus Lucretia aims for a pleasure in life which accepts libertinism, however, as recommended by his Master, without excess. Some sophists like Antiphon practically share this type of hedonism with the aim of happy ataraxis.

The Cyrénaïques, them, like Aristippe, a character known as "couch" in colors, aspire to the pleasure and not to the simple ataraxia or the controlled pleasure. Conversely, *Plato and Socrates* (at least as seen by Plato) vilify these sophists and these pleasure-seekers. According to them the main goal in life is not ataraxia or happiness but good, virtue, justice and the salvation of the soul. Death for them is not that important and even, at least in the case of Plato, an excellent thing since the soul will survive and allow bliss, if its salvation is accepted by the gods. Physical pleasures are therefore to be prescribed or avoided: true love, for example, according to Plato, should be sublimated.

Thus, very diverse philosophies of life appear which lead to divergent social behaviors, especially with regard to political action.

Social behavior and political action of the Greek philosophers

They can range from total withdrawal to the most active participation, and in this case, from very different perspectives. Among the most radical supporters of withdrawal from social and political life are *cynics* like Diogenes and Pyrrho. They want a total break with the city. They even engage in social provocation by adopting "animal" behaviors (such as defecation or masturbation in public) and refuse any work activity, practices which obviously do not promote their social integration. This most often leads them to a problematic, if not miserable, life. In order to subsist they are forced either to beg or, if this solution fails, to accept strict survival occupations: Hadot shows that Pyrrhon, like Lao Tseu, keeps pigs. These cynics are the opponents of all legislation (nomos) and, more generally, of all the artifices of civilization. Hadot (173-5), for example, presents Diogenes as a Socrates gone mad, indifferent to everything.

The Cyrenaics, like Aristippus, also want to get out of collective affairs and live alone, but for very different reasons: to be able to seize the opportunity (kairos) of pleasure. As for the Epicureans, they do not share at all this provocative vision of the total withdrawal from society. However, they tend not to participate in political and social activities in order to better be able to concentrate on their quest for ataraxis or controlled pleasure. Thus Democritus wants to stay away from public affairs and asserts his distrust of general rules. His taste for loneliness and ataraxia even leads him to advise against starting a family in order to be able to be 'easy'. *Epicurus,* for his part, says that we must change ourselves rather than change the order of the world and criticize those who, like Plato, want to impose general social norms. However, less "savage" than Democritus, he accepts to live in a community, preferably free, and hidden in the countryside. He professes advanced social principles by advocating, in this community at least, equality between of men and women. But he only wants to participate in politics by instructing kings on the basis of his philosophical precepts. Lucretia, too, favors withdrawal to the countryside[7]. Only Philodemus of Gadara and Diogenes of Oenanda clearly admit participation in politics. The first wants to educate good kings and the second dreams of a community extended to the whole of society. Some *sophists* like Antiphon also find little pleasure in the social order, but for different reasons: the laws would be detrimental to freedom, that is to say to the nature of man. Indeed the sophists consider that what happens in the nature is the product of chance and that man must play with his technique (techné) to impose his

---

[7] Larrère and Larrère (2009,55-6) raise the question of whether withdrawing from the public scene to cultivate one's garden does not lead Lucrece to seek more the reflection of oneself than nature, but believe that it does not: "his ethics unites us to nature."

strength in a hostile world where competition reigns, which goes totally against the theses of Socrates.

But there is also a clan of philosophers favorable to political life with two schools that have very different justifications and objectives. The *Stoics,* faithful to their cosmic conception of the world, have concern for others (Hadot, 209). They therefore want to take part in political life for the service of the community. Not only, and this is remarkable, of the human community but also of a larger community. Indeed they consider that man is in harmony with nature and, on this basis, develop an ethic of "oikeosis," that is to say a perspective of the close, familiarity, kinship with others beings of nature. Nowadays some philosophers will even consider that they announce the ideas of the current of ecocentrism in the 20th century (see below). The *Platonists,* on the other hand, are followers of a community of life extended to the city on the basis of severe laws which are supposed to produce the order of justice and good. These laws, according to them, must be established by philosophical kings and their respect ensured by guardians subjected to a Spartan regime. As for the *skeptics,* they too accept to respect the laws but in a completely different spirit. Their goal is, like Democritus, to be "easy-going," but with different reasons: they feel that everything is relative. As a result, they even want to give up philosophy: for them no one thing is worth more than another. In this context as well, they believe, to comply with the laws.

Such is the extraordinary variety of behavior offered to us by the philosophical legacy of the ancient Greeks.

Several conclusions can be drawn from this brief analysis of their conceptions as well as those of their Latin successors. First, their attitude towards the Gods is extremely variable, ranging from total respect to absolute indifference, including a sort of neutralization of their importance. It is difficult in these conditions to say, on this philosophical basis alone, that among the ancient Greeks the characteristics of the Gods could have a general bearing. As to whether these differences of the philosophers relative to the Gods had any influence on the practices of their contemporaries is even more difficult to know. Let us underline, moreover, that the current of atheistic materialists, resulting from the ideas of

Democritus, can generate as well a pure mechanism which sees the cosmos (nature) as a simple machine with clashes of atoms in a vacuum as well as an Epicurean conception of the universe of a mechanism corrected by the clinamen: a conception in which man and nature interact.

It is therefore difficult, again, under these conditions, to make materialism, and even "Greek mechanism," a fundamental element of the question of the relationship between man and nature. Conversely, is it obligatory to think that the Greek theists would have a pre-established vision of the relation man-nature? "Pure" theists like Socrates and Plato seem to believe that man and nature can go hand in hand. But then what difference with the mechanistic theists "softened" by the concept of clinamen that are the Epicureans who follow Epicurus? What about non-mechanistic theists such as the Stoics? Should we conclude from this that the question of religions is not fundamental in the context of ancient Greek philosophies, even if the 'sophisticated' theists consider man and nature as adversaries?

Despite this complexity of Greek philosophy, however, it is often said that, for the majority of Greek philosophers of this classical age, man is part of nature and has peaceful relations with it. It is generally added that this would be due mainly to the characteristics of their gods: unlike the Christian or Jewish religion, these gods did not create man in their image and, therefore, man, a priori, has no superiority over the other members of nature. Plato and his followers, in particular, recognize that it is the Gods who rule the world and forged it from a perspective of concord. Thus, Socrates, in the Gorgias, tells us that gods, heaven and earth and men form a community, that they are bound by friendship, love of order and a sense of justice. The cosmos, in this type of philosophy, is therefore not disorder: it has a meaning, a purpose for the good of all its members.

In this context of osmosis between men and the rest of nature, the *Stoics*, as Larrère and Larrère (2009) underline, form a particularly remarkable current for their conception of man in harmony with nature. As we saw it, they develop an ethic of "oikeosis." But it is above all the Epicurean Lucretius who attracts the attention of philosophers who want an agreement with nature. For them Lucretius would take up the first ideas of the presocratics of phusis as an autonomous ongoing process and would like a pact with nature[8]. He would enounce the principle of fluid dynamics (everything flows) and reconnect with the ideas of pre-Socratics like Thales (focus on water), Anaximander (focus on vortices) and Anaximen (focus on air).The fundamental element of phusis would then be a *process*, a story, a continuous flow from which tangible bodies appear at random with two tendencies: one towards death and the other towards resistance to dissolution. Our human world, according to this vision, would be mortal but history would continue without it: De rerum natura, of Lucretia, does it not end with catastrophes including the plague which ravages Athens? It would still be a mechanical model (that of the foedera naturae) of a double natural humanity: biological(including soul, which is made of atoms) and historical, with a history of fears and religions that would allow them to be overcome while generating other fears. The physics of Lucretius would then be a means of making the history of fears and of substituting for these fears, like do it the pre-Socratic, rational causes. This would make it possible to distinguish what amounts to myth and to nature and to live in harmony with it in order to go towards ataraxia: to stand near the clinamen, to the small gap, to live on little with a few friends in a remote place according to an ethics of the local, in a garden. In short, a humanist and naturalist ethic, at the service of man, but not anthropocentric. But, as Larrère and Larrère (2009, 56) recognize, Lucretius's physics is no longer ours, although we can find in him the idea of negentropic resistance to universal entropy. Serres, meanwhile, is a philosopher who was very inspired by these theses of Lucretius for the writing of his book dedicated to the "pact with nature" (1990). He appreciates that in him there is something linked in nature and above all no anthropocentrism, this within the framework of a humanist position. But as Larrère and Larrère also say (id 233-4),the Epicurean solution of return to nature and to the local is no longer possible: even the garden is not immune to the greenhouse effect. However it is remarkable that this Epicurean school, despite certain influences a priori not very favorable to a conception of man linked to nature, such as the mechanism of Democritus, ends up developing ideas which favor a "pact" with nature.

[8] The development that follows owes a lot to Larrère and Larrèrre (2009, notably 53-6).

But, it would be wrong to think that all the ancient Greek philosophers were in the same vein. This is particularly the case with Aristotle, who is complex. Indeed, the philosopher of the Academy distinguishes between formal and final causes (while Plato confuses them in a single intelligent design) and gives a particular status to individuals who can pursue their own good: he advocates a kind of teleonomy in action[9]. Pellegrin et alii (Le savoir Grec p.17)quoted by Larrère et Larrère, 2009,42) speak in this regard of an autonomy of human being. For this philosopher, therefore, there would be room for manoeuvre for men to develop standards. Aristotle logically distinguishes the theoretical sciences ("pure" knowledge, such as physics) and the practical sciences (ethics and politics). According to Larrère and Larrère (idem, 44) he seems to push the decoupling between ethics (including politics) and physics so far that he "may appear in some ways closer to the sophists than to Plato." For him human activities continue to be part of nature because of the production and exchange activities which are essential. He therefore has a strongly anthropocentric and utilitarian view of nature (idem, 46). Taylor[10] (1981, French trad. 145) goes even further: he considers that "the idea of the inherent superiority of men over other species is contained implicitly in Aristotle's definition of man as a rational animal," and even that "this view begins to appear in the whole tradition of classical Greek humanism. Our animal nature has already been reduced to the rank of bestial desires which require order and the control of reason to regulate them. Rationality is thus, in this tradition, the key to our superiority over animals." He then believes that the Greeks "were not able to see that rationality is basically only one capacity among other of human beings" (146-148). In view of these considerations it appears that while "Plato looks at the sky, Aristotle, he, looks at the ground" (Larrère and Larrère, idem). It is this anthropocentric focus that leads Aristotle to consider that politics must first appeal to prudence, a

[9] Larrère and Larrère (239-40) believe that Jonas (1979) would have a comparable approach because he identifies mechanism and science and develops a metaphysical biology: conscious human finality would be the summit of an unconscious finality that affects all living beings and their flourishes in man: an ontology of the Aristotelian type opposed to modern mechanism. There would therefore be in this approach ends in nature, active teleonomies. But Jonas' goal is mainly to preserve future generations and to consider them as a subject towards whom we have a non-contractual obligation.

[10] See also Larrère et Larrère p. 240.

fundamentally human quality that he emphasizes, as we have seen previously. So, for this philosophe, the right decision is not in the sky. To make the right decision is for man to choose the right use of things.

With him we toured the main actors of this Greek philosophy which will mark the minds for centuries and still today. All these famous authors of classical Greece have one thing in common, however. Despite their differences, they practically all have the idea of a world without landmarks, except Democritus who anticipates the ideas of the 18th century mechanism. However, to conclude, it seems impossible to us to consider that they have the same ideas on the place of man in nature. It is even more difficult to say if their divergent ideas could have had any influence on their fellow citizens, especially on the farmers who represented the most important part of them. It would also be adventurous to say that the ideas of prudent management and good use of the natural resources of Aristotle could have inspired these farmers and even other professions more mercantile, all the more so since, as we have shown, these ideas are vague. What we do know, however, is that at that time the Greek economy was based essentially on two pillars: farms of independent peasants and slaves who worked for all citizens. In this context it was difficult to see the emergence of a modern capitalism of the type that we described before, in the first part. We have moreover proved, with the preceding developments devoted to the notions of capital in antiquity and to the dissociation of commercial and agricultural spheres, that the ancient Greek world is characterized by a predominance of agricultural activity which obeys to economic and moral principles that have nothing to do with that of the modern capitalists of the late Middle Ages. It remains to be seen now if the Romans changed this situation.

Chapter 8
The question of an emergence of modern management in the Latin era

We are going to see how the Latins, despite being reputed to be pragmatic and already much more "advanced" than the Greeks, both economically and technologically, never invented a modern management system comparable to that of the capitalists of the late Middle Ages. Their approach to business management remains anchored in a very agricultural and family framework which is hardly conducive to the development of a system focused on the subject / object relationship. However, as demonstrated by Petrazucky (1893) and Reichel (1901, der Begriff der Frucht im römischen Recht: the concept of fruit in Roman law) the Romans had already conceived, often in a remarkable way, the concept of consumable fruit by opposition to a kind of concept of capital (something to conserve), this as well within the framework of private civil law (case of individual farms, mainly agricultural) as even of companies law.

The framework of civil law

Roman jurists gradually developed a civil law aimed at preserving the different items of the owner's patrimony, first in the field of usufruct, then in the management of dowries and their restitution: it was a question of knowing what the manager of this patrimony[1] (usufructuary or husband) could consume or not (Petrazucky,[2] 227). At the beginning, the question put to them mainly concerns the management of herds and slaves. The first jurists to debate the problem, such as Scaevola, Manilius and Brutus, believe that when it comes to herds, certain fruits should be preserved. With regard to the party ancillae ('fruit of slave'), after some hesitation (Reichel, 219), the rule must be even stricter: it is that of systematic conservation. Later jurists interpreted the latter position as an ethical

[1] The term patrimony (patrimonium, which is the property of the father) is used to designate a thing to be used and not to be conserved.

[2] Referenced P thereafter except exceptions.

attitude inspired by stoic philosophers, but Petrazucky (245) believes that the solution was fundamentally dictated by economic motives: the fruit of the slave was not a regular fruit. Subsequently, with the development of the monetary economy, Roman jurists were led to define a much broader concept of consumable fruit, and this with even greater difficulties. Unlike the common people, they initially tended to keep the use of the word fructus itself to designate non-consumable things such as money (interest and rent received): this is how Cicero does not use yet the word reditus. But they too, starting with Julianus (P, 242), ended up making extensive use of the word reditus, especially in the Institute, keeping the word fructus only for the oldest texts such as the Codex (P, 240)[3]. On the other hand, under the pressure of the circumstances, they more quickly changed their vocabulary relative to the use of a patrimony carrying different incomes: while at the beginning they spoke of *enjoying* (frui) the fruits of a patrimony, as in the case of a tree, they will gradually talk about using it (uti), which testifies to the abstraction of the concepts of patrimony and income (P, 242-3)[4]. These principles will be applied in particular as regards usufruct. The fundamental rule is that the usufructuary (the user) can only consume the fruits (fructi), that is to say only what allows to leave the patrimony intact: this is the principle of "salva substantia." Let us underline the appearance of this specific term "salva substantia" which can be translated by intact capital and which refers specifically to the conservation of a thing. Although more research is needed on this point it appears that the Romans already made some distinction between things to be used (a patrimony) and things to be preserved: a substantia, it means a capital in the sense of classical accounting. Modern Roman jurists like Labeo and Papinianus will end up applying this rule of conservation as well to sets (universalities) of physical things (herds) as well as to a patrimony in money (fundus) (Petrazucky, 248). In both cases, it is recognized that the usufructuary is not obliged to reconstitute the patrimony identically but in

---

[3] It should be noted that when it comes to income from work, Roman jurists generally use a special word, that of quaestus: the quaestus is the 'fructus servi': fruit of the slave (P, 254).

[4] Note, however, that the words "brauchen" (to use in German), xraomai (to use in Greek) and fruor (to use in Latin) are related (P, 247).

equivalence: for example a number of heads of cattle unchanged[5]. This systematic conservation rule is, according to Petrazucky (116), a common-sense economic rule that any reasonable paterfamilias should observe. In the event of loss of capital, the rule, with some exceptions, is that of replacement (substitutio or summissio): any other consideration would put the economy at risk. Thus a good paterfamilias, just like a usufructuary, cannot consider that the animals he slaughters are elements of income if the herd is not reconstituted[6]. So, according to Petrazucky, Roman jurists appear to be realist practitioners: the concept of fruit (fructus) apparently allows them to effectively manage the economy. This all the more so since this concept of fruit can be in kind or in money: Reichel (224 and following), shows that a landowner Titus who has Coneliani fund can rent his domain and receive rents (Pachtgelder) which will be considered as fruit[7]. He underlines that we are moving to incomes (loco fructuum) which are no longer based on direct exploitation but on legal relations: it is the triumph of a monetary economy. In this context of monetary economy, income (fructus) can be gross but, more often than not, in most cases, net. In general, indeed, the Roman civilians of the Juris corpus, in particular in the case of the distribution of the monetary fruits of an inheritance, of a dowry or of a company, do not conceive that one can give back the fruits without having deducted the expenses (impensae) associated with the obtention of these fruits: "fructus intelligentur deductis impensis." They therefore devised a concept of net income to which, in late literature, they gave the special name of "reditus purus" (or "xatar prosodov" in Greek ecclesiastical literature). The Romans therefore generally deducted from the fruit (or of its monetary expression) the expenses relating to its production (impensae

---

[5] Reichel (215) stresses that to speak of the fruit of a herd is already an aberration ("monstrum der Herdenfrucht"). Indeed the herd is an abstract university (abstrakte universitas) (Reichel, 213). He adds that to speak of wool as the fruit of sheep is bizarre (213). Girard, 1906 (G, thereafter) (367) indicates that the edict of the lender obliges the usufructuary to promise to enjoy the patrimony as a good father and to restore; hence, artificially, a contractual obligation for the usufructuary. He also speaks of a systematic mandatory inventory (inventarium) of property during inheritance and guardianship, this at the time of the empire (268).

[6] "Si gregis usum fructum quis habeat, in locum demortuorum capitum ex fetu fructuarius summittere debet" "recte enim colere debet et quasi bonus paterfamilias uti debet" (§38 J.de rer.div.2,1) (P, 116).

[7] He quotes Ulpian: "mercedes a colonis acceptae."

fructum). For example, in the case of managing a herd, they deducted the cost of its feed. The usufructuary could then dispose of the net income subject to respecting the capital conservation rule (non-consumption of certain head of cattle to maintain the herd).

But this already remarkable conception of physical and even monetary conservation would fail in some very important cases. Indeed, in the case of domains with buildings, they encountered a very complicated problem. What can be done so that these buildings which are inexorably wearing out are conserved? The Romans then distinguished two categories of expenditure: expenditure on building maintenance, which they considered to be charged against the fruits received by the usufructuary ("impensae in fructus"), and expenditure on the purchase of new buildings or reconstruction (impensae in rem), which they considered to be the responsibility of the owner and deducted from his capital (P, 154). But this solution did not really make it possible to determine a consumable net income after conservation of the capital invested in real estate. Indeed their accounting was a simple cash accounting. Only, therefore, the maintenance expenditures were the responsibility of the usufructuary, which absolutely did not guarantee the effective conservation of the building insofar as simple maintenance does not generally make it possible to ward off the ravages of time[8]. It was the same for the slaves: their maintenance (food, care...) was the responsibility of the usufructuary (onus fructuum) while the purchase of the slave to replace the exhausted slave was the responsibility from the owner (onus dotis). Certainly, within the framework of this "cash" accounting, the Romans ended up distinguishing, within the expenditure on gross fruits, the current expenditures of production, maintenance and even transport (Ulpien), which were deducted from these fruits, and the extraordinary expenses of reconstruction or repurchase which were charged to the owner of the patrimony (capital) (P, 249). They had named these last type of

[8] This classic accounting problem will persist for a very long time, especially in the context of public accounting which will most often remain cash accounting until the end of the 20th century. See also in particular Lemarchand (1993) on the question of the simple maintenance of railway tracks which could not compensate for their wear. Only the modern capitalist double entry accounting was able to solve this problem thanks to the revolutionary concept of systematic and regular depreciation.

expenditures “necessary expenditures” (impensae necessariae) as opposed to expenditures relating to fruits (impensae fructum) which were qualified as useful impensae (Ulp.fr.VI 14-17). But that didn't answer the questions they were asking. We can first note that with this principle there was a difference in fate in the case of the herd and the building. In fact, by taking care of the herd and setting aside animals for its continuity, the usufructuary took account of the effective conservation of the capital. On the other hand, in the case of the building and the slaves, it only took account of their simple operational maintenance. Neratius, a very perceptive jurist, had already criticized the naivety of this classification but could not find a solution (P, 253).

Thus at the end of their remarkable reflections, the Roman jurists had ended up conceiving a very pragmatic concept of income,[9] in terms of cash flow, and already very elaborate. But the latter, as we have shown, did not make it possible to determine a correct permanent net income and even less a rate of return. The Romans did not have the concept of depreciation at the time or *did not have the motivation to imagine it*. Furthermore, they could not follow the movements of capital to be kept separately from those of "capital" to be used (the patrimony), for lack of invention of the double entry accounting system. This may be explained by their framework of life

---

[9] Reichel (250-254) believes that with their definition of the fruit in relation to a preserved patrimony and their theory of the salva substantia (Substanzschönung) the Romans define the substancia not from a materialist view but from a more abstract, philosophical view: the essence of the thing (Kernwahre, Natur des Dinges, cf substantia obligationis). According to his thesis, this is done with reference to Aristotle (his “ousia”) and the stoic philosophy of substance (upoxeimenon: what is at the base of the thing, das innerste Wesen). But he concedes that this ontological vision was too theoretical for the Roman jurists: these jurists then gave it a concrete coloring.They put an idea of purpose (Zweckgedanke) into the concept of substance. For example, for the concept of fruit tree (Obstbaum): what is substantial for this tree is that it fulfills its economic function (wirtschafliche Bestimmung) of fruit tree: it is therefore a matter of a teleology conservative in an economic context. The substance of a thing in this Roman law is what is necessary to allow it to fully exercise its economic function. Hence the definition of fruits: income that a thing guarantees without its ability to fully continue its economic function being endangered. Based on this Roman definition Reichel (250-1) rejects both the theory of fruit which is based on regular income (that which is based on a restrictive production of a thing) and that which is based on the permanent return of the fruits.

The framework of the life of the Latin people and the agricultural economy

The word fruit (fructus), from the root frug, which we have just analyzed among Roman jurists, existed long before in popular language and in agricultural economics, the basis of Roman civilization. It had three possible meanings. According to Petrazucky the triple root of this word fruit referred to the whole of the life of the Roman: his rule of life, which is that of frugality, his goal, that of nourishing himself, and his means (objects) which are also fruits. The first meaning is therefore that of frugality, retention, economy (cf. Cicero, Verr: 2,3,27,67). Thus the life of a slave who does not consume too much will be called "frugi vitae or bonae frugi." This first meaning, according to Petrasucky, would be due to the fact that for the oldest Romans, these small farmers who are not very rich, frugality is required in the management of property. But, with economic development, we see the emergence of a second meaning that we find in the root "frui" and which is that not only to feed but also to enjoy. Note that the German verb "freuen" refers to jouissance while the French word fruit does not have this connotation. Finally, in an even later meaning, the word fructus was used to designate concrete products coming first from trees, then from plants and even from harvests (hence the word frumentum which is found in French froment): here we are already in a rule of life oriented towards more elaborate agricultural management where the initial frugality gives way to that of management with a good paterfamilias (father): we no longer speak of frugi vitae but of homo diligens (Petrasucky, 224). We note, however, that the term frugi vitae will remain the hallmark of the attitude of slaves (ibid). There are therefore two distinct types of life in "modern" Roman times. The fact that the word fruit in everyday language no longer designates the product of trees but that of broader sources, such as wheat, shows that it is becoming an abstract concept. Petrasucky (225) points out, however, that the extension of the concept does not initially concern young animals: there is no question then of considering them as fruits. The Romans use the term "fetus pecorum" for them, just as for slaves who give birth we speak of "partus ancillarum." Indeed they are well aware that if they "consume" the newborns without thinking about the reconstitution of the herd the economy will perish. When the monetary economy develops and a monetary or rental patrimony appears the Romans, accustomed to seeing concrete things in fruits, will have difficulty using this word fruit to speak of rents (mercedes) or of interest (usurae): the "fruits" of these new types of financial patrimony are indeed strange. They will then "forge" the word reditus which will gradually replace that of fructus to characterize all the consumable income of any patrimony (P, 239)[10]. It was on the basis of this evolution of popular language that Roman jurists forged their remarkable concepts and terminology. But before them, in popular agricultural activity, the notions of fruit and patrimony were mainly linked to problems of conservation of the children of animals and possibly of the children of slaves who were assimilated to them. In any case, we are still a long way from the goals, techniques and applications of the modern capitalists of northern Italy in Datini's time. But there were also in Rome associations much more "evolved" towards modernism than the small agricultural holdings: the companies.

The question of management in the context of Roman companies

Trumpler (Die Geschichte der römischen Gesellschaftsformen, 1906, 1-6) shows that in ancient Rome, at the beginning, the only company is the community of goods (CG) which is established in the form of a community of inheritance between the brothers (cohederes) at the time of the father's death: the "heredes" then become "patres" with land, slaves and herds to be managed (see also Del Chiaro 1928, 9-10). At that time, in this case, there is joint possession and it can only be broken by a special legal action (actio fundiliae erciscundae) which results in a distribution of the inheritance. But, in principle, the cohederes stay together with jus fraternatis relationships and continue family life together in the house. Wieacker (1966, 130),(W later), shows that these family companies are not established on the basis of a contract but by legal obligation with the swearing of the blood of the members before the praetor which obliges them to respect a rigorous solidarity.

[10] It is this term repeated that will be borrowed by many European peoples to designate the net products of the activity: income, revenue, rendita.

What particularly interests us is that, in this context, as Wieacker emphasizes, the cohederes do the accounts only in the event of a liquidation, otherwise they do not count, notably, no doubt, because the asset base is family property that is not valued. According to Wieacker and Del Chiaro (1928) (DC later) it is this type of family community that will later be the basis of the Societas Omnum Bonorum (SOB), the fundamental society of Roman law. This kind of company no longer brings together men from the same family but partners who know each other well, without necessarily being parents. Thus the SOB will borrow the features of the family company (the consortium) (W, 113,194). Del Chiaro shows that, generally, in these SOBs, at the origin at least, there is an equality of contributions as in the case of relations between brothers. As such, Papinien qualifies the SOB as a voluntary consortium (DC, 148). In the beginning, moreover, there may be an SOB with the children of brothers and however common goods. Of course the SOB has differences with the family company, in particular the need for a contract, and the dissolution in principle in the event of the death of a partner. This whereas one can only leave the consortium by action "familiae erciscundere" as in the law of the twelve tables (DC, 11). But this SOB retains features of the family community of goods (CB). In fact, it is a joint property with a jus fraternatis of socii and an equality of shares in the event of sharing (actio communi dividendo). Del Chiaro (118) says that in an SOB the partners bring all their fortune, with contributions probably equal to the origin.

So, at the beginning, the Roman partnership contract was not a capitalist type contract but a community with co-ownership constituted for the realization of a service. Even in Justinian's time the goal was not to share profits but mutual assistance. This society is a community of partners and goods, formed by contract (of common life), in which debts are common. It is a group of individuals, not a legal person (DC, 222). Another peculiarity that sets it apart, and which testifies to a certain degree of openness, is that the co-owners can be workers. But what shows the community character is that this contributor of labor is also entitled to share the patrimony at the end of the company (DC, 12). We are then dealing with a company for the common use of things and not a simple company of co-owners. Things

(Sachen) are res communis[11]. In this framework there is a community of gains and losses (DC, 15). Another striking feature of this type of company is that the determination of an actual net income is made at the end of the life of the company, at the time of the liquidation of assets (DC, 135). This actual final result is then obtained by making the difference between the value of total assets and the amount of final debts. This is through the action of the praetor known as "separantur communi dividundo," and not the prosocio action (DC, 276). Liquidation, which only targets tangible property, is therefore the only means that allows a firm to be given value (DC, 281). The death of a partner leads in principle to dissolution except, (Justinian's right), if it is provided for by contract and continuation of a new company (DC 294). Hilaire (1986,169) insists on "the personal character of the company," on the "participation of all the partners in the management" and on the fact that affectio sociétatis involves the risk of dissolution of the company by unilateral will.

Thus, all Wieacker and Del Chiaro, Trumpler and Hilaire show that at the beginning Rome was an agrarian state (Agrarstaat) with family businesses in form of companies of co-owners.

But, with the orientation towards commerce, we will see the development of particular types of companies, adapted to this evolution. These include publican companies (SP),[12] first public, then private. According to Del Chiaro (25), they would be the ancestors of commercial companies and of all current modern capitalist company law. This author also claims that they are the earliest examples of commercial companies (53). What is more, they can have legal personality (DC, 223) with partners who are only responsible for losses in the limit of their share of capital (idem, 227). Indeed Del Chiaro (81) also shows that these companies have a social capital distinct from the patrimony of the partners and that they are not dissolved by death of the partners. In addition, they may admit unassociated contributors. We would therefore, according to this thesis, have a sudden transition from the old SOB to a form of capitalist company

[11] Cicero (Pro roscio) speaks of the slave Panurge brought by Fannius while Roscius brings his talent. Del Chiaro (119 -12) shows that Gaius admits the contribution in industry: "opera alicujus pro pecunia valet."

[12] The first mention of such companies dates back to 215 BC (Livius).

comparable to the shareholders companies nowadays. But this thesis of the sudden evolution of Roman societies is not shared by Wieacker (237-8). The latter proposes another longer and more complex evolution with four types of increasingly capitalist SOBs. First, a pre-capitalist type of partnership: the "Quae ex quaesta veniant" SOB which has a long-term management. Then short-term companies oriented towards the search for short-term profit: the "Societas unius negotii" as well as the company "Operarum," wich allow the hiring of salaried workers. Then the "Vectigalium" type companies whose object is the execution of tax receipts under an agreement with the State (Steuerpacht). And finally the famous publican companies (PC) which are no longer SOBs at all.

According to Wieacker (261) the nodal point in this evolution is the time of Servius when the principle of equal distribution between associates, that is to say equal shares per head (Kopfteile), is undermined. Hence the unevenly distributed profits and losses and therefore a totally different philosophy of management and economic calculation. This would be another view of the evolution of Roman societies. But this other view does not question that there was a kind of revolution with the emergence of publicans societies. The latter, indeed, anticipate modern capitalist societies on certain points. But, whatever the debate, there remains in all cases a stable element which characterizes all these types of possibly capitalist companies: whatever their forms, the calculation of their results (incomes)is never done permanently, as it may already be the case of modern capitalists like Datini in the 14th century: it is always carried out during the final *liquidation* of these companies by comparing the value of the assets liquidated at the end of their life with the initial stake. Thus Mucius always calculates the profit as the difference between two initial and final "stakes," this during the actual final liquidation[13]. So even the Romans, assuming they really needed it, which is not obvious from their agriculture-based society, never invented the "weapon" of modern double-entry bookkeeping. It was not until the Middle Ages that the conditions for such an invention appeared, which leads us to the next point.

[13] Whereas modern capitalists will invent a sort of periodic fictitious liquidation or a succession of periodically renewed company contracts.

Chapter 9
The emergence of new concepts of capital and interest towards the end of the Middle Ages[1]

The Middle Ages obviously inherited the conceptions of antiquity, notably Greco-Latin. In particular, the central medieval doctrine rests on the Aristotelian perspective of prudence and hostility to chrematistics. On the other hand, "capital" (in the economic sense of the term it means assets), in the form of "pars capitalis," is exclusively money lent. Under these conditions, the question of interest raises two issues and even two definitions. Interest, which merges with usury, is, from a purely practical point of view, anything that exceeds the principal, it means the money lent (Wood, 2002): it is thus opposed to the notion of "pars capitalis" or of "caput pecuniae."

But the interest also lies in an attitude: the desire to have more than what one has lent (Wood, 2002). In line with ancient representations, the interest is therefore not linked to a problem of return on "capital" (or principal). In its medieval sense of surplus, interest was condemned as early as the 4th century (Wood, 2002). The reasons for his ban can be summarized as follows (Wood, 2002):

1. interest corresponds to the sale of something that does not belong to the usurious lender: time, which belongs to God;
2. money is sterile and therefore cannot reproduce: only animals have this possibility and an animal never reproduces in the same way, but in a different form;
3. the interest corresponds to a double "sale": that of the principal and that of the use of the principal. Indeed, money is considered to be fungible. Now, a fungible thing is consumed during its use; one cannot therefore separate the use of the property, unlike land for example. Under these conditions, " the usurer selleth together the

[1] This chapter also owes a lot to Rambaud (2015).

thing that he lendeth and the use of the thing and therefore usury cometh of selling of the use "(Wood, 2002,10);

4. money should only be used for exchanges and not for loans, so to collect interest is to use the money incorrectly;
5. interest breaks a balance, that of the fair price: " the rapacious merchant and the usurer both violated justice by ignoring the balance between the two parties. The difference was that the price agreed by the sale contract was the result of free bargaining, and was assumed to be just. In the case of a loan contract, however, there was little opportunity for bargaining. The borrower had to take it or leave it " (Wood, 2002);
6. Interest corresponds to the grabbing of a profit obtained by work, not by being inactive: only activity makes it justifiable.

Several of these reasons clearly refer to western Christian cosmology, that of the western middle ages. This cosmology is indeed based on the notion of Caritas (Le Goff, 2010; Wood, 2002). As Le Goff (2010) underlines: "medieval western society is dominated by religion and by the church [...] In the western Middle Ages, money was not therefore an economic entity: its nature and its use come under other conceptions. [...] If friendship, love, caritas, peace existed in ancient Rome and still exist here, the realities that these words covered in the Middle Ages are not at all the same. These are different social logics which each have their own coherence. [...] The economy does not exist [...] but only an economy of charity [internal to Caritas]. [...] In this system, the only event that can be compared to those today is bankruptcy, and indeed, most of the establishments that were called banks in the Middle Ages went bankrupt. As for money, or rather currencies, cash is used for the communication of goods which is an expression of charity." Therefore, the fact that time belongs to God (reason 1) or that money cannot be reproduced (reason 2) comes directly from this idea of Caritas. Reason 5 refers to an ideal of a fair price, of a fair measure. In this connection, we can note that this notion is itself taken from the internal logic of Caritas. As Guerreau (2013) underlines, the notion of mensura in the Middle Ages "combines [in general] a quantitative consideration (moreover rather crude) with a prescriptive aim, one would be tempted to say axiological." Thus, while "[...] in our system of representation, the link between concrete quantitative aspect and metaphorical moral aspect is conceived, and functions, under the regime of the arbitrary and the optional, in the medieval system, on the contrary, the two aspects were structurally linked and inseparable." The mensura is therefore not based on a dichotomy between what is objective and what is subjective, central questioning of modern thought[2] (Latour, 1997). The search for a fair measure, a fair price is based on the search for a 'good order', in connection with the good Christian life. The balance of justice is therefore not a simple metaphor, it is an intrinsic dimension of the experience of medieval life. As Guerreau (2013) underlines the number is moreover apprehended, in this medieval universe, as the main model in the mind of the Creator, as thus sharing "[…] eternity with God […] or part of his plan of creation." It is thus "[...] on the side of the intellectus and the spiritus, this substantia higher than the lux itself" (Guerreau, 2013). The number is therefore a spiritual substance: it is not a rational entity but a fundamental constituent of the Cosmos. Thus the right price is well embedded in Western Christian cosmology and cannot be confused with the search for an objective and / or socially accepted price.

These are the fundamental rules which in principle lead to a condemnation of the interest. However, it should be noted that certain types of interest, in the sense defined above, as simple excess of the principal, were nevertheless accepted in the Middle Ages (and this in line with Roman law),to restore a balance: in particular a fair measure granted to the lender

[2] Modern measure can be defined as follows: "1) The various meanings [of the term] are perceived as different and each used without the relation to the others even being underlying; 2) Physical, objective, precise and universal measurement constitutes the semantic center of gravity of the word […] current languages are organized to implement the best possible distinction, univocity is the ideal" (Guerreau, 2013). This perspective is directly opposed to that of the "mensura," in which: "1). the totality of the meanings that can be identified forms a compact whole, fairly clearly articulated, but where precisely each use, with the nuance specific to the context, is incomprehensible if one does not see that the totality of the structure is at stake at each moment, the meaning resulting precisely from the interaction between the various aspects 2). The center of gravity of this term resides in the relationship between a physical appreciation, rather approximate and relating only to a few categories of objects, and a consideration of the good order of things, a good order which refers, directly or indirectly, to this which is considered as a divine prescription […].. The ideal lies in the linking of diverse and hierarchical perspectives [… and] could perhaps be defined as a search for the systematic leafing through of the senses'" (Guerreau, 2013).

in the event of default by the debtor. In fact, as Wood (2002) underlines the very term interest originates etymologically from this perspective: interest "meant something which is between [Inter-est]: it meant difference [...] and payment to restore the balance of justice."

But, at the end of the Middle Ages (from the 13th century), as we have already sketched at the very beginning of this book, a set of converging conceptions will substantially modify these doctrines and initiate the passage to the modern concept of capital. Among these more or less conscious or clearly defined revolutions, we can retain two fundamental elements:

1. the emergence of the subject (De Libera, 2015) in the 13th century, resulting in a self-awareness, a new awareness of his individuality, no longer relational (Sahlins, 2009) but more atomic, more introspective too. Aho (2005) moreover makes this introspective vision of man (and in particular of the merchant) one of the foundations for the appearance of the "double entry" in accounting, as an expression of a sort of market confession, of "business scruples."
2. The idea that time does not really belong to God, but ultimately (or more and more) to men, which calls into question the reason 1 for the ban on interest.

The consequences of these postures are multiple and will lead to modernity, through the Renaissance. The point 2, relating to the control of time by man, will give rise to the humanist idea that man is master and architect of his destiny, which will draw the outlines of the central notion of progress,and of linear time (Ariffin, 2012). The point 1, the emergence of the subject, results in a new awareness of property, law, etc. Thus social phenomena will be considered in the light of the emerging subject and his individuality. In particular, as Robert (2013) points out, "to explain how Caritas (the cornerstone of western Christian cosmology according to Le Goff) can vary from individual to individual [...] theologians of the 13th / 14th century were among the first to accept [...] the quantification of qualities prohibited by Aristotle." Thus, continues Robert, "as a quality of the soul, charity is susceptible of more or less independent of any bodily quantity." Caritas, a central principle arising from the Christian imagination and referring to a life experience, then becomes an individualized attribute of emerging subjects: this individual charity is then subject to the subjective variations of these subjects and it is advisable to establish a measure for it. While Caritas was not individual but a cosmological link between Christians, it is reduced to a personal subjective quality, subject to inter-individual variations.

All this will lead, according to Robert, to the new physics developed as early as the 14th century at Merton College (Oxford) based on "[...] the use of the mathematical theory of proportions to consider a calculation of qualitative variations." It will serve as a basis thereafter for Newton's work. Among the directly visible consequences of the development of the subject in the Middle Ages we can mention the fact that new links appear between possession, work and individual subjects. For example, a perspective defended by some late Middle Ages theologians, in anticipation of Locke's ideas, was that man, by joining the work of his body to something, made it his property (Wood, 2002). In this reflection, the mendicant orders, and in particular the Franciscans, will have an important role. Todeschini (2017) explains that among the central players in the transition from western Christian cosmology to modern thought, we find these Franciscan orders which will make Caritas evolve towards a more materialist vision, where the use of things will become central. They are in fact redefining the virtues of poverty through very specific "good management" of the uses made of things. It was about "making use of things to dominate and know them." This, according to Wood (2002), will lead to the idea that possession is the work of God (who owns the Earth and its resources) and that Men manage in "holding by stewardship […]the Pope or the King being able to ensure the role of an intermediary between God and the Christians administering the earth." These concepts are associated with the notion of "work and industry," introduced by Guillaume d´Auxerre (1150 - 1230). *I*ndustry corresponds to the intellectual and entrepreneurial capacity of Christians (especially merchants), able to make good use of things (Todeschini, 2017). It is thus through work and industry, terms adopted overwhelmingly by the Franciscans in particular, that it is possible to properly manage the things of this world and to derive 'good profit' from them. As the Franciscan Richard of Middleton (1249 - 1308) points out, " of a sterile thing no one ought to demand a fruit, but money of itself is sterile thing, for it can bring forth no fruit except by the labor and solicitude of the user; therefore you ought not to demand any fruit of your money if you have neither labored nor been solicitous for that profit "(Wood, 2002). Industry is therefore the escape route from the sterility of money. In these conditions, we see a shift in the meaning of the concept of capital. Indeed, Bernardin de Siena (1380 - 1444), another Franciscan, known for his work Tractatus de contractibus et usuris where he justifies private property and defends the place of the entrepreneur in the Christian world, declares: "money was truly worth more to its owner than itself because of the industry with which he would have use it [...] and therefore the receiver of the money not only deprives the owner of his money, but also of all the use and fruit of exercising his industry in it and through it "(Wood, 2002). Thus, according to this thesis, totally contradictory with the previous Christian doctrine, the borrower withdraws by the loan not only the principal but also all that it would have been possible to do with labor and industry of this principal by the lender. In this conceptual revolution, we cannot fail to recognize here a beginning of "economic" reflection in terms of opportunity cost. But Bernardin de Siena goes even further (at least as far as our questions are concerned): he explains that the lender should get more in return (therefore an interest) because, as indicated above, he could have obtained a profit with this money, and so he had to assume a loss of potential profit. And for this, Bernardin de Siena affirms that the lender "does not give money [pecunie in the original text] in its simple character, but also gives its capital [capitalis in the original text] "(Wood, 2002). Bernardin de Siena therefore introduced the idea, revolutionary for the time, that capital was therefore not simply money, it was money capable by "labor and industry" of producing a profit. Capital therefore becomes productive money.

Moreover, alongside the evolution of the very concept of capital, the 13th century begins with an equally revolutionary work: "A quantum leap above existing [financial] knowledge" (Goetzmann, 2005). This is Leonardo Fibonacci's (also known as Leonardo of Pisa) Liber Abaci, published in 1202. This book paves the way for the principle of capitalization and the mathematical calculation of present values (Goetzmann, 2005.The valuation of capital in the Fundist sense[3] of the term therefore also emerged at this time. It should be noted in passing that the Catholic Church has tried to resist these subversive ideas or techniques. Indeed "the Church's attack on the charging of interest was, in fact, an attack on exactly the kinds of operations described and analyzed in Leonardo's book " (Goetzmann, 2005). But Fibonacci's ideas were nevertheless to assert themselves and flourish,especially in the new modern capitalist world that began in the 14th century. It is therefore, according to Bernstein (1998),by conceptualizing another relation to time and to the future, in connection with point 2 mentioned above, by making them controllable and probable in particular, that Leonardo of Pisa will be able to really consider this way of approaching the calculations of debts and loans and offer new computational horizons to these capitalists[4]. His discovery of discounting is indeed fundamental to the future of modern capitalism. In particular, it can be used to calculate a theoretical resale value of any invested capital if we know the future profits it generates, or, more exactly, the operating cash flows (net of salaries, taxes and materials paid): for this, it is 'sufficient' to discount these future cash flows, on the basis of a rate of return deemed minimal (the famous cost of capital)[5]. This is how we proceed nowadays to

---

[3] This is the Fisherian theory of value (Fisher 1906) which conceives the assets of the company not as isolated physical things which are used for physical productions but as a fund of value generating interest, the value of the fund being calculated on the basis of the discounting of future interest that it generates (see in particular Rambaud and Richard 2015b and Richard and Rambaud 2022a).

[4] Goetzman (2005) points out, however, that "about seven centuries before Fibonacci Hindu mathematicians were calculating interest rates and investment growth. Thus,closer to the Fibonacci era and in a spirit very close to that of the financial problems of the book of this Pisan, we already find the work of Lilivati of Bhāskarācārya (1114-1185).

[5] For example, suppose for simplicity an invested capital of 1000 in T° and a single expected (future) net operating cash flow of 1320 a year later in T1 after total use of the invested capital for one year. If the minimum annual rate of return demanded by the capitalists is 10%, the theoretical value of his capital is 1320 divided by the factor 1.1, i.e. the maintenance rate to which is added the rate of return minimal. We then obtain an estimated value of the capital in T° of 1200. Thus from T° the capitalist could resell his firm with a profit of 200 because the expected profitability of this firm (13.2%) is higher than the profitability " demanded" by the market (10%). If things are "normal" ones in T1, he makes a profit of 320, whereas the normal market profit is only 100. The discounted super profit of 220 (220/ 1.1) does indeed correspond to the expected capital gain of 200 in T°.

calculate, within the framework of what is called financial capitalism, the theoretical stock market value of companies in order to compare it with their real quotation and to gamble on the stock markets. The theorization of this theoretical stock market value was only completed at the beginning of the 20th century, notably with the work of the neoclassical economist Irving Fisher, especially his famous work "Value and capital" (1906)[6].

But our fundamental question here is whether from the early Middle Ages the first modern capitalists knew and especially used this type of tool. For a long time it was believed that this was not the case and that it was necessary to wait until at least the 17th century to see practitioners or theorists of economics to grasp it. But Rambaud (2018), in a fascinating article, proved that at the end of the 15th century the Franciscan monk Pacioli, author in 1494 of a sort of mathematical encyclopedia for the use, in particular, of the merchants of his time (the Summa mathematica) explained how to use discounting to determine the theoretical values of an invested capital. More pragmatically it was to help merchants who were reluctant to enter into a business calculate the maximum amount of capital they had to invest (given the expected cash flows of that investment) to have minimum profitability. It is therefore clear that, from that time on, the most advanced fringe of these new modern capitalists had the theoretical and practical means to calculate the value of their business[7]. What is more, one of the most famous chapters in the world of this encyclopedia, chapter 22 devoted to accounting, which makes Pacioli the spiritual father of accountants, has certain characteristics which suggest that this avant-garde Franciscan monk would have a preference for a valuation of unsold assets (and capital appearing as liabilities) in terms of price value and not, as we have shown, in cost value. We have previously shown that with regard to their accounting modern capitalists, despite certain inflections, have never ceased to continue to favor this optic of cost value in order to be able to measure a "real" result achieved. This does not mean that at some point of history they did not start using the "Fibonacian" weapon, at least in

[6] However, from the 18th century Cantillon carried out discount calculations to calculate the value of certain agricultural operations (Richard and Rambaud, 2022a).

[7] Whereas, as we have shown (Richard and Rambaud, 2022c) for centuries and even practically until today, they will not use this tool to measure the value of their business in accounting.

companies. Indeed, practically during the 20th century, in these large companies they started to ask their financial services to systematically let them know the value of their business on the basis of the kind of actuarial calculations initiated by Leonardo of Pisa.[8] Thus was born the dichotomy between the world of accountants and that of financiers which characterizes in particular the large modern capitalist firm. It is clear that financiers (linked to neoclassical economists), over the past 50 years have had an increasing influence on the management of large firms. We can therefore logically qualify this "deformation" of modern "classical" capitalism with the expression "financial capitalism," a capitalism even worse than that imagined by the Italian founders of the Middle Ages. However, the double-entry accounting with its cautious principle of cost valuation that arose at this time was a landmark innovation unprecedented in earlier history, including by comparison with the ancient Greek and even Latin worlds.

Conclusion of the second part

We have just proven that, for various reasons, modernity, in the sense in which we have defined it, could not have arisen before the invention of modern capitalism at the end of the Middle Ages. We have also shown that this appearance of modern capitalism was going to trigger massive, systematic and permanent destruction of nature. We will now see what the reactions of economists and philosophers to these new problems has been.

[8] See Richard and Rambaud (2022a) for more details on this evolution.

Part Three
The Solutions of Economists and Philosophers Facing Modernity

First we will examine how the "mainstream" economists, whether classic or neoclassical, will "grapple" with the problem of modern capitalism's destructive relationship with nature. Then we will deal with the attitudes of philosophers facing these same questions.

Chapter 10
The reactions of economists

The gap between the modern "reality" perceived by capitalist managers and the real world will increasingly cause problems of sustainability of natural resources (NR). Economists will then have to deal more and more with the phenomena of scarcity of these resources. Their reaction will begin in the 16th century with the current of "sustainable management" of forest economists. But that will not be enough to solve these problems. Therefore, in the 20th century, new proposals compatible with modern ideology and neoclassical economics will emerge, notably with the famous "theory of externalities" and the lesser-known concept of "existence value." We will study in turn these three fundamental moments of the emergence of a neoclassical "environmental" economic thought.

The emergence of the concept of modern sustainability of nature with forest economists (16th-17th centuries)

From the 16th century (Williams, 2006[1]) and even more at the beginning of the 18th century, forest managers had to face problems of scarcity of timber resources. They will try to answer it with their concept of "sustainability" and will thus be among the very first economists to evoke the principles of more 'rational' management of nature. The difficulty is that, like the Aristotelian concept of 'good use', the concept of 'sustainability' is vague (Daly and Farley, 2004; Du Pisani, 2006; Jabareen, 2008; Gray 1990; Gray and Bebington, 2001). Basically, it's about knowing what we want to conserve, for whom, in what way, and at which level. But each set of possible answers corresponds to different visions of sustainability.

This notion appears for the first time in the work of H.C von Carlowitz "Sylvicultura oeconomica" (1713) (Richard and Plot 2014, 71). The author, a

[1]This author asserts that, as early as the 16th century, "the amount of wood needed to bake bricks and burn lime to build a house was greater than the timber needed for construction" and that "it was metallurgy that was considered the most destructive of forests."

German mine administrator, introduces the concept of sustainability (Nachhaltigkeit in German) in the context of rational forest management. From this perspective, woods should be worn with care (pfleglich in German) but with a particular concept: that of a possibility of long-term use (Grober 2014). It is true that, as we have seen, since antiquity, some authors such as Aristotle have developed a notion of prudence and care towards nature (Du Pisani, 2006) but none has developed a notion of sustainability associated with a concept of "sustainable yield" (nachhaltiger Ertrag) such as that of Von Carlowitz. This concept was first adopted by German foresters towards the end of the 18th century, then by other European countries during the 19th (Grober, 2014).We must then admit that the forest administrators, these 'managerial economists', saw the need for a careful use of nature long before the 19th century. Cournot and Marx are therefore *not at all the "first economists"* to raise this point.

The expression 'nachhaltiger Ertrag', associated with the concept of 'Nachhaltigkeit', was translated into French as early as 1820 as 'rendement soutenable', a type of yield which remains today a central concept in the management of the so-called natural resources (Conrad, 2010; Dedeurwaerdere, 2014). This is particularly the case in Anglo-Saxon countries with the concepts of 'sustainable yield' and 'maximum sustainable yield.' For Von Carlowitz, like his successors, the forest appears as a "collection of raw materials" where trees are "resources to be used" (Caradonna, 2014). This forest visibly corresponds, from a modern perspective, to simple objects: a cluster of trees, a volume of wood, a forest area, a rate of growth, a form of which it is possible to understand the laws of its growth and of its rational exploitation to meet the requirements of production, especially those of capitalist companies. It is then a question of "managing"[2] the forest in such a way as to make it last long enough to meet the needs of industrious subjects over a period planned by them. As Harrison (1992) shows, from the 18th century, "the Germanic forest became the archetype of the submission of a disorderly nature to the rigorous constructions of this 'science': this forest appears as a rational arrangement of trees. It is thus the reign of management based on the 'maximum

[2] This term goes everywhere being susceptible to several acceptances: we put it in parentheses.

sustainable yield'. This vision of forest management will inspire many economists, and even their critics, later. Flipo (2014b, 56-8),for example, will use this case of "economic" forest management to criticize the theses of Foster (2000; 2002) who attributes a precursor ecologism to Marx. He affirms indeed that Foster, just like his object of study Marx, do not have an ecological conception of the treatment of forests but a vision similar to that of forest economists: "Foster does not really problematize the ecological question: he remains in the managerial and conservationist perspective of the forest as a renewable resource and takes up the thesis that he attributes to Marx according to which the degree of civilization of a people can be determined by looking at metalworking." Flipo (ibid), moreover, also refers to works by Tanuro (2005 and 2010) on the absence of a real ecological theory from the part of Marx.

But back to this "science" of forest management. Let us transpose this reasoning into accounting language, the language that the large German forestry companies could very well use during Kant's time, especially in Prussia, one of the most advanced states in terms of accounting technique and legislation[3]. So the typical balance sheet of "Carlowitzian" forestry operations could be schematized as follows, limiting ourselves to the items that interest us in this analysis (without quantified data to simplify):

Assets (Means or objects)	Liabilities (Subjects)
Forest to manage (cost of use)	Capital of capitalist X

In this vision of long-term exploitation, and no longer short-term, the forest object to be exploited is now an asset and considered as an investment. The latter could be valued on the basis of the purchase costs of this forest increased by management expenses which allow its maintenance over the planned duration of its "rational" use (pruning, brush, clearing, etc.). The depreciation expenses for this forest would then be registered as and when the cut timber is sold. In the context of this reasoning, which essentially aims at long-term production of wood for humans, ecological issues, particularly that of biodiversity, are not taken into account (MacNeely,

[3] See Richard (2001) for an in-depth study of the Prussian Code of 1790 which, the first in the world, establishes an obligation for companies to practice depreciation of their assets held for the long term.

1994).One could, however, object that the solution for such problems of forest complexity could be solved by considering and entering more data in the calculation of foresters. But this approach still denies the fact that forests or biodiversity are entities with very complex ontology and a source of unpredictability (Maier 2012). To take this situation into account from a truly ecological perspective, these entities should be considered 'for themselves' as much as possible, which amounts to questioning the foundations of modernity and adopting an ecological and non-economic positioning of the forest, greening being seen as a not only social but also cosmological process denying the subject – object relationship, this without going back to the case of pre-modern civilizations. We would then leave the context of modernity with its subject-object dichotomy and its desire to impose its rational solutions on the world of non-humans (and even some humans). But this is not the path that the mainstream economists will take in the 20th century. In line with Von Carlowitz, they will continue to defend the precepts of modern 'rational' management of natural ressources, while incorporating certain inflections. The major contribution of this current consists in particular of the famous theory of externalities, which was developed in the 1920s.

The Modern Orthodox neoclassical approach to the theory of externalities

With this type of approach it is a question of achieving 'modern sustainability' taking into account the 'externalities' that the capitalist management of the company entails. To continue with the case of forestry, we can cite the example of forest degradation caused by industrial pollution and human-induced global warming. Problems of polluted forests, that is to say of hybrids, to borrow a terminology from Latour, arise which call into question the uses that man derives from these forests, even in the context of their 'rational' management. The notion of externality will then be invented by neoclassical economists like Pigou (1920) (Gladwin et al, 1995; Daly and Farley, 2004). It will be an illustration of a conceptual instrument - the key to modernized neoclassical economics which will largely influence not only first the economy but also, subsequently, management, including so-called 'environmental' management. We can even say that it will practically become the standard vocabulary and the essential, if not uncontested, reference of any economic approach in favor of the environment. With it the neoclassics have undoubtedly won a battle of words. It has indeed become very fashionable to invoke the 'internalization of externalities': it is the ultimate in 'environmental' management and it is even often a vocabulary used in philosophy of nature[4].

A rigorous definition of this concept is as follows: " an external effect exists when an actor's (the receptor's) utility (or production function) contains a real variable whose actual value depends on the behavior of another actor (the supplier), who does not take this effect of his behavior in his decision-making process "(Verhoef, 2002). With such a notion of the externality, non-humans disappear completely. By definition, the stakes are transferred to questions of variations in the utility (or production) of humans and quantification of the variables of their utility functions. The externality is therefore a very efficient purifying machine[5]: any hybrid problem must be divided, reframed, on the one hand into quantifiable, determinable and predictable variables and, on the other hand, into subjective or inter-utility functions (case of utility) or in technical functions (case of the production function). So the externality doesn't have much to do, to put it mildly, with non-humans or hybrids themselves, like pollution. It is not fundamentally a question of looking at pollution as such, its root causes, the relationships it implies between humans and non-humans and the measures to be taken to stop it, but, in the first place to the subjective appreciation of the economic damage which they entail, mainly for the subjects who have economic and political power in the capitalist world. As Pearce (1976), one of the few neo-classics to have the honesty to recognize the fundamental flaws in this concept, put it very clearly: "we need only remember that externalities are defined with respect to sufferer's utility functions, so that any physical measure of pollution may be positive without any externality being present: if people do not care about biological changes in species (or, indeed, in themselves) no 'economic' effect can be said to exist." Thus, with this type of reasoning, there is no externality without damage (or benefit) to the well-being of human beings, and this eventual damage involves a

[4] See notably Dalsuet (2010,149).

[5] In the sense understood by Latour (1999): apparent elimination of real problems.

primarily monetary valuation of these losses of wealth from the point of view of humans, a task, as we have seen, generally reserved for economists, and not for traditional accountants who gravitate in another world. Insofar as there is a damage to the wealth of capitalists which is often delayed in time,[6] therefore, in this perspective, massive use will be made of the concept of present value, in particular to quantify the costs of future losses of wealth due to future ecological phenomena. With this economic reasoning of the stock market type,[7] the economic decision in the face of the manifest and dramatic degradations of the state of forests and their biodiversity will be taken not exclusively, or even mainly, on the basis of the observation of the figures of this degradation provided by ecologists, but according to the subjective assessment of future economic damage caused by these degradations, an assessment depending in particular on a capitalist profitability standard. Transposed in terms of double entry capitalist accounting this economic taking into account of the foreseeable additional costs engendered by foreseeable future damages, assuming that it takes place, will give rise to provisions for depreciation of investments which will reduce the 'economic value' of these investments and, therefore, the profits of capitalist enterprises. In the previous case of our forest, its cost value recorded as an asset in the following balance sheet will undergo the following reduction corresponding to what is called a provision[8]:

Assets (objects)	Liabilities (subjects)
Forest to manage (cost of use *less provisions for externalities)*	Capital of X
Other assets	Net profit of X (after provisions)

Table 10-1 *Recording of the forest*

[6] This is for example the case of damage resulting from foreseeable long-term sea level rises.

[7] Estimates of stock market values are indeed based on expectations of future profits, discounted on the basis of a standard of profitability required by capitalists (see all finance textbooks).

[8] Unlike amortization, which is a definitive reduction in the value of an asset, a provision is an anticipated reduction in value which is only probable and therefore provisional, and can be revised and cancelled.

Insofar as decision-makers are in fact generally shareholders and managers of large multinational groups and the political forces that support them, these practices emanate from the fraction of the subjects who dominate the capitalist world. As the current actions of these actors show, some of them believe they can escape future disasters while continuing to enrich themselves, in particular by sheltering their families in Nordic countries believed to be spared from global warming. So there is already little chance that they will seize this type of instrument proposed[9] by the most advanced section of neoclassical economic 'science' at their service. But anyway, without placing himself in this extreme context, an entrepreneur who strictly applies the externalities model will hardly ever succeed in solving the ecological problems underlying the losses of utility, assuming he intends to do so. As Pearce (1976) and Ulrich (1977) eloquently show, the entrepreneur who will integrate externalities (-it means discounted future damages to capitalist properties) into his costs will not take conservation measures as long as the costs of conservation of the nature concerned are greater than these discounted damages. With such a reasoning we come to make the conservation of nature depend on the level of profitability imposed by the capitalists. Only a "miracle" could then change the situation of this cost-benefit method which is based, as its name suggests, on a comparison of the possible costs to be paid for the utility losses of the economic actors concerned. This miracle would be that the potential victims of negative externalities, with the help of legislators, fix the price of marginal damage at a level at least equal to the cost of maintaining the ecological function involved. In this case, and only in this case, the capitalists would have an interest in taking measures to avoid pollution and not to compensate for the damage assessed through the prism of subjective utilities. Pearce (1976) and Ulrich (1977), joined by Godard (2010), consider this miracle illusory and, therefore, deem that the internalization of externalities inevitably leads to a final environmental catastrophe. For them, the search for the neoclassical optimum constantly leads to a level of activity that exceeds the ecological limits that should be respected to ensure 'normal'[10] stability in the functioning of ecosystems.

---

[9] Especially if it is a question of long-term forecasts which these capitalists will be able to qualify as uncertain.

[10] See below for an explanation of this adjective.

But, despite these critical observations which emanate in particular from the very heart of neoclassical economics (and which are very little known to most people), the choice and the "hammering" of such reasoning by the main-stream economic explain that it has influenced a growing number of people who are interested in the environmental cause, in both the economic and accounting fields, if not the general public. In the economic field, we can cite in particular the works of specialists in 'green capitalism' such as De Perthuis,[11] who take as a reference for their reasoning the consideration of environmental damage and its impact on production. In the field of management, the main applications can be found in the work on eco-efficiency of Schmidheiny and the Business Council for Sustainable Development (Schmidheiny-BCSD, 1992),the approach of the "Natural – Resouce based view of the firm (Hart, 1995),the theses of Porter and Van der Linde (1995) or the famous "Triple Bottom Line" by Elkington (1997). In all these visions of management, mainly American ones, the goal is to manage to reconcile the maintenance of the capitalist rate of profit with certain actions known as 'environmental'. Thus, eco-efficiency is perceived as allowing companies not to act against its own financial interests (Savitz and Weber,2006). All these actors are well aware that they have to show that they are doing something for the environment in an increasingly critical context. To justify their concern for an 'environmental' response from capitalist firms, some of them do not hesitate to invoke, in the face of certain ecological movements, the threat of a (re) -emergence of a communist ideology. For example Elkington (1997) talks about the problem of "ecological communism" while K. Yonezawa, of the Japanese Global Guardian Trust, states in 1996 that " now that the world's communist movement has gone, I think that the only one circulating around the world is the extremist environmental movement of Greenpeace and the like "(Murphy and Bendell, 1997,148-9).

This whole philosophy of 'environmental' management is therefore based on the fear of claims from certain stakeholders harmed by capitalist practices, claims that could lead to actions for damages and, even more serious, on a questioning of the capitalist order. In all of this there is never a question of considering nature for itself. Of course, this type of reasoning

[11] Notably his "capital vert" (2013).

has its limits and is increasingly criticized, especially by those who have precise knowledge of the issue. It is for this reason that other currents, within neoclassical thought itself, will propose approaches that claim to better take into account the reality of natural phenomena. So it is with the economists who initiated the concept of existence value.

The Modern Orthodox Neoclassical Approach to 'Existence Value'

Existence Value (EV) is in mainstream economics the modern orthodox version of an attempt to take into account environmental entities "for themselves." We first present the concept before showing its integration within the framework of a total economic value and dealing with the problem of its valuation. To better highlight its specificities, we end this description of EV with a comparison with a very different concept proposed by opponents of the neoclassical view: that of "intrinsic value."

The concept of Existence Value (EV)

This concept was introduced in 1967 by Krutilla, a neoclassical economist (Hargrove, 2000). As its inventor himself says, this is a value that results from "the pure knowledge that a resource is preserved or continues to exist"(Krutilla, 1967). Strictly speaking, it is not a new value but the recognition of part of the usefulness of the subject which comes from the valuation of an object-resource simply because of the knowledge of its presence and condition. This conceptual contribution can therefore be considered as an improvement of neoclassical theory.

Krutilla worked on land management in the US and was concerned with the application of the cost-benefit method in the case of conservation and exploitation of land or parks (that of the Yosemite, in particular). Its perspective is that of optimizing the management of natural resources: it is about "providing for the present and future the amenities associated with unspoiled natural environments, for which the market fails to make adequate provisions" (Krutilla, 1967). This in the case of non-substitutability of certain natural resources.

Experimentation with this method dates back to the 1980s (particularly on mouflons and grizzly bears). There are many definitions of EV. Among them that of the WBCSD (2012): "value attributed to knowing that specific environments are preserved even if they are not used directly or indirectly." The UNEP (2013) proposes another definition which puts more emphasis on problems of price to pay: "it is the result of people's willingness to pay for something with no expectation that they themselves will benefit from it."

Hence a controversy among economists as to whether something not used can have a value in use and, in addition, give rise to a willingness to pay, therefore a monetary valuation. Note that although created within the framework of "environmental economics" this component of utility can appear for other types of resources such as artistic ones and even for any type of resource, for example an era of skiing (Epstein, 2003). Either way, this is a purely utilitarian concept independent of moral choices other than the utility of the subjects. With the "Blueprint for a green Economy" by Pearce et al (1989), EV will become a key concept of "orthodox" sustainability (Randall and Stoll 1983). Pearce and his co-authors stress that "environmental quality is part of the wider development objective of an improved quality of life." So it is not the natural (or other) object itself that is a source of concern but what it is capable of providing to the subject (gain of power, subjective gain of well-being, etc.). This type of sustainability requires increasing the "values" and in particular the motivations of the subject and his total utility. It is part of a larger concept: neoclassical total economic value.

EV and the concept of total economic value (TEV)

The neoclassical economic approach is based on an axiological monism: there is only one value, the value in use for the (economic) subject. But there can be various reasons for this usefulness. Hence the need for a taxonomy of these values in use. The general framework proposed is that of the TEV with its two main areas: use values (UV) and non-use values (NUV).

Use values are first and foremost, classically, direct use values (DUV) linked to productive and consumerist uses, but they can also be non-consumptive use values as well as aesthetic values. Neo classical economists also consider indirect use values (IUV) which relate to the enhancement of certain environmental functions necessary to maintain the use of the object in question. They even have conceived option and quasi-option values that can be attached to these use values. The concept of option value was introduced in 1964 by Weisbrod to take into account the fact that consumers might agree to pay something to have the option of consuming a good in the future and therefore to guarantee future use of the good concerned. The quasi-option value (Arrow and Fisher, 1974) is a kind of option value but in an environment of high uncertainty, in particular a context of irreversibility of certain actions leading to a loss of future use of the object considered. If the option value is static, the quasi-option value is dynamic because it depends on "the possibility of reacting to new information, independently of our current preferences and knowledge" (OECD, 1999). We can give as an example the potential use of biodiversity, in particular the possible discovery of plants allowing the manufacture of new drugs.

Non-use values (NUVs) concern three types of values: altruistic value, bequest value and existence value. These values can potentially be manifested in any subject even very distant from the good or the service in question. Altruistic (or philanthropic) value "is associated with the satisfaction derived from ensuring resources are available to contempories of the current generation" (Turner et al. 2001). Indeed, according to this view, the access of other subjects to the use of objects within the framework of intra-generational altruism gives the subject concerned more utility. The bequest value[12] is a kind of altruistic value transposed into the future in the context of an intergenerational altruism: knowledge that our descendants will use the resource in the future. Thus, in that case, subjects rationally derive a benefit, that is, an increase in their usefulness, with an unused object. This concern for a quality of life for future generations would testify to a "post-materialist" questioning (Inglehart, 1977).

But these new types of values cause some neo-classics uneasiness mainly because of the difficulty in differentiating them. For some, altruistic and legacy values are indeed use values but not for the evaluator, while existence value (EV) is the only non-use value. For others, altruistic and

[12] Krutilla invented this concept at the same time as the EV.

legacy values are also non-use values like the EV, the latter being, in a very broad sense, synonymous with non-use value for the evaluating subject. This last extensive understanding of EV explains the turmoil in neoclassical economics: recourse to altruism to explain value(Randall,1997) An object in itself (without use) could then be a source of special attention on the part of subjects! The only possible orthodox explanation would be that this altruism is not aimed at the object but at other subjects. Then the subjects – objects dichotomy would remain.

In this context, some authors cite two main reasons to explain the EV: paternalistic and non-paternalistic altruism. Non-paternalistic altruism means that the usefulness of the subject depends positively on the usefulness of other subjects who are users of the considered object: under these conditions the EV includes the altruistic value. Paternalistic altruism (the most plausible case for Mc Connel, 1997), is not based on valuing the utility of other subjects but on the services that the valued Object can provide to these other subjects. In both cases of these visions we see that the preservation of the object must ultimately rest on the use that can benefit other subjects.

To sum up, in a broad sense, EV would encompass non-paternalistic altruistic values and paternalistic altruistic values as well as option value and quasi-option value. Non-paternalistic altruistic value would concern the usefulness of other subjects in the present. Paternalistic altruistic value the usefulness of an object for other subjects in the present. The Option Value will concern the preferences of a subject in the future (low uncertainty) and the Quasi-option Value the irreversibilities relating to the evolution of an object in the future (high uncertainty). Hence the definition of EV: part of the utility function of a human subject linked to the maintenance over time of her/ his subjective representation of the essence of a given object (environmental or not), independently of its direct or indirect use by this subject, and that only according to the subjective representation of the purposes attributed to this object by this subject.This brings us back to Krutilla's original idea (1967): that of a representation of simple knowledge (see also Gowdy 1997). But this knowledge is not enough. It is still necessary to give it some substance. The next step for the subject which determines the EV is therefore to inscribe a mark on the object concerned (and not to enter into discussion with the other subjects): it is in fact a question of giving a monetary expression of the existence value.

Monetary Assessment of Existence Value

The usual method of valuation is normally based on the market. However, some goods, services or securities may be off-market. Under these conditions it is necessary to have recourse to the willingness to pay (WTP) or receive (WTR)) of the subject. The EV is typically located in this situation because existence services have the attribute of being both non-rival and non-excludable: pure public goods (Tisdell, 2004; White, 1996). Curiously, we would then be leaving the principle of capitalist property[13]. But the choice between the WTP and the WTR depends in theory on the question of property rights. If a subject does not hold property rights over a resource R, then it is relevant to know his willingness to pay to acquire a right over this resource, in order to guarantee an improvement or avoid degradation. Otherwise, when the subject has such a right, it is necessary to know how much he is ready to receive (WTR) to accept a degradation of the resource which modifies its utilities.

With this evaluation question we have presented the fundamental characteristics of the EV of neoclassical economists. To refine our analysis and better understand the essence of EV we will compare it with another concept defended by supporters of what is called Environmental Ethics, that of "intrinsic value (IV)."

Link between EV and the intrinsic value (IV) of environmental ethics

IV[14] refers to three main interpretations: first as a non-instrumental value, second as a value based on properties specific to a resource considered, and third, as a value owned independently of the evaluation of a human appraiser. This latter value is referred to as an objective intrinsic value

[13] The dominant neo-classical conception makes ownership of productive goods one of the fundamental characteristics of capitalism.

[14] Or inherent value (Callicott 1995, in Afeissa, 2007, 199) defined as the value that belongs to the essential nature of a thing.

(OIV). It is the one that truly forms the basis of environmental ethics. It appears that the EV can in no way be compared to the OIV (Callicott, 2005; Crowards,1997) although these two concepts are based on the modern attitude (see below). For the EV the subjects are human beings while for the OIV it is a question of extending the domain of the subjects to non-human entities. Thus, for the neoclassical EV the entity to be evaluated remains an object depending on the evaluation of the human subject while in the perspective of the OIV this entity is in itself an almost subject which "should not be subject to pricing of any kind, shadow or otherwise(Callicott, 2005).

So the EV remains above all a human subjective value (Turner, 1999): it is based on subjective representations leading to a subjective benefit for the human evaluator. On the other hand, the OIV has no link with subjective representations or any benefit for humans: the preservation of this non-human entity is a moral duty which is imposed on human beings because the essence of this entity must be absolutely preserved. Thus an entity can have a OIV without having any EV, as shown by the example of the rat inviting himself into Callicott's kitchen: there is a moral duty not to kill him, without any idea of profit. Attfield (1998-1999) does highlight the aspect of human quality of life in EV. It is thus an instrumental valuation of the knowledge that something continues to be present in this world, without being interested in the living conditions of that thing, its development. We cannot therefore assimilate the EV to the OIV (a non-instrumental value).

If we are now interested in the meaning of the OIV as a value based on specific properties of the object concerned, we must admit that this is also the case of the EV. The fact that this value is based on non-use then tends to suggest that the EV would be purely non-instrumental, even if the evaluated entity is conceptually an object. But on analysis, it appears that the question is whether or not it is possible to conceptualize a variation in utility outside of all use. In fact EV can be interpreted as a particular use value, a passive use value (Arrow et al., 1993). This value comes, as we have pointed out, not from the use of the object directly but from knowledge: from information related to the state of preservation of this object (Davidson, 2013). Instead of using the object itself, the subject would use a service rendered by the object: the information that this object continues to be in a given state, this level being subjective. This is compatible with the definition of EV that we have given: an EV as part of the utility function of a human subject linked to the maintenance over time of the subjective representation of the essence of a given object (environmental or not), regardless of its use and this only according to the subjective representation of the purposes attributed to this object by this subject. This view is reinforced by the fact that the EV is found to be extremely dependent on information brought to the subject about the state of the object.

In conclusion: the real EV is indeed this economic EV, partially instrumental, resulting from neoclassical theory, while other types of "existence value" like the OIV gravitate in the periphery of the economic EV but outside the neoclassical theory. Another example of such a neoclassical EV appears when a subject attaches moral value to the existence of an object because it is valued by another subject. In this case again, the preservation of the object is based on a priori respect for this other subject and not on that of the object itself: therefore nothing to do with the OIV which is based on a deontological approach to the preservation of an object. In practice, however, this neoclassical EV can neither be dissociated from an ontological questioning of the evaluated entities, nor be de-entangled from a tangle of different types of anthropocentric, non-anthropocentric moral, citizen relations, etc.. This makes permeable the barrier between objects and subjects, between facts and values, between individuals and society and between subjective and objective. We thus see the hybrid, relational ecological character of these questions within the neoclassical 'Orthodox' approach itself.

Accounting representation of the EV

We have underlined that the neoclassical EV remains in the modern movement with its subject / object distinction. What's more, it does not extend the domain of subjects: subjects remain humans only. In this context, an accounting solution for the companies concerned would then consist in taking into account the probable subsequent losses of the existence of the resource due to non-compliance with certain thresholds of existence of this resource. This deterioration would lead to the recognition of a compensatory obligation towards all subjects considered to have a right to these services (but not using them) on the liabilities side of the balance sheet, by assigning an EV to this resource. In fact it will be, for example, for the subjects of a willingness to receive (WTR) to accept a degradation of their former well-being due to the only knowledge of the integrity of a forest and the threat which weighs on her. We are therefore dealing with a modern balance sheet with an object / subject cleavage where the liabilities always refer to obligations towards human subjects. Let us take the case of a forest of which a firm would not be the owner and would not have the control either, for example a forest of a region of country Y which begins to be "concerned" by smoke from a firm X located in another country. Suppose there is no legal obligation on this firm X in this regard. As part of the reasoning of the EV X should recognize a liability on its balance sheet in the form of a provision (conditional debt) corresponding to the amount of the WTR estimated by the subjects of the region of Y and this even though these subjects are not users of the forest. The corresponding asset (which could be considered as expenses to be spread over several years) should be depreciated to take into account the annual degradation of utility linked to the environment (and not the degradation of the environment), knowing that as long as the pollution does not actually occur no depreciation should be registered [15]. The corresponding balance sheet could be as follows:

Assets of X (objects)	**Liabilities of X (subjects)**
Miscellaneous assets of X	Capital of X
Expenses to be spread over several years	Conditional debt towards the subjects of Y

Conclusion on the consequentialist anthropocentric modern orthodox approaches of neoclassical economists

In all of these orthodox economic approaches, whether it is the old foresters approach, the theory of externalities or the existence value, nature is a simple means, having no fundament, no finality. As lawyer Jacqueline Pruner (2005) says about the Exxon case:" legal and environmental injuries are tainted by three factors: an anthropocentric perspective (motivated by

[15] Except taking into account the increase in the probability of the occurrence of the maximum risk of deterioration.

human interests), an overconfidence in objective and rational formulations for determining the earth's sustainability thresholds (science and methodical data) and an emphasis on private property entitlements and individual liberty over the greatest interests of the community (individual liberty). These three fallacies lead to an illusory legal concept of environmental injury. In order to correct these fallacies a normative conscience needs to be infused into the legal system." The philosopher Grange (2012,57-62) speaks precisely about the errors evoked by the lawyer, of a green capitalism who, under the guise of the term sustainable development,[16] aims only to limit the damage of capitalism without to tackle the real problems. We will now abandon these dead ends proposed by mainstream economics and examine very different approaches, which, although remaining in a modern vein, come mainly from the circles of philosophy and ecology.

[16] This term has been used according to completely different philosophies: like the term capital, it can have opposite meanings. For lack of being able to avoid it, the reader, to know its meaning, has the only solution to read completely the works of those who use it in order to know its particular meaning. The use of this term should therefore not be condemned a priori: what matters is the objective pursued by the authors and their concrete solutions.

Chapter 11
The reaction of the philosophers: 'Environmental ethics' and its limits[1]

During the 20th century, due to the intensification of ecological problems, we see the emergence of attempts to partially question the systematic subject-object divide within the modern approach itself with the desire to subjectify certain non-human entities, all this without being able to get out of the frame of the modern approach. This is the case with the current of Environmental Ethics whose conception will be theorized mainly by philosophers. In opposition to the 'orthodox' approach of economists, this approach, to deal with the problems of the ecological crisis, starts from an ethic which wants to take into account environmental entities for themselves without, however, seeking to infer new concepts from them in the fields of economics and business management.

Whatever criticisms we can make and that we will make against this current, we must recognize that it had the great merit and the courage to go, from the years 1960-70, against all those who have denied and who, often even today, doubt the existence of a deep ecological crisis caused by men (or rather, according to us, some men, chiefly the capitalists).

Among the critics of this current and of the ideas that it defends are also philosophers: philosophers in court who clash with deviant 'green' philosophers. One of the prominent examples is Luc Ferry. For him, concern for nature would contradict humanism. In his diatribes against the 'green' philosophers, he went so far as to compare ecologism and Nazism, a regime which would have had one of the "most elaborate legislations...in terms of the protection of nature and animals"[2] (1992, 25). His hostility to all that is green will even lead him to declare that the IPCC (Inter-

[1] This section owes also a lot to Alexandre Rambaud (2015).

[2] In fact, as Hardouin-Fugier (2002, 51-70) shows, at the time of Nazism the legislation which best protected animals was that of Great Britain: why did Ferry not then compare the Environmentalism to English Democracy?

governmental Panel on Climate Change) is "a group in which are co-opted the bosses of associations who are often ecological ideologists"[3]. In the same vein, but less aggressive, Gauchet (Le Debat N° 60, May –August 1990, 247-50) believes that ecologism, with its love of nature, would mean "hatred of men." All these accusations by philosophers who defend modernity, and with it capitalism (which is an inseparable element), are unfounded, as shown by Simmonet (1979). Before resuming this debate, we will first state the general principles of environmental ethics, then describe its different schools.

The 'Environmental Ethics' approach: General view

Environmental Ethics, as we have underlined, is based on the modern attitude. In this it differs from older forms of ethics, such as the ethics of virtue and pragmatic ethics.

The ethics of virtue, or of good, as we have seen, finds its roots in ancient Greek thought (Fieser, 2000), in particular in the Nicomachean Ethics of Aristotle. This type of pre-modern normative ethics is characterized by a focus on the individual himself, that is to say on his particular characteristics, such as generosity, honesty, loyalty etc (Burgh, 2006). The moral finality, according to the ethics of virtue, is based on the development of habits, of lifestyles, which would lead to a fulfilling life of such or such an individual: " the virtues are clearly not ends in themselves, but means to the end of achieving the individual's telos [...] the good for man " (Beadle, 2006). It is therefore a quest for a particular individual in search of his own goals, which entails certain specific consequences in terms of the objectives sought. Primarily:" there is within the concept of the quest the idea that it is a search for something that is not adequately characterized and that it is through the search itself that the goal of the quest is finally to be understood. So the telos is both partially known and unknown, and in the quest for the unknown we also refine our understanding of the known "(Beadle, 2006). One of the current advocates of this ethical perspective is Alasdair MacIntyre (1981).

[3] Le Figaro (8 July 2008).

The second non-Modern normative ethic is *Pragmatism* which is directly opposed to modern dualism and, in particular, to Cartesianism. Pragmatism "does not take a stand for any particular position," it "is only a method" (James, 1968: pragmatism), or a "philosophy of action" (Joas, 1993). This with a search for truth within the framework of the experience of the reality at the bottom, especially during an interaction between living things and their environment (Debaise, 2007). It is therefore not a question of pre-framing reality in order to purify it according to general inter-subjective principles, but of re-inscribing and re-locating the question of our relationship to the world and of our actions in these vital interactions (Debaise, 2007). This approach favors "investigations," paths to be constantly repeated, on facts and values. We go from objective facts, radically independent of any human influence, to facts, which are somewhat fabricated, and we go from radically subjective values, outside the objective world, to values, that is to say concerns, non-indifferences (Lavelle, 1950), which are somewhat anchored in the non-human environment in which humans live. We therefore go from an ethics of the purity of the subjective to an ethics of the impurity of daily and uncertain mediations, where are mingled facts and values, local and global, etc.

Pragmatism is therefore an ethics of the dynamics of the world as opposed to the contemplative statism of the moderns (Farinelli, 2004).

Modern Ethics aims to overturn these two ancient approaches to normative ethics. It is no longer a question of focusing on the individual and his telos: these specific ends of each must be prohibited. It is a question of what the subject does and not of what the human individual is or fully experiences. His act can thus be broken down into two central elements: the causes (intentions) and the consequences: a duality that should be purified and interpreted through the subject / object dichotomy, the causes being the domain of the subject and the consequences the domain of the object. We can then define two main types of Modern Normative Ethics structured around this dichotomy: consequentialist ethics based strictly on the subject / object and causes / consequences dichotomy and non-consequentialist ethics (but also modern) admitting that certain features of acts humans have intrinsic value (Burgh, 2006).

Consequentialist ethics like ethical selfishness assert that all subjects must choose acts that will produce the best consequences for them. In general, they aim to define whether an act is good or not by focusing only on the optimization of the consequences of this act regardless of the underlying intentions of this act. The most typical example of such an ethical perspective is utilitarianism or rather utilitarianisms (Sen, 2003) which will inspire many economists (notably JS Mill).

Non-consequentialist ethics, on the other hand, are organized around two other poles: that of rights and duties, a division which nevertheless remains marked by the subject / object distinction, the duties referring to the subjective and the rights to the objective (Everett, 2004). An example of normative ethics based on duties is that of deontology associated with the name of Kant. This author emphasizes the notion of duty and intention, where duty is anchored in reason and intended to be universalized. Kantian deontology is thus based on a single principle, that of the categorical imperative: "Act in such a way that you treat humanity as well in the person of any other always at the same time as an end and not simply as a means."(Kant 1788). We can see there the notion of proper finality, which will constitute the basis of the concept of objective intrinsic value of human subjects, in the original Kantian perspective, then of non-humans in theories relating to environmental ethics (Callicott, 2007). We are aiming for an end in itself, an objective end from which an absolute value. Within the framework of these deontological approaches, it is a question of apprehending "the deep moral nature" of a situation. As Bloomfield (2003, 499-500) says: "if situation S is present that has the deep moral nature of the N kind then apply the Rule R." In other words, the deontological approach absolutely ignores the consequences: it is simply a question of enacting general principles making it possible to establish ex ante whether an action is fair or not, ethical or not. The goal of much of environmental ethics will be to combine these modern ethical theories with an extension of the moral center, therefore of the subjects, and with concepts such as objective intrinsic value (OIV). Before addressing this type of so-called environmental ethics, we will first show that there is an intermediate stage between it and orthodox economic theory with the modern approach of Non-Consequentialist Anthropocentrism (NCA)

The Modern approach to Non-Consequentialist Anthropocentrism (NCA)

Within the framework of this philosophy, natural capital corresponds to things which "have value or are good for other people and we think they have moral standing so that what is good for them is relevant to our moral decisions, then we have a moral reason [...] not to deprive them of it "(Cox, 1997, quoted by Rambaud, 2015). According to this type of value the thing concerned has no objective intrinsic value (OIV): it does not constitute a moral center in itself. On the other hand, it can be valued in one way or another by human subjects who are recognized as having such a OIV and having a source of universal duty. In this framework there will be a preservation of the thing concerned because there is a duty towards other subjects, and not towards this thing. Thus, according to this particular Kantian deontological vision, one could explain that the fact of destroying a thing valued by other subjects cannot be elevated into a universal law and that it is therefore not right to destroy it in a particular situation. Passmore (1980) is a typical author of this anthropological perspective. In his "Man's Responsibility for Nature" he notably defends the idea that pollution is bad because it degrades the health, and even the rights of certain human beings, through the deterioration of the quality of the air. We recognize in this example the idea that the moral subject is indeed the human being and not the air, and that the ethical attitude to be adopted is based on rules situated in the intention of acts and not in the a posteriori analysis of the consequences: pollution is in all circumstances a source of injustice towards certain subjects and this, in particular, independently of a cost-benefit analysis (Desjardins, 2006). Regan (1985) (critically) gives another example of non-consequentialist anthropocentrism through the animal question. He cites the case of thinkers who favor a kind of contractarianism: "the root idea of that morality consists of a set of rules that individuals voluntarily agree to respect, as we do when we sign a contract. Those who understand and accept the terms of the contract are covered directly: they have rights created, recognized and protected by the contract." As animals cannot sign and understand a contract they do not have rights. From this point of view the fact of not making a domestic animal suffer, for example, is based on an implicit moral contract with the owner of this animal: since the suffering of the animal would cause injury to the owner who has rights protected by this moral contract this prejudice should be avoided whatever the situation. But the animal itself has no place in this type of ethics[4]. Take the example of a cow C operated on a farm F to produce milk and meat. Consider that consumer subjects are concerned about their health and have a right to 'good health'. Under these conditions from an NCA point of view, if we focus on the 'environmental' non-human entity C, notably its breeding conditions, it is because they condition the health of consumer subjects, and need to be investigated. In addition, the notion of 'good health' refers to a normative construction of the concept of health. Suppose we focus on the particular problem of antibiotics given to C: in these conditions the question of the use of these antibiotics arises, not because of a concern related to C itself, but in relation to the problem of public health. Therefore, in this situation, what is 'capital' happens to be public health, that is to say the rights of consumers, and not the cow C. Thus the essence which founds the right of the moral subject in our example - and which is to stabilize - is the health of individuals through C. The characteristics of this essence must be established ex ante on the basis of the definition of human 'health capital', close to the concept of natural capital of orthodox environmental economists. So the 'environmental' entity is a simple support, a simple means, on which are grafted inter-subjective questions. There is therefore no question of taking C into account 'for itself'. From this perspective of the NCAs Ethics, it is possible that the authorities decide to totally ban antibiotics (-when the health of C requires a certain dose but less than that practiced by the farmer F-) to avoid that she does not fall ill. In particular, as Carolan (2013) says: antibiotics are used to produce cheap meat ": this is a utilitarian view.

What then becomes our integrative accounting model(IAM) within this framework of the NCA? First of all, it is necessary to recognize a particular capital: capital-health. This capital is evaluated at its maintenance cost. More precisely, this capital is "used," and potentially degraded, indirectly, in the same way as the utility of the subject in the case of a certain vision of natural capital, since the cow C is exploited in one way or another by F. The integrative accounting model then allows to specify the types of uses of this capital-health in order to highlight the different farming practices

[4] Thus in France until 2014 the Civil Code considered the animal as movable property.

according to their impact on people's health (we can in particular differentiate the case of children, adults and the elderly). These different farming methods may induce additional costs recorded as usage costs on the asset side of the balance sheet as a consequence of the rise of the costs of human capital-health. In all cases, the cow C remains a resource object not taken into account for itself: it does not appear on the liabilities side of the balance sheet as capital to be kept but only as an asset. In conclusion in all cases the NCA cannot integrate the idea of an environmental unit for itself. It is an approach halfway between the orthodox economic approach and non-anthropocentric environmental ethic. We will now approach the latter by starting by studying its key concept: that of intrinsic value.

The concept of intrinsic value (IV) in environmental ethics

This question was the subject of an intense debate between the members of this 'community', in particular between Taylor, Callicott and Rolston. See in particular Callicott's article "The intrinsic value in nature: a meta-ethical analysis" (1995) in Afeissa (2012,187-225): this article retraces the stages in the development of this concept.

Initially Taylor (1981) was inspired by the work of Schweizer (1923), himself influenced by the post-Kantian Schopenhauer (1859)[5]. Kant, in his Fondements de la Métaphique des Mœurs (1785), posits that "the human being, and in general every reasonable being, exists as an end in itself, and not simply as a means for the use that could make such or such a will of it." He adds that "these ends are not simply subjective ends but they are objective ends, that is to say things whose existence is in itself an end." He posits this general principle that if each one subjectively represents himself this existence as an end his subjective value becomes in a certain way objective provided that others value themselves in the same way as ourselves, which leads to a sort of moral community of humans. As for Kant, only reasonable autonomous beings are capable of valuing themselves in this way, this poses the problem of the exclusion of non-rational human beings, in particular children.

[5] Schopenhauer proposes a noumenon at the root of all phenomena: the will to live (while Kant seems to make universal reason this fundamental noumenon).

Schweizer(1923)uses Kant's logic by substituting the Schopenhaurian criterion of 'wanting to live' for that of rationality:it is above all a question of "preserving life, promoting it, bringing to its highest value life capable of development, that is what is good." It is on this basis that Taylor(1981, in Afeissa 2007,210) will propose a conception of the inherent (intrinsic) value of nature. But he will hesitate between two arguments. In a first article (Taylor, 1981) he considers that it is human cartesian subjects who assign this inherent value to plants and animals, however under the constraint that they only take into account what is good for these plants and animals regardless of what is good for them. On the other hand, in his later book on environmental ethics (1986), he asserts that this value inherent to living nonhumans does not depend on a human subject, which makes it "a mysterious sort of objective property belonging to living beings." We would then go beyond the subject / object dichotomy and the derived dichotomy formulated by Hume (1739) between what is and what must be (Afeissa,2007 212). Following the example of Kant Taylor confines himself to asserting that the beings who have a good which is their own have an inherent, objective *'worth'*, reserving the term of 'value' to the evaluations of things by men (Afeissa, 2007 213).

Rolstom (1988) will later generalize this approach to include non-sentient living beings. His stratagem will be to use the generalization process of Kant (1785-88). It will start from the fact that all living beings, including plants devoid of consciousness, defend their life and deploy strategies for this that have value for themselves: an instrumental value. And thus, by virtue of the teleological proof of the existence of an intrinsic value, the existence of instrumental value in plants and animals implies the existence of their intrinsic value. It therefore seems that the latter does not need a Cartesian subject to exist. But what then for non-living entities as there are with ecosystems? In this case the argument no longer holds. So Rolstom has not shown that an intrinsic value can exist independently of any kind of self-valuing subject. However, Callicott praises Rolston for not only having stepped out of Kantian and Cartesian perspectives (Afeissa, 2007, 217,223), but also for having been aware of the limitation of biocentrism which is limited to granting moral status only to individual living organisms. Rolston (1994, in Afeissa,2007, 218) recognized that one cannot give an intrinsic value to ecosystems based on a "fountain of life." [6] Callicott, influenced by him, will then abandon the Kantian perspective of the biocentric optic. As he declares, he will "base environmental ethics on the capacity that is ours as humans to value non-human natural entities for what they are, independently of both the services they can provide us, and the question of knowing whether or not they are capable of valuing themselves "(Callicott in Afeissa,2007, 219). This leads him to consider that, under these conditions, "intrinsic value cannot be said to be fully objective" (idem, 221). It seems to us that, fundamentally, he then agrees with the anthropocentric thesis of Norton (1992, in Afeissa,2007,221) according to which "the respect we owe to human beings is more than enough to justify the protection of nature, consequently anthropocentric and non-anthropocentric environmental ethics would converge." However, finally, Callicott (1992, in Afeissa 2007, 221-223) believes that this not the case. He argues that like Heisenberg's relativistic physics, [7] which goes beyond Newton's and the rigorous divide between subjects and objects, his position is no longer that of the cartesian context. As he underlines the context changes: "it may be that the cartesian subject, like the platonic form of Good, or like Aristotle's Intellect agent, one day becomes a historical curiosity, having lost all hold on the western mind." He therefore claims, unlike Norton, it seems, a post-modern approach according to which intrinsic value cannot be said to be fully objective.

Environmental ethics are therefore based on the central concept of "intrinsic value" (Taylor,[8] 1981; Norton, 1992; Callicott, 1995,2005 and 2007; E. Katz, 1997). But the very term "intrinsic value" is not without ambiguity (O'Neil, 1992; Krebs, 1999). It can refer, as seen above, to three main meanings: (1) a non-instrumental value, (2) a value based on proper properties and (3) a value possessed independently of the evaluation of a human evaluator.

---

[6] Rolston (1994, in Afeissa, 2007, 219 and 222), will develop the specific concept of "systemic value" at a level where the subject no longer plays any role; this contrary to Descartes (see below).

[7] In quantum physics we recognize that there is an inevitable interaction between the subject and the object of study.

[8] Paul Taylor, professor of philosophy, was one of the founders of the "biocentric" current within environmental ethics.

O'Neill (1992) indicates that "to hold an environmental ethic is to hold that non-human beings have intrinsic value in the first sense: it is to hold that non-human beings are not simply of value as a means to human ends. However, it might be that to hold a defensible ethical position about the environment, one needs to be committed to the view that they also have intrinsic value in the second or third senses." In fact, the intrinsic value that really underlies the issues of Environmental Ethics is the third one, which is also called "objective intrinsic value" (OIV) (Norton 1992; Katz, 1997). By conferring intrinsic value on a non-human entity, it is a matter of giving it the status of a moral subject or a subject of law (Regan,[9] 1985; Faucheux et al, 1995; Katz, 1997; Norton, 2005). Under these conditions, with intrinsic value, we are always dealing with a modern notion. As Katz (1997) confirms with the objective intrinsic value "nature is an autonomous moral subject analogous to the traditional subject of modern ethical theory." The goal is in fact to attribute a part of the subject's domain to non-human entities: hence the latter remain *a priori* considered to be totally objects. But what complicates things is that with this status of subject these entities can no longer be treated as simple means available to humans. Subjectivation therefore makes it possible to place the debate on an ethical and no longer technical level. Humans and non-humans are then treated on common moral bases. The objective intrinsic value thus allows a clarification of the ends/means dualism.

But it is on the condition of finding a solution to conceptualize this value, which is not obvious. To do this, the supporters of this approach will objectify the recognition of the status of the (almost) subject of the non-human entities concerned. Depending on the type of non-human entity concerned or the understanding of the notion of objectivation, different lines of argument will be proposed ranging from pathocentrism to ecocentrism, the latter point of view being the most extreme with which environmental ethics is often confused (see below). In all these cases, with this objective intrinsic value, we come to the point that non-human entities are perceived as pursuing certain "pre-established" objectives which precisely define in an objective manner what is supposed to permit the

[9] Tom Regan Professor of Philosophy is one of the leading theoreticians of animal rights.

recognition of an entity as an (almost)subject. It is a question of objectivizing certain essential characteristic forms of certain non-human entities and of imposing the recognition of the stabilization of these forms on other subjects by means of an attribution of a part of the domain of the subject to these entities via the objective intrinsic value. Callicott (2007) attempts to give two "proofs" of intrinsic value as a concept in its own right. The first is phenomenological: "the question which asks how can we know that intrinsic value exists is analogous to the question which asks how can we know that consciousness exists? We experience each other introspectively and irrefutably." [10] The second proof, "teleological," [11] inspired by a type of Aristotle's argument,[12] refers to the idea that the existence of means (like a tool) implies the existence of ends and that of pure means can be means of other pure means thus forming an instrumental chain of pure means. But the world being finished this chain must necessarily have a beginning because otherwise there would be something which would be a pure means of nothing. Hence the idea that there is at a given moment an end in itself, and therefore an intrinsic value that appears at the end of a chain of instrumental values. The problem with this argument is that it tends to make objective intrinsic value a complement to instrumental value. Now, in principle, objective intrinsic value is the opposite of instrumental value: it is a radical finality and not just a going beyond mere instrumentality. Besides, once we have decided that such and such a thing has an intrinsic value, what do we actually do to ensure that it is preserved? In particular, what are we doing against the economic systems that threaten this thing? Should a value be given to the intrinsic value and if so which one? This question is going to be the big problem of environmental ethicists. Before tackling it we will study the different currents of this school.

---

[10] Pister (1995, 85) to the question what are the Cyprinodon diabolis fish that he wanted to save from extinction good for, answers his interlocutor, inviting him to a phenomenological response: "and what are you good for?."

[11] Callicott relies in particular on Sylvan and Plumwood (in Routley and Routley 1979).

[12] This philosopher seeks to demonstrate that happiness, the end in itself of human existence, exists because a chain of means (including various tools) must end somewhere.

The different currents of environmental ethics

As stated previously three moral centers-types, therefore three major categories of attributions of objective intrinsic value (OIV), can be retained depending on whether one refers to pathocentrism, biocentrism and ecocentrism.

Pathocentrism (non-consequentialist)

This current wants to attribute an intrinsic objective value (IOV) to all sentient beings [13] . It is against the utilitarian and consequentialist pathocentric current defended in particular by Bentham (1789)[14] and then by his godson J. Stuart Mill (1909)[15] which, from the 18th century, (case of Bentham) has a strong inclination to include in the community of moral subjects (or in any case moral patients) sentient beings of which animals are part. According to Singer (1975) (in Flipo, 2014a, 41) this old point of view can lead to "recognizing the inherent value that individuals possess, including non-human animals" but on the other hand it does not tend to " grant rights, but rather equal consideration to animals." As a result, this pathocentric utilitarian perspective does not imply the abandonment of intensive husbandry practices (Lusk and Norwood, 2011) or animal testing (Hess 2013). Indeed the decisions in this framework depend on the global

192 This is unlike a consequentialist or utilitarian pathocentrism which reasons according to a cost-benefit analysis between the advantages and disadvantages for human beings of practices that generate pleasure and suffering.

[14] "Under the Gentoo and Mahometan religions the interests of the animal creation seem to have met with some attention. Why have they not universally, with as much as those of human creatures, allowance made for the difference in point in sensibility? ...The French have already discovered that the blackness of the skin is no reason why a human being should be abandonned without redress to the caprice of a tormentor. It may come one day to be recognized, that the number of the legs, the villosity of the skin, or the termination of the os sacrum, are reasons equally insufficient for abandonning a sensitive being to the same fate. What else is it that should trace the insuperable line? Is it the faculty of reason, or, perhaps, the faculty of discourse? But a full-grown horse or dog is beyond comparison a more rational, as welll as a more conversable animal, that an infant of a day, or a week, or even a month, old. But suppose the case were otherwise, what would it avail? The question is not, Can they reason? Nor, Can they talk? But *can they suffer*? (Bentham, 1789).

[15] For Mill (1909) "The reasons for legal intervention in favour of children apply not less strongly to the case of those unfortunate slaves and victims of the most brutal part of mankind, the lower animals."

analysis of the costs - benefits relative to the advantages and disadvantages with regard to the pleasures and sufferings generated for the animals taken as a whole: "aggregate utilitarism is not interested in suffering per animal but in total suffering (Lusk and Norwood, 2011). This pathocentric utilitarian (consequentialist) point of view is therefore strictly opposed to that of the non-consequentialist pathocentrism which is the object of this development. This is shown in particular by an author like Regan (1985). He posits as a principle that animals are subjects of a life and that there is a fundamental commonality between human beings and animals: a shared sensitive experience. He deduces the existence of an inherent value that can be compared to a IOV of animals. The question for him is not do animals have inherent value? But is it possible to prove without adding arbitrary assumptions that they do not have (or less)? According to Singer (1975) this approach is not incompatible with the utilitarian approach. But Regan (1985) believes that the recognition of such an inherent value in animals must imply the recognition of special rights of these animals[16]: unlike utilitarianism this view in principle denies that we can justify good results by using evil means that violate an individual's rights, for example that it could be moral to kill a bear to harvest beneficial consequences for other species. Thus for Regan animals must have rights guaranteeing that by principle they cannot be mistreated or killed. To which Singer (1975), replies, as a convinced utilitarian, by explaining that the main fault of these theories is a kind of rigidity which makes them incapable of responding to the various circumstances, real and imaginary, in which we are led to form moral judgments. We clearly recognize in this opposition the modern dichotomy between Singular and Universal, avatar of the singular and universal dualism. If we take again the case of the cow C, it appears that the pathocentric approach, whether non-consequentialist or not, really allows C to be taken into account for itself because it is "the subject of a sentient" life. So the essential form which constitutes the point of attachment of this value is indeed, in the theory of Singer or Regan, the capacity of sentience. In these conditions, what appears to be essential in this context is precisely this capacity. There is, however, a fundamental

[16] Ferry (1992) differs from Regan regarding the attribution of rights to animals but agrees with him that they have their own dignity, that is to say an inherent value. As such, humans must protect them. But he is not going, like Regan, to advocate an elimination of commercial ranching and, virtually, of hunting.

difference between these two pathocentric approaches. In the case of utilitarian (consequentialist) pathocentrism of Singer C can be exploited as long as his interests, based on his experience as a sentient entity, are considered into the overall cost benefit analysis. Thus it is possible to proceed to compensations for the level of suffering of C. In this case it becomes possible to exploit this cow, that is to say to use its capacity for sentience, from the moment when the maintenance of a certain level of interest, of utility in the utilitarian sense, of C is guaranteed. Under these conditions, we can then define a capital-sentience whose ontology is based on a description of observable elements in connection with C's sentience capacity. For example, provide C with living conditions in such a way that it can compensate for the pain suffered as a result of its exploitation. This can lead to changes in costs associated with C: additional 'utilitarian animal welfare costs' (Lusk and Norwood, 2011, 511). In contrast to this view, Regan's non-consequentialist Pathocentrism would imply "animals to be viewed and treated not as resources, which implies nothing less than dissolution of commercial animal agriculture "(Regan, 1985). This declaration therefore means the impossibility of maintaining C as a resource and therefore the abandonment of its exploitation. Thus, in the case of this author, from an accounting point of view, the cow C appears to be a real subject on the liabilities side of the farmer's balance sheet. On the other hand, in the case of consequentialist (utilitarian) pathocentrism, a whole herd would appear on the liabilities side of this balance sheet for its new "conservation" costs such as costs for alleviating the pain of animals during dehorning and costs of compensating for the suffering caused by their exploitation.

However, despite these important differences, in both cases we remain in a modern approach. It is towards subjects that the company has obligations. The difference with the orthodox approach is that these subjects are non-humans to whom the company has these obligations. Thus, for the first time since the Middle Ages, a non-human entity could appear next to capital when taking this entity into account for itself. This extension of moral centers will be even greater with the cases of biocentrism and ecocentrism knowing that in these cases too it is quite possible that these positions can be incompatible with any exploitation: as Krebs says (1999: Ethics of

Nature) beyond pathocentrism, ethical demands become too strong to allow the relationship between man and nature.

Biocentrism

This current extends the status of the moral subject to any living entity. Two of its main authors are KE Goodpaster (1978)[17] and P. Taylor[18] (1981).[19] Goodpaster as early as 1978 emphasized that trees and plants in general have "interests" to remain alive and that the interests of these senseless living beings had to be respected no matter what,[20] thus stigmatizing purely hedonistic or quasi-hedonistic theories of values and their vectors (80-4). Taylor (1981), as we have seen, provided a rational case for this protection [21] . He starts from a Kantian deontological ethics (not consequentialist) to extend the respect of humans among themselves to respect for nature, on the basis of a new philosophical vision of the world that he believes rationally acceptable (but not necessarily demonstrable). This is because of the interdependence of all living things within an organic order, which he says ecological science show[22] (125-126). He bases his biocentric perspective on four universal principles (129):

1. Humans are thought of as members of the earth's community of life, holding that in such a membership, the same terms as apply to all the non-human members.

---

[17] On being morally considerable, Journal of Philosphy, Vol 75, 6, p 308-325 reprinted in Afeissa (2007, 61-109).

[18] The ethics or respect of nature, Environmental Ethics, Vol 3, 3, 1981, p 197-218; reprinted in Afeissa 2007 (111-152).

[19] One can wonder about the knowledge of these authors of the book of Jonas (1979) on the principle of responsibility. There is a similar approach to the moral responsibility of man towards sentient non-human beings (like that of parents towards their children). (199) In particular, he shows that the objection that nature does not respect life does not hold: "gratuitous murder rarely occurs in nature" (90).

[20] He was influenced, it seems, by the ideas of the partisans of "industrialism." He denounces "the ends pursued by technology, which are hedonistic"of having "gradually hardened the heart of a civilization with regard to the biotic community" (85).

[21] According to Afeissa (2012, 99 note) Taylor would have found his inspiration in the thought of Schopenhauer and Schweitzer.

[22] He also makes a reference to justice as Rawls' equity by extending its duties to nature (122).

2. The earth's natural ecosystems as a totality are seen as a complex web of interconnected elements, with the sound biological functioning of each being dependent on the sound biological functioning of the others[23]. This is the component referred to above as the great lesson that the science of ecology has taught us.
3. Each individual organism is conceived of as a teleological center of life, pursuing its own good in its own way.
4. Whether we are concerned with standards of merit or with the concept of inherent worth, the claim that humans by their very nature are superior to other species is a groundless claim and, in the light of elements (1), (2) and (3) above, must be rejected as nothing more than an irrational bias in our own favor.

The point 3 permits to clarify the notions of bio-centric approach and of the objective intrinsic biocentric value to be preserved[24]. The protection of living beings is not based on a moral appreciation and duties defined a priori but on the existence of an intrinsic property of development in certain units, this development being seen as essential for the latter[25]. If we take the case of our cow C, it is therefore a question of taking her "for herself" according to her own ends: taking into account her telos (her blossoming) and no longer starting from her sensitive experience as a sentient entity. So this goes far beyond issues of monitoring one's level of suffering and issues of compassion. One can then wonder if this philosophy is compatible with the exploitation of C.

---

[23] Taylor speaks of an "organic whole" in balance, of a holistic perspective and insists on this factual aspect of our dependence on nature as the basis of our attitude to take towards it while emphasizing the role of science in this awareness (in Afeissa 2007, 133-5).

[24] This perspective is also found in the Consequentialist Biocentrism of R. Attfield (1999). This type of biocentrism is consequentialist insofar as the moral appreciation of an act on a living being is judged in relation to the consequences of this act vis-à-vis all the capacities concerned of this being.

[25] Taylor points out that this attitude of respect towards non-human living beings, which is disinterested, is analogous to the attitude of respect for the fulfillment of the interests of persons within the framework of the ethics between men (In Afeissa, 2007,120).

Anyway, the balance sheet of the Integrated Accounting Model in this case should reflect the damage caused to the development of C on the basis of a new type of capital. Likewise, as far as plants are concerned, biocentrism allows a tree to be taken into account "for itself," through the recognition of its own life, which has implications for the way it is pruned.

With biocentrism, it is indeed the trees and the cows which are individual subjects, entities whose vital telos is to be preserved. One can wonder about the possibility of considering or not the felling of the tree: the consequentialist vision would allow it but not, a priori, a non-consequentialist vision. But these practical problems are hardly addressed by Taylor in his seminal article (1981 in Afeissa 2007). He simply states that "there is no reason to deny plants and animals legal rights" and that "we could consider granting them legal protection." However, despite this legal excursion, he never mentions the problem of regulating capitalist enterprises. Also influenced by industrialist ideology, he speaks only of "containing technological development" without further precision. Rightly, Afeissa (2007) believes that the biocentric individualistic ethic "shows itself incapable of transforming intrinsic value into environmental norm and of providing criteria for decision." This review does not prejudge our respect for the laudable intention of these pioneers in the protection of living non-human beings. Our critique of the means they use has nothing to do with that of, for example, Ferry (1992).

Ecocentrism

This environmental ethics can be subdivided into three major sub-categories (Ten Have, 2006): Earth Ethics, introduced in 1949 by Aldo Leopold, but later developed by J.B. Callicot from the 1970s; the Deep Ecology initiated by Arne Naess (1973, 1989) and the Theory of Intrinsic Value of Nature developed by Holmes Roston III (1994-2007)[26]. These three approaches are of the non-consequentialist type (Callicott 2007; Hess 2013), even though the Earth Ethics allows for a consequentialist interpretation

[26] But Afeissa (2012, 102) considers both Rolston 3 and Callicott to be direct heirs of Leopold.

(Fieser 2000)[27]. To different degrees they tend to conceive of ecosystems under the aspect of a certain stability, possibly homeostatic, typical of a systemic vision, and of a bodily metaphor of biotic communities. It is therefore a matter of preserving this whole in its integrity, possibly dynamic, especially in its ability to organize itself. In this case the capital to be protected is therefore an essence.

The Ethics of the Earth (developed by Léopold then Callicott) is the basis of ecocentric thought. The goal is, in the words of Léopold which have become famous, to "think like a mountain." This means to fully understand a member of an ecosystem, no longer as an isolated being but as an entity forming part of a whole. So a total difference from the classical pathocentric and biocentric approaches based on a principle of individualism (the source of intrinsic value is a given individual).

With this approach we are moving towards the other side of modern dualism: the collectivism / holism. The latter, in the environmental context, becomes 'Eco systemism'. His rule of thumb then is: "a thing is right when it tends to preserve the integrity, stability and beauty of the biotic community; it is wrong when it tends otherwise" (Leopold, in Callicott 1989). Insofar as the target of conservation is a whole (holistic perspective), conservation concerns this whole and not, as is the case with Taylor's biocentric individualistic conception, separate entities. We are therefore dealing here with a consequentialist ethics which aims for the good of the whole and which is no longer purely deontological (Afeissa,2007,101).

It is for this reason that this approach has often been criticized for sacrificing members of the community to the "interests" of the latter, some going so far as to speak, in this regard, of ecofascism (see below).

Naess's Deep Ecology, for its part, revolves around two major ethical principles (Ten Have, 2006): biospheric equality and the principle of self-realization. According to the first principle all the units of the biosphere are equal in intrinsic value, because they are elements of the whole that is this

[27] Fieser draws a parallel between Leopold's maxim and that of Stuart Mill (1863): "actions are just in so far as they tend to promote happiness; unjust insofar as they produce the opposite of happiness."

biosphere. The second principle is a condensed expression of the unity of certain social, psychological, and ontological hypothesis: the most comprehensive and deep maturity of the human personality guarantees beautiful action. This is based on the human nature. Indeed "We need to develop our self ...Increasing maturity activates more of the personality in relation to more of the milieu. It results in acting more consistently from oneself as a whole "(Naess, 1989[28]). Thus, according to this view, the authentic self would be the one which would tend to make one with nature: integration of humanity into the all that is the biosphere thus guaranteeing that human nature itself is oriented towards the development of this holist self.

Hence "to harm nature is to harm ourselves, and to defend earth is self defense" (Ten Have, 2006). Such is the principle of ontological realism connecting the part and the whole: each entity exists and has an intrinsic value because, being part of a whole, which itself is in fact the real holder of the ultimate intrinsic value, and which constitutes the real subject, the other existences being in fact objectivated, subject to the force of this supra-subject. The realization of human beings consists in being one with this All.

Such are the main theses of Naess. This author, who influenced Ellul (1954-1988), who also claims to be in deep ecology, aroused violent reactions from some, notably from Ferry and Bourg (1996, 11) (see Flipo 2014a, 89). Ferry, let us remember, defends the thesis that man asserts his morality by tearing himself away from nature: man, to be man, must be "anti-nature." He therefore considers the supporters of deep ecology, and more generally of American environmentalism, as well as the importers of their ideas in Europe, such as Jonas and Serres, as antihumanists. In a book very hard on environmentalists (1992), he believes that a right can only be carried by a subject in the proper sense, that is to say a human being who has a capacity to judge, a reason. If not, he asserts, after the foundational advances

---

[28] For Naess "organisms are nodes in the biospheric network or the field of intrinsic relations" but his holism links him to a more systemic conception. In his type 3 relational ontology "every thing is connected to all the others." In particular, objects in the forest are considered as interaction anchors." We are therefore taking a global perspective (Leary, 1985, Interaction theory in forest ecology). Indeed in this context the relations are determined by a whole which is the system. This type of relational ontology, close to the conceptions of Naess (1973), is also called "Deterministic Relational" (Dépelteau, 2013).

towards humanism of Descartes and Rousseau we would regress to animist views or to Christian or Aristotelian representations of nature with a multiplicity of entities, all placed on an equal footing provided that they pursue their own ends. As already said Ferry even goes so far as to compare this "regression" with the ideas and practices of Nazism. But Flipo (2014a, 90) shows, with supporting evidence, that "the gap between what the French debate said about Naess, based on Ferry, and the reality is staggering[29]." Ferry is in fact an advocate of capitalism and liberalism for whom all means are good to defend this system of thought,[30] including by caricaturing the thought of its adversaries.

The Theory of Intrinsic Value of Ecosystems

Holmes Rolston III (1994-2007) emphasizes the life of eco-systems in which the violent death of individuals which "constitutes a necessity for the species" (167). More generally, for him, the eco-systems themselves constitute inclusive communities, and thus fundamental units of development and survival (171). There is therefore an intrinsic value of an ecosystem which would result from certain specific capacities, referring in particular to a spontaneous order, a self-organization. As Rolstom underlines (idem, 171) "an ecosystem has no brain, genome, skin, no capacity to identify oneself through time, no telos, no unified program... however an ecosystem generates a spontaneous order which envelops and produces the richness, the beauty, the integrity and the dynamic stability of the parts which compose it." He draws the consequence that "men are not so much those who ignite value in a world of purely potential values, as those who psychologically join the ongoing planetary natural history in which value is found wherever positive creativity asserts itself. This creativity can be present in the subjects considered with their interests and

---

[29] He points out in particular that Naess was a Nazi resister and a follower of Gandhi's ideas.

[30] Ferry, who compares environmentalism so well with Nazism, and who defends liberal modernity, is careful not, in this "German affair," to mention the pact of the German liberals with Hitler: he denounces the authoritarianism and the regression of the environmentalists whereas the latter never had power and said nothing about the serene if not friendly relations of his modern liberal friends and German "humanists" with the creator of the concentration camps. See in particular on this subject Maxime Izoulet's post "How liberalism brought Hitler to power" (online, 04/28/2017).

preferences, but it can also be present objectively in living organisms which defend their own life and in systems capable of self-organizing "(idem). He concludes that an eco-system is "the result of a balance of values" (173) which "is the deep source from which the individual and species spring up" (175) and which has, beyond its "intrinsic value," a "systemic value" (176).

In response to an accusation of a naturalistic fallacy Rolston replies that "it is properly by committing the subjectivist fallacy to think that all value rests on subjective experience that we commit the anthropocentric fallacy by thinking that all value rests on choices and men's preferences "(166). He cites Leopold's famous phrase in support of his reasoning: "One thing is right when it tends to preserve the integrity, stability and beauty of the biotic community.It is unfair when it tends to be the reverse "(171). Thus Rolston extends in a way the telos of living beings, which would, in the case of Biocentrism, impose an intrinsic value on an organizing capacity of certain beings to found a notion of objective intrinsic value: in short, an extension of the value of men to ecosystems, seen as communities.

Thus, to follow this type of reasoning, if we take the example of company F using a forest as an ecosystem (and therefore its trees), the tree appears as a particular element of capital-debt since we are located in a holistic perspective. It is then the ecosystem (the forest) as a whole which becomes the subject to which the company has an obligation to maintain the capital of "biospheric integrity "[31]. Unlike Taylor's individual biocentrism, there is no longer any question of normative egalitarianism: the existence of a plurality of values does not exclude their hierarchy. It is therefore conceivable that the destruction (felling) of a tree does not necessarily call into question the integrity of the ecosystem and even is necessary. To

---

[31] Rolston (in Afeissa, 2007, 156-8). clarifies that "to say that n can be valorized does indeed mean that a man M takes an interest in a natural object n, but it is not necessary that this means that n satisfies the desire of M, insofar as M can take interest in trees for what they are in themselves, and not just to satisfy M's desires. That being said, "there is no value until consciousness enters the scene.." the arrival of men corresponds to a sort of ignition of value but not to something that the object would gain.." "Value is extrinsic for n insofar as it is conferred by M and..it too is extrinsic for M because conferred by M on n as far natural data..potentially possess intrinsic value." He also specifies that "although things do not matter to plants, there are things that matter to them: trees benefit from light"…and "actively defend their own life" (idem, 163-5).

transpose these principles into accounting, the capital-debt in the corresponding balance sheet will be made up of a specific forest, identified as a community, and considered and preserved for itself. In the context of this holistic reasoning E, an element of this forest is neither a subject to whom the company has an obligation, nor an asset.

Overall conclusion on the four approaches to environmental ethics

Katz (1997) defends the idea of a radical difference between pathocentrism and ecocentrism in the sense that " ecological holism reinforces the proper role of pain in organic life. Since pain is as necessary as pleasure in a successful organic life, it cannot, and should not, be considered a moral evil." For him an ecocentric vision can only be opposed to a vision based on a certain rejection of animal suffering: this suffering being an essential element of the self-organization of biotic communities. Nevertheless attempts to reconcile Pathocentrism and Ecocentrism exist. Callicot (2010) thus draws the outlines of such reunification, in particular to reconcile holism and individualism. It does this by separating the wild and domestic species: "domestic animals are members of the mixed community and should benefit from all the rights attached to this condition;wild animals are members of the biotic community: the structure of the biotic community is described by ecology." Callicot wants indeed a truce and a common front of the various environmental ethics.

But the question of the separation between individualism and ethical holism also marks a conflict between biocentrism and ecocentrism. Callicot (2007) explains that "environmental ethics has little to do with the well-being of bedbugs, shrubs or earthworms, and on the other hand has everything to do with larger groups (such as species and ecosystems) and with the abiotic aspects of nature (such as the atmosphere and the ocean). In these conditions, for him, biocentrism would not ultimately succeed in taking into consideration the supposed real issues of environmental ethics, the purpose of which would be to linger on questions of a global nature. There would therefore be a certain normative point of view on what environmental ethics should be: a philosophy of bodies as a whole, almost a kind of "bio -philosophie," comparable with the expression of bio-power of Foucault. Above all, there is a presupposition according to which the ecological crisis is a crisis of the global masses, in which the particularities are ultimately more anecdotal. Moreover, there is the problem of the question of "entities for themselves": is it an individual or a community (or even an environment)? More broadly, this question again raises questions about the type of capital (in the accounting sense) to be conserved: is it the capital relating to a given tree or to a forest ecosystem? This fundamental choice leads to different indicators and obligations.

In the end, anyway, as the balance sheet structures show in the cases analyzed, the four approaches to environmental ethics remain based on the separation between subjects (liabilities) and objects (assets), which remains consistent with the fact that the approach to environmental ethics is resolutely modern.

At this stage of reasoning we have seen that both the orthodox approaches of neoclassical economics and that of environmental ethics remain based on modernity due to the object / subject dichotomy.

However, it must be recognized that if, in economic approaches, non-humans disappear completely, the stakes being transferred to questions of variations in the utility of humans (or of production), the same is not true in the case of optics of environmental ethics. In this context, the notion of subject tends to be extended to other non-human beings or entities. But, as Grange (2012,59) underlines, in addition to the fact that these ethics remain in the field of modernity, they also have the major flaw of being ineffective because they do not lead to proposals for concrete political and legal measures to counter the misdeeds of capitalism[32]. One of these practical questions is that of realizing intrinsic value. To move forward towards the solution of these aporias we are going to leave (partially) this intellectual framework with the approach of relational ecology.

[32] Grange (2012, 59-60) goes even further in severity. For this philosopher, who cites in support of her opinion the works of Larrère and Larrère tending to dismiss science and ecology in favor of moral considerations, it is necessary "to get out of decades of sterile ethico-philosophical speculations to tackle the real problems. The point of view of environmental ethics like that of Hans Jonas [..] seems ineffective.

Part Four
The Relational Ecology Approach and its Economic and Accounting Translation: Towards a New Practical Ecological Philosophy Against Capitalist Modernity

In the conflict between biocentrism and ecocentrism the central question is to know whether the current ecological stake is to be found on the side of individual entities or of large global masses. We can argue that it is indeed important for ethical reasons to focus on each entity, which has a right to life, to flourish and develop. But, immediately, we also have the feeling that, to an objective point of view, the real problems concern global questions. In particular, climate change, the biodiversity crisis, the pollution of ecosystems, etc are essential points in any truly moral behavior and / or act. However, at the same time, we keep the feeling that we cannot objectively subject all beings on this planet to this single paradigm.

In fact we are confronted with the central problem of the modern attitude: we are condemned to switch tirelessly from the local to the global, from the individual to the universal, etc., without ever being able to bring them together and take the time to think differently outside the framework of these two fictitious extremes. To get out of this dilemma, it seems to us that we need to take another ecological approach, thanks to an ontology of our world called 'relational'. This approach is based on the question of what should we preserve or conserve, that is, what is important. It leads to an ontology of capital-debt allowing a new type of economy based on a new accounting management. We will therefore devote two chapters to these two fundamental questions of relational ontology and its implementation by a new economic system.

Chapter 12
Relational ontology: General notions and positioning

We will start with a general presentation of this notion and then position it in the debate on the concepts of modernity and pre-modernity[1].

General presentation

The reference to ontology corresponds to a preliminary questioning of what our world is and the entities populating it: it is therefore not a problem specific to such or such field of knowledge but rather a general question. on our universe. Following Eckersley (2004) and Humphrey (2007) for example, it can be argued that we have to decide about the nature of the universe before we can begin to think sensibly about ethical and political matters. In the same way that modern ontology performatively models our universe, in particular by affirming that only financial capital is worthy of systematic conservation, similarly the notion of relational ontology tends to put forward another particular type of relationship to the world.

But any notion of ontology, relational or not, can be approached in different ways. Leary (1985 and 2012) defines these types of ontology (in an application to forestry) according to four approaches to reality.

A utilitarian type 1 ontology, as in the orthodox economic vision of natural capital: the tree is then a simple marketable good (trees are timber). *A naturalist (individual) type 2 ontology* where each tree is seen as a natural thing in its own right, and no longer as a medium (trees are more than timber). This ontological perspective is close to biocentric individualism because it is centered on an individualized thing, characterized by its natural state. These first two ontologies have the common point of not being relational unlike the following two.

[1] This development owes a lot to the doctoral dissertation of Rambaud (2015).

In type 3 (systemic relational ontology) everything is connected to everything else: forest objects are anchors for interaction. We are therefore in a systemic perspective and, in this context, relationships are determined by a whole which is the system. This type of relational ontology, close to the conceptions of Naess (1973),is rightly called "deterministic relational" (Dépelteau, 2O13 cit).

In type 4 (*interactions as a basic element of the populations of a set, such as a forest*), on the other hand, we find an ontology where relations are on an equal footing with things in forestry decision making. We therefore see with types 3 and 4 that relational ontology can already refer to two different concepts, one of which, type 3, is clearly affiliated with the modern attitude and the other not.

We can also define weak and strong relational ontologies with Slife[2] (2004): according to the first weak category persons, places and things, as well as practices, begin and end as self-contained individualities that often take in information from the outside. Relationships and practices in this weak sense are reciprocal exchanges of information among essentially self-contained organisms. This weak form of relational ontology is ultimately a type of modern ontology, of an individualistic type.

The second (strong) perspective is comparable to Leary's type 4 ontology. In this case, things are not first self-contained entities and then interactive. Each thing, including each person, is first and always a nexus of relations.

We can therefore observe that there is a certain confusion of relational ontologies. Some, of the modern individualist type, are ultimately determined by the essence of subjects. For example in the ideal neoclassical mode what matters are the individuals who act on the markets (Bénicourt and Guerrien, 2008).

In the case of holism (type 2) the relationship is just as secondary and acts as the internal cement of the system. The initial subject is the system which conditions the entities composing it. The reference to relationism means that "the network replaces the society of the holists" (Dépelteau, 2013).

---

[2] This author is a psychologist.

Instead of networks of individuals we are dealing with structural networks in which objectivized entities are encysted.

But how then to conceptualize the strong relational ontology? It is, in our opinion, the one which admits that the relation is primary and that the main entities are the different knots (nexi) of relations (Leary, 1985; Sidorkin, 2002, Castree, 2003. Wildman, 2010). Wildman, in particular, insists on the great possible variety of relations: "How can a philosophical theory of relation simultaneously embrace fundamental physics and the valuational contexts of flags and nations?" This type of difficulty explains why it is tempting to slide towards a substantial posture and modern purification.

Thus, according to Sidorkin (2012), we must consider the total plurality: "relation is the aspect of reality brought about by plurality. Admittedly, a certain reality comes from unity and sameness of being. However, another and more important aspect of reality is determined by the differentiation of being, by otherness of being. This second aspect of reality can be described as relation." It means according to Sidorkin that "existence itself is a relation… the quality of existence does not belong to the thing that exists… existence is an honor, bestowed by others."

The conclusion to be drawn is that it is impossible to conceptualize a thing that has no edges and no limit, made up of a single unit. Something exists because it is relationship. As Sidorkin points out "when I see a goat and think: the goat is there, who is doing the thinking?"[3] Where should we attribute this thought? For Sidorkin " the relation thinks and I am only a part of the relation that happens to have a better brain." This whereas, very differently, the modern positioning attributes the thought to a fictitious subject, pure intellectual emanation situated outside any material universe. This is what Latour (2007b) shows in particular with his "brain in a jar."

Sidorski and Wildman therefore oppose atomist views and their simplifications: there are generally and even systematically co-determination, co-creation within relational fields. In this respect, we can give a few examples in very different spheres of activity, such as that of the pianist. Who feels the piano in his fingers? It is indeed a co- experience, of

[3] This remark can be compared in physics from the quantum point of view.

an entangled state but which does not mean an equi-distribution in relationality: certainly for this pianist it is more a question of fingers and creativity than of piano keys, but what about the role of touch? In the field of cost accounting we also find the case of the distribution of indirect costs[4]: it is neither entirely objective nor entirely subjective. Note that relational ontology is not a simple relativism either: not everything is admissible in the reality of relationships. Thus the existence of the pianist depends on his relationship with the piano, which does not mean that he merges with it. This type of ontology therefore encourages us to conduct an investigation into the modalities of existence offered by the plurality of relational fields. As Latour (2012) puts it: "in order to exist a being must not only go through another... but also in another way, by exploring other ways of altering itself." All existence takes place through the relationship and therefore, indirectly, through the other items of this relationship to be followed over time. So the relational ontology is of variable geometry because it is not substantial: a knot (nexus) is a trajectory. Each actant has a unique signature in a dynamic space where humans and non-humans intermingle. For example, a tree can appear as a nexus in a tangle of dynamic reactions with various connections: visual, physical, biological, cohabitation, economic relationships. So a multitude of relationships and concerns, uncertainties. There can be no closed debate ex ante on the things that make up the world: there is perpetual discussion and politics. This brings us back to the question of modernity.

Relational ontology, pre-Modernity, Modernity, and post Modernity

There is a link, even if it may seem tenuous, between relationalism and pre-modern worlds (Sahlins, 2009). As Turner and Atleo (1998) testify, the cosmological system of the early peoples of North America held that " the creator made all things are related and interconnected. All things are sacred. All things are therefore to be respected." Likewise, Poirier, in his book 'Three ethnographic examples from Aboriginal Australia' (2014),

[4] These are expenses, such as the pay of a CEO, the amount of which is difficult to attribute to a single activity of the company. We are obliged to distribute them between the activities with approximate means (for example the time spent by the CEO on problems of strategy, marketing, lobbying, etc.).

shows " how being a human and social being means embodying relatedness; engaging in relations of exchange and reciprocity and assuming responsibility webs of relatedness." Wildman (2010), for his part, positions certain religious traditions within the framework of relational ontology: " non-theistic religious traditions such as Buddhism speak centrally of relations, and some Buddhists claim that it is liberating to realize that we have no substantive being of our own but are only ephemeral bundles of relations." These religious references are based at least in part on spiritual or magical bases (Slife, 2004). We have also shown that, to a certain extent, the positions of certain philosophers of ancient Greece, especially those of the Epicureans and Stoics, were not incompatible with the approach of relational ontology. But, as Jeffrey Brower (2001),[5] a specialist in medieval philosophy, observes, a rupture took place towards the end of the Middle Ages: "the fourteenth century marks an important turning point in the medieval discussion of relations." Indeed, according to him, at this time," philosophers are increasingly willing to say that substances themselves provide the ontological grounding for relational situations. Thus instead of thinking of relations as the items responsible for relating two or more substances they now begin to think of them as items existing only in the mind- that is, as mere beings of reason or concepts." This judgment confirms our thesis of a rupture at that time, a thesis which however enriches that of the historian by adding the fundamental datum of the birth of modern capitalism. It is indeed at this time that will appear, to use expressions of Latour (1997), 'ghosts' only present in the subject's mind. Latour indeed considers that with modernism there is a recomposition of reality, because the interrelational networks of mediations are replaced by intermediaries who faithfully claim to represent and figure a totally determined, stabilized and rigidified relationship in an ideally infinite temporality. The modern attitude is to assume that any relationship can be decomposed into a leaf of ultra stable and ultra unstable relationships. Anything whose (relational) existence is part of totally stable, rigidified, relationships is objective. Conversely, on the contrary, subjectivity would correspond to relations in permanent radical change, which corresponds to the ideal of progress. This dualism is an arbitrary

[5] See the Stanford Encyclopedia website (http: plato.stanford.edu/entries/relations-medieval/).

hypothesis on our world which refers to ideal fictitious types: a relationship cannot be stable ad vitam aeternam, everything is a bit of a means and a bit of an end in itself. The fact of bringing reality to two unreal extreme forms of relations in fact allow us to define in the absolute a kind of 'automatic pilot' gradually replacing any discussion on the modalities of relational existence of things populating our universe. On the contrary, in order to paint a full and entire existence, it is necessary to articulate essence centered on permanence and contingent existence. For example, in the case of a human being, his appearance could be contingent and his structural physical organization (his skeleton) rather stable. We must therefore oppose the Moderns and especially the modern capitalists and their artificial vision of the world which boils down to absolute contingency and total essence. As Slife (2004) shows, failure to take the 'relationism' of our world seriously leads to a host of conceptual problems.

But how can we preserve the relational ontology inherent in our world while possibly preserving certain positive contributions from modernity? For Latour, the solution is to keep the relationism of the pre-moderns and borrow from the moderns the notion of reflexivity inherited from the ancient Greeks: the questioning of meaning of life and of self as well as the possibility of conceiving networks of associations of humans and non-humans. But this within a specific framework: as in the pre-moderns under the constraint of taking careful account of the consequences of acts, in particular by discussing several of these consequences[6]. According to this author, it would therefore be a question of replacing the cartesian cogito by a cogitamus (Latour, 2010). Therefore, think of several to define a common relational reality (Pickering, 2009) and not reason at the purely ethical or individual psychological level. So political activity. In this regard Eckersley (2004), proposes the foundation of a "green state," Bourg and Whiteside (2011) an "ecological democracy." As for Latour (1997), he advocates the establishment of a "Parliament of things"[7] whose goal will be to allow a common learning pact on our world. He poses four demands for this Parliament in order to establish a common world, a new Demos.

---

[6] As Turner and Atleo (1998) say about cutting down a tree: talk to it.

[7] See also, in the same sense, Castree (2003): "extending political reasoning to include non-humans."

1. "Do not simplify the number of human-non-human associations. This implies perplexity: asking the question how many are we? Instead of having a single actor legitimize a network of actors. Where the moderns want to simplify more and more by going up the progress staircase, going from complicated to even more complicated" (Latour, 1999).
2. Concretely, for example, we must not freeze the relational investigation of a forest: as a relational nexus it is constantly evolving with the rest of the world (in particular with the migrations of species). So no a priori purely causal order between it and its environment, be it environment towards forest or vice versa: that would then be returning to a weak relationshipism.
3. "Do not bypass the number of voices that participate: consultation (living together) with a parliament of things as an informal mechanism or even a particular method of pragmatic orientation. The natures will be present but with the scientists on their behalf. One of the representatives talks about the ozone hole, another about the loss of biodiversity. So a parliament made up of mediators, spokespersons for things: this is in a way an application of political rights to non-humans, which does not in itself imply an anthropocentric vision of this parliament. An atmosphere of research, of controversy to say something about the mandate attached to the members of this new institution."
4. "Discuss the compatibility of the new proposals with the old ones. In this context, therefore, there is no closing of the decision by a scientific or political authority, but reversible decisions, possibilities of recovery. So we will move from a culture of science to a culture of research. Indeed, science is cold produces objectivity, research is warm: creates controversies." (Latour, 1998). Thanks to this we will have a more realistic appreciation of the uncertainty, the future being assumed not to be probable in principle. The use of probability will intervene only as a mediating element to say something about our reality. It is thus a new processual, iterative conception of political ecological activity. Admittedly the moderns can revise their judgment but the problem lies in their permanent will to close something and to obtain indisputable facts or totally subjective values within the framework of an immutable world (as

regards the objects), the subjects which dominate being radically free and singular. Unlike these moderns, in the parliament of things, time is no longer linear and controllable. Indeed, relational recovery (of our interrelationships) is directly opposed to the concept of linear progress: fundamental uncertainty is at the heart of mediation networks[8].

5. "Once the proposals have been established, no longer discuss them until the next iteration and establishment of essences for each entity at the end of a process." (Latour, 1999).

These are the four requirements set by Latour for the institution of a new policy of nature which deserve some comments. In this approach to the relations of humans with nature, the great deal of disciplines is called upon. Literature and history remind us that everything (or almost) has already been said[9] but still it is necessary to be able to operate syntheses with the help of the collaboration of the various fields of knowledge. Natural sciences are essential to approach the reality of ecosystems and the impacts of human beings on nature. Philosophy enjoins us, normally, to love nature and act wisely towards it. Sociology and political science help us understand the nature of the social systems that led to modernity and the current crisis. Artistic disciplines, such as theater in particular, feature the actors of these systems. Economics, of which accounting is an integral part according to Proudhon,[10] allow us to make proposals to reconstruct the current capitalist system, and legal sciences allow us to inscribe these proposals in new norms. It is therefore a co-reconstruction on the basis of a plurality of disciplines. Note that this point of view is not shared by all those interested in this question. This is particularly the case with Serres. The great merit of this philosopher, with his "Natural Contract" (1990), is to have underlined the undeniable importance of the physical and natural sciences in this reconstruction. But his work is marked by a sharp criticism

---

[8] See for more details on this point Callon et alii (2001).

[9] But we may not be too late!

[10] Proudhon, who had the art of striking formulas, affirmed that "the true economist is the accountant from whom a coterie of false litterateurs has stolen his title." We leave it to the reader to judge the relevance of this impertinence of the author of the "Philosophy of misery" (1846). Marx, he, the economist, made a clear cut in 1847: "Poverty of philosophy"!

of the social sciences, especially sociology[11] and economics in general. It is with this type of bias that Serres comes to speak of a new natural contract without having at any point dealt with economic and social issues in his book. He even succeeds in the feat of never uttering the word capitalism during his fresco, moreover interesting, on the history of conflictual relations between natural sciences and law, the latter being visibly treated with suspicion[12]. The cleavage is clear: on the one hand the scientists (those of the natural sciences) who fight for the recognition of the truth and our good and, on the other hand us,[13] all the other citizens, who are all responsible for the situation. This whatever our social status of dominated or dominant.

Our position is both more ecumenical and more differentiated. Regarding the disciplines, we believe that there will be no possibility of changing the current economic system without a precise analysis of its functioning, which is also, fundamentally, a matter of social and political sciences. When it comes to responsibilities, we believe that the capitalists in charge of the economics (and the politicians and economists who support them) and the rest of the population, especially those who regularly challenge their actions, cannot be put in the same basket. Serres asserts that the "Earth holds us" (133) and that if there is not a new natural law based on the natural sciences (the real ones) it will win over the laws of men. But we can reverse the reasoning. If the earth "holds" us (or takes revenge) it is because the dominant system for centuries, modern capitalism, "holds" us: a reality which Serres does not see or does not want to see.

---

[11] One example among many others on this theme: his Sage, the Third Instructed, is an expert in the natural sciences and likes action "away from the social sciences with truths that are more critical than organic and banal information and not uncommon" (1990, 147). Clearly, sociology is useless. According to this author, it is better to act than to talk and criticize as sociologists do.

[12] Although Serres claims to want a "pax" between science (reason, truth) and law (judgment) (146), often, in his text, he claims that science will win (especially pages 101, 128,133). He also frequently and clearly opposes those who are in the "clan of law," like Sartre and the moralist politicians, to those who, starting with Anaxagoras, a true philosopher, are fortunately only interested in the natural sciences and not to those of the city: for him the social sciences are "police" (106-113). Very logically, his Sage, the educated third party, is, practically, a scientific expert who makes the law.

[13] The term "We" is omnipresent in Serres' work.

To close this development we add that all these discussions and research imply that spokespersons for nature, especially scientists, will enable the firms concerned to know the ecological limits to be respected in order to have a sustainable economy. In this regard, the concept of resilience of systems developed by Walker, Holling, Carpenter and Kinzig (2004)[14] could play a fundamental role. Let us specify in this regard, to respond to the justified fears of Carton (2013, 172-5) on a problematic use of this concept that, in the CARE model that we will propose (see below), this approach is absolutely not intended to deny the responsibilities of social actors in the struggle for nature conservation in the name of ecological fatalism. On the contrary, it is a question of identifying these responsibilities precisely. Take as an example the case of greenhouse gases (GHGs) and examine how, according to this CARE model, a firm should proceed in practice. Six steps will have to be completed by this firm. The first is to do a carbon footprint to measure its current emissions. The second is to take into consideration the IPCC's requests to reduce these emissions over a given period and apply the requested reduction percentages to the current mass of emissions to determine the overall reduction volume of these gases under the period considered. The third is to find the least costly measures to achieve this goal within the time limit. The fourth is to enter the corresponding cost budget as natural capital-debt (concerning GHGs) on the liabilities side of the firm's balance sheet and, simultaneously, according to the double entry system, on the asset side of the balance sheet as usage costs of atmosphere. The fifth, each year during the period, to depreciate in annual fractions the cost of this asset and to pass the corresponding expenses in less of the profits, which will ensure a retention of funds in the firm in an egal amount. The sixth and final step will be to use the corresponding funds to finance the planned measures to reduce GHGs.

This serious system results in a multiplicity of "carbon costs": as many carbon costs as there are firms. It has nothing to do with the price of carbon, a concept invented by neoclassical economists, inspired by the theory of the internalisation of externalities, and therefore totally inefficient (see Richard

[14] These authors define resilience as the "ability of a system to absorb a shock and to reorganize itself while retaining essentially the same function, structure, identity and reaction capacity."

2012a, Rambaud 2015, Rambaud and Richard (2015a), Rambaud and Richard (2016), Richard and Rambaud 2020, 2021b, and especially Richard 2022d). Such are the main characteristics of this appliance of relational ontology which can be used for multiple elements such as soils, plants, animals etc. We therefore prefer to base ourselves on Latour's philosophy rather than that of Serres to achieve our attempt to replace the capitalist system with an ecological economy. But that does not mean that we agree with all of this philosopher's propositions. Our concern for putting into practice the ideas underlying relational ecology will lead us to modify somewhat, even substantially, the Parliament of things, in particular because of the consideration of a new ecological accounting model and social support for ecological co-management for firms and States.

Chapter 13
Putting relational ecology into practice: a new economy and a new management of firms

Introduction

We have shown previously that the modern capitalist system has been the main cause of the progressive destruction of the ecosphere since the late Middle Ages, and that the priority is to wage an (intellectual) war against it. The major problem with the principles formulated by Latour, like those of most philosophers of nature, is that they are not associated with proposals for concrete reform of the capitalist economy and, in particular, of its governance, of which accounting law, is at the heart of it[1]. The thesis that is defended here is that there can be no rapid and effective change of the current situation without a new ecological and social governance of the big groups which lead the world. This is what does not figure in most of the propositions which are usually made by philosophers. As we have shown, it is not a question of a deficiency peculiar to philosophers: since the time of Datini, there has never been, in practice, any serious questioning of modern capitalist accounting and, more generally, of its system of governance. Not even, as we have explained, on the part of economists with a Marxist tendency, starting with Marx himself. It is true that certain authors like Foster (2000, 2002) have sought to demonstrate that Marx would have had an ecological concern. But others, like Tanuro (2010), Benton (2003) and more recently Flipo (2014a, 185-190) dispute this point of view and believe that Marx only dealt very superficially with ecological problems and instead encouraged the use of nature as a source of wealth for industry. Regardless of this controversy, it is clear that Marx never

[1] Grange (2012, 70) adds to this type of limit to Latour's work the fact, according to her, that they would cast doubt on the value of scientific evidence, which would send "shivers down the spine" because it would be the "door open to all climatic and other populisms." This interpretation of Latour's thought seems to us, to say the least, highly questionable. In any case, if this were the case, it would not be ours: the CARE model is based on scientific knowledge provided in particular by ecology.

proposed an economic model that would allow the conservation of nature, or even, for the conservation of humans. He could not, supposing that he wanted it, since as a 'classical' economist he did not have the concept of capital-debt. The only attempt which could have constituted the beginning of an alternative is that of accounting for Yugoslav self-management inspired by Kardelj's work. But we have underlined its limits: it remained anchored in a modern perspective. It has been also shown in Rambaud (2015), Richard and Rambaud (2020) and Richard and Rambaud (2022b) that recent attempts to develop what is called the famous "Integrated reporting" of the IIRC (2013), which certain works such as those by Gleeson-White (2014) improperly qualify as "six capitals accounting," absolutely do not meet the demand for genuine ecological accounting, for three main reasons. The first is that this is not a real accounting, but, as the name suggests, a simple reporting tool. This is not at all the same thing because a simple reporting does not make it possible to calculate the profit of the firms in a systematic and permanent way and, more generally, is not an instrument of management of these firms. That is to say, in this regard, that those who offer "environmental" reporting as a solution to the ecological crisis want to fool those who do not know the mysteries of accounting: they want to pass off simple fragmentary information for real accounting. In this respect we stress that the creation of the International Sustainability Standard Board (ISSB) at COP 26 has not for goal to modify the today's international accounting standards but only to establish common disclosures (notably concerning information on the types of energies used).The second is that, under the guise of an apparent equality of treatment of these six capitals (financial, natural industrial, human, social and intangible), this type of reporting is based on the idea that only financial capital is real capital to conserve while the other 'capitals' are in fact simple means at the service of the subjects holding financial capital. The third, which corroborates the previous ones, is that there is not the slightest allusion in these pseudo "accounts" to the respect for ecological limits, starting with those that the IPCC asks companies to respect in terms of GHG emissions. However, as Simmonet rightly emphasizes (1979,70), "environmentalism calls for awareness of limits." Unlike Integrated Reporting, the ecological and human management model that we propose is accompanied by real accounting entirely based on this idea of limits, with the help of data mainly provided by ecological sciences at different levels, macroeconomic[2] or microeconomic,[3] as the case may be (see Richard and Rambaud, 2020 (67-100); Richard and Rambaud 2022b; Richard 2022d). This model therefore does not simply invoke the principle of resorting to these limits but systematically includes them in an accounting practice[4]. The basic works in this field are that of specialists in ecosystem resilience, in particular those of Holling (1973, 2001). The situation is quite different with integrated reporting: this type of initiative, which remains fully anchored in modernity, and which continues to make the financial capitalist the only real subject in the company, is in fact a delaying means which allows the capitalist class to make believe that it acts for the environment while continuing to pay the dividends of its financial management of companies. Therefore, we can say that currently there is no serious offer of ecological accounting that could constitute a real alternative to the IFRS, those international accounting standards which dominate the world. More generally, there is no alternative economic system that can encompass both a new governance of large firms and a new management practice from an ecological perspective. The only proposals that are made generally revolve either, in terms of management, around a generalization of traditional workers' cooperatives, or, in terms of the economics, around the taxation of the rich, in a perspective of redistribution of the Keynesian type, or finally, more generally, around simple catalogs of disparate measures of the type proposed in France by citizens, under the presidency of Emmanuel Macron. None of these measures targets the essential, even those which aim, more seriously, to propose a kind of state ecological planning[5]. They all indeed absolutely do not tackle the fundamental cause of current ecological and human problems: the governance of large firms, in particular their accounting system which is, let us underline, the basis of any model of national accounting and, hence of any type of planification. It is to fill this gap and allow a concrete alternative to the current system that we are proposing a new model of ecological accounting and governance in line with the principles of relational ecology: in short, a new imagination

---

[2] This is the case, for example, of the limits to be respected in terms of greenhouse gases.

[3] This is particularly the case for pollution and soil degradation limits, which must take into account the specificities of the different soils and the most varied types of crops.

[4] See the appendices for examples.

[5] As is particularly the case with the political current of France Insoumise in France.

based on a new reasonable calculative reason[6]. This is the CARE[7] model, which enables a "management revolution" to generate a new ecological economy based on a new social and political contract. We will present its philosophy first, but we will not stay there. It is in fact relatively easy to state fine general principles, as Kant did, in particular. It is not enough, for example, to transpose his famous formula "act in such a way that you treat others as an end and not as a means" by substituting, as Birnbacher (1994, 19) practically does, nature for man; or like Heidegger to advise not to "forget Being" or to say, with Gorz, that "only what is good for all is worthy of you, only deserves to be produced what neither privileges nor does not lower anyone." All this is fine and relatively easy to say but much more difficult to apply in practice, notably to the economy and to the management of firms[8]. We are therefore going, beyond the statement of general principles, to 'get our hands dirty' and analyze the consequences of these principles for corporate governance, particularly concerning the concepts of cost and profit and, more broadly, economy and world politics.

Philosophy of the new ecological management model CARE/TDL

The priority of men, before any search for their individual happiness, should be to conserve the natural capital which is the basis of everything on earth and the human capital of their colleagues: these capitals are indeed

[6] The term reason comes from the Latin ratio, the first meaning of which is calculation.
[7] CARE: in French "Comptabilité Adaptée au Respect de l'Ecologie"; in English CARE/TDL: CARE"Comprehensive Accounting in Respect of Ecology"; TDL: "Triple Depreciation Line."This type of accounting was initiated by Richard (2009-2012a) and developed by Rambaud and Richard (2015a) based on the thesis of Rambaud (2015). It has been presented to various institutions, particularly in France to the Accounting Standards Authority (Rambaud and Richard, 2016). It has also been quoted as a convenient device to reform the financial system in a report to the International Monetary Fund: see Bhattacharya, Ivanyna, Oman, Stern (2021).
[8] Let us stress in passing that Kant, to our knowledge, never mentioned either the capitalist practice of the Prussian firms of his time or even Prussian accounting law, one of the most advanced laws in the world at his time, although these practices and laws were totally at odds with his beautiful principles. All he had to do was read the ALR code (Algemeines Landrecht) but he did not do it or wanted to do it or, last more serious hypothesis, he read it but did not take it into account.

capitals. CARE[9] is precisely an accounting model that cares about people and nature in general. This model is based on a practical philosophy of the coexistence and conservation of living and material elements of the terrestrial ecosphere which is based on a non-dominant and inclusive conception of the human being and which, thanks to the use of the concept of capital- debt, leads to a radical change in the current economic and political system.

This definition has four main elements. *First,* the human being, particularly the capitalist, within the framework of this philosophy, contrary to the liberal-capitalist conception, is no longer a dominant subject: he must 'compose' with the other elements of the ecosphere which ensure his own conservation.

Second, to be able to achieve this objective of 'composition', CARE / TDL, unlike most previous philosophies, which privilege only one of the faculties of the human being such as reason (case of Descartes and Kant) or compassion (case of pathocentrist ethics), appeals to all human faculties: understanding as well as reason, vision, sensation, compassion, etc. However, in this model, a particular focus is given to understanding, that is to say the faculty that man, placed in adequate information conditions, can have to comprehend (cum prehendere in Latin) all of the phenomena which condition its existence. The primordial importance of comprehension (understanding) is underlined by an ecologist like Barbault[10] who affirms, about the problems posed by the ecological crisis, that "as in all matters, it is first necessary to listen, to analyze and to comprehend" (2006, 11)[11]. It is on this basis of a global comprehension that human reason can and must function to become reasonable and opt for the

---

[9] Care means care, concern; it gave in French the derivatives ' curé ' (one who takes care of others). The term comes from the Latin verb 'curare ' which means to take care.

[10] Director at the time of the ecology department at the Museum of Paris.

[11] Barbault (2006,211) himself refers to a book by Osborn (1949) who, to resolve the ecological crisis, believes that "the ultimate solution lies in understanding the long-term functioning of nature."

conservation of the biosphere, an act which, as Barbault (2006,37) shows again, is "quite simply to ensure the future of life." [12]

Third, CARE / TDL, unlike other approaches, especially those of traditional ecological economics, takes as a basis[13] for the realization of its philosophy the concept of capital-debt retained by modern classical accountants, a concept which, as we have seen, is a fundamental means of a systematic and permanent conservation of a thing.

Fourth, CARE / TDL leads to a complete transformation of the entire capitalist economic and political systems, which is rarely the case with the proposals that are being made today. This transformative action is made possible precisely by the use of the concept of capital-debt, which refers to the institutionalized relations that must be stabilized and preserved during the period of time between the two iterations of a device such as the 'Parliament of things'. We can indeed say that the relational ecological perspective requires the establishment of such a device: there can be no real ecological management without the possibility of a political activity, in the sense defined previously, capable of debating attachments from the business to the things it gets to use. All this is concretized in the recourse, adapted for the needs of the cause, to the concept of capital - debt (Ornaf and Rambaud 2012; Rambaud and Richard, 2015b). Thus things themselves are sources of worries, preoccupations, uncertainties and the institutional essences to be respected and preserved, more exactly their cost of preservation, form the capital in this approach of relational ecology. The reference here to the concepts of "preservation" and "preservation costs" rather than those of simple conservation (in the case of financial capital) is due to the fact that the degradation of biodiversity and the habitat of many populations of the globe, particularly in Africa and the Amazon, is such that simple conservation efforts are no longer enough: we must now at least preserve what remains of biodiversity and wild habitats that allow this biodiversity. On this point, we agree with the theses of the ecologist Waller (2010) regarding the famous debate which in the United States pitted supporters of preservation against those of simple conservation. Moreover,

---

[12] Hulot, in his preface to this book, takes up this key idea in another form: "diversity is nothing other than the life insurance of the planet" (page 9).

[13] Note: taking as a base doesn't mean that changes aren't made, which they are.

another argument in favor of this choice, to distinguish the case of the conservation of financial capital (relatively simple) from that of human and natural capital (more complex), the term preservation is also preferable, this concept being broad enough to encompass the conservation of financial capital (see below for more details).

The CARE model is therefore based on an ethics of preservation[14] extended to three types of capital (natural, human, and financial) and no longer reduced to financial capital alone, as is the case in the current capitalist perspective. To use a 'Spinozian' formula, this involves integrating the concern for preservation into the conatus. This ethic of extended preservation aims at and endorses what is essential on earth for all living things, namely their longest possible preservation[15]. It is supported and institutionalized, as we will show in more detail below, by a constitution subject to democratic approval and by laws, notably new company laws and new accounting laws drawn up by new political bodies. These laws will allow a systematic participation of citizens in the management of firms and countries with representatives of the three types of capital. Let us underline in this regard that before posing and approaching ontological problems in their detail (that of the essence of the various entities that make up nature) it is first for us, human beings, to say democratically what we want to preserve on earth[16]. Is it, as modern capitalists propose, only financial capital or should we also, as most ecologists advise, systematically preserve natural capital, which is itself the basis of the conservation of human beings? [17] Such is for us the fundamental choice. The main

---

[14] Unlike the feminist "Care" movement, CARE/TDL does not aim so much to repair the damage caused by the capitalist world (which is respectable) but, much more, to prevent this damage through conservative accounting.

[15] This need for preservation begins to manifest itself with the first cries or cries of the baby, human or animal, just born, as soon as it is hungry or threatened.

[16] It is a banality to say like Heidegger that we are there and that we have a "Dasein." Once we have seen it, we have to decide on our preservation, which certainly seems more difficult to achieve but more important.

[17] In a broad sense the concept of nature encompasses everything on earth including humans; In the restricted sense, chosen here for convenience in dealing with the problem, nature and natural capital encompass everything on earth except humans. These definitions of nature are not those found in particular in the nature/culture opposition where the focus is on a concept of nature untouched by any human influence.

characteristic of the human being, which totally distinguishes him from other species, is that he has, in principle, the possibility of making a choice on the evolution of the earth on which he lives. As we see it, this choice consists of the following alternative: either to let the modern capitalist system eradicate human life, even life on earth, or to prevent it from carrying out this destructive work. It is this freedom to choose that makes human beings responsible, unique in the world. Our hypothesis, which is based on the rationality and common sense of most human beings, with the exception of the fringe of the hard-hitting capitalists and their unconditional followers, is that the political response of the democratically consulted citizens, will go in favor of the second branch of the option. This optimistic hypothesis is based on the rationality of (informed) women and men and their desire for preservation in nature. It is therefore a question of preservation extended to three types of capital. Its realization through political responses, in particular the peaceful overthrow of capitalism, has nothing to do with the ideas of the search for well-being, virtue and happiness that mark ancient philosophy, in particular that of Aristotle. It has also nothing to do either with the speculations on the being or the essence of the man of the type of those of Heidegger which are completely disconnected from the concrete realities, starting with those of his time: in particular his "forgetting" of the misdeeds of the German capitalists who supported Hitler. Our proposals go beyond the simple general formulations without practical support of the Kantian style "act so that the effects of your action are compatible with the permanence of an authentically human life on earth" (Jonas, 1990, 30). They also have nothing to do with liberal attempts of the type proposed by Rawls which seek to maintain capitalism while softening its devastating effects. This is the reason why, while we may largely agree with Pelluchon (2015,244-250) on his goal of the primacy of sustaining life, we cannot accept her solutions. In fact, these aim to reconcile the liberalism (even modified by taking into account the satisfaction of primary goods) of Rawls (1987) with the eudemonism of Aristotle to lead to a kind of "alliance between enjoyment and justice," this justice remaining of a liberal type.[18] We also believe that

[18] Although Pelluchon (2015,251) considers that the primacy of freedom and equality is emblematic of Rawls' theory, the latter, as a true liberal who endorses capitalism, stops this freedom and this equality at the door of the companies that he sees as part of the private world.

the main cause of the current problems is a mode of production before being a mode of consumption, the latter being closely dependent on the former. It is not therefore, as Rawls does, to take as a basis a vague situation of "ignorance" but, on the contrary, to make a critical analysis of the reality of capitalism in order to succeed in its replacement.

Thus CARE proposes to start from the observation of the existence of the concept of capital-debt in the service of only capitalists to propose to extend it to other capitals. If we make this choice, economic and political actors will have to rely on ecological science which gives indications allowing to take into account the limits to be respected to ensure the conservation of these three types of capital. Then, accounting discipline and accounting law will make it possible to operationalize everything in a new type of ecological management of firms based on new balance sheet and income statement models. This last point clearly separates CARE ecological accounting from ecological economics which cannot lead to such fundamental indicators for the management of companies (Richard, 2009; Richard 2012a, in particular 74-84; and especially Richard, 2022d). CARE also sets itself apart from the traditional philosophical principles inherited from Enlightenment: neither Locke's rule (do what you want with the land you own as long as you work it) nor Kant's very vague rule (your physical possession or legal must respect the universal principle of law) are suitable for dealing with the crucial issues with which we are currently faced. On the contrary, CARE is based, concisely, on accounting conservation laws which cover both simple possessions (rentals for example) and possessions accompanied by a title deed. These general laws are intended to concern all firms on the planet, replacing the dangerous IFRS. CARE is therefore a model based on law, a fundamental instrument of any civilization. Thanks to the law, in particular the accounting law derived from the CARE model, the conservation rules proposed are precise and demanding: they go far beyond simple slogans such as "renaturing the human" or "saving the economy." CARE is therefore situated within the framework of a practical philosophy based on an observation of the reality of things, in particular of capitalism.

In this framework of reasoning, what is essential is the use of the concept of capital-debt understood, like traditional accountants, as something to be preserved and applied to things other than just financial contributions.

Before going into detail, let us consider, to give more clarity to our approach, our traditional example. Company E operates a forest F, the existence of which must be taken into account. In this context, a system of the type of the parliament of things type must be set up to monitor, among other things, this forest (and the other entities called upon to gradually compose a common world with the company). During the first round (at the beginning of year N) are invited spokespersons such as, for example, scientists, associations, foresters, residents, elected officials, enthusiasts of animal and plant observation of this forest, including members of the company who have shown their concern for these issues. From the debates about what this forest is, it emerges a deepening of the company's attachment to F (Berrier-Lucas and Rambaud, 2012). The essence of this forest thus becomes a capital for this company, which is learning to be attached to this entity not only as a provider of services but as a complex and variable essence. At the end of this first round, which gave rise to discussions, if not controversies, it is decided, on the one hand, that a second round will take place in two years, but also that to preserve this essence it is necessary provide a budget for costs to be borne by E, depending on the intended use. Let us suppose that this budget provides for the following expenditure schedule: in year N 200, in N + 1,700 and in N + 2,600. In accordance with the CARE / TDL method, the "value-cost" of the capital - essence of F will be equal to 1500 (200 + 700 + 600). We emphasize that the necessary existence of a repeat of these numbers, especially in the second round, prevents the costs of conservation from being definitive. Moreover, these costs are obviously neither objective nor subjective but collectively instituted, which, in the ecological framework, makes them legitimate. Thus these planned costs may be revised, even before period two, if additional information is obtained. In general, the actual conservation costs will be different from the expected costs: the usual pragmatism of classical accounting is therefore in order. This 'relational ecological' perspective leads to a completely new accounting balance sheet which allows us to escape the subject/object / structuring which characterizes the accounting of modern capitalism. In place of the subjects of the models of 'orthodox' approaches and 'environmental ethics' we have on the liabilities side of the balance sheet debts for the preservation of ecological capital, here the essence of F, towards multiple human and non-human entities. In the other orthodox and environmental ethics approaches, capital, with regard to nature, referred to substantial notions disconnected from the very reality of the entities concerned: these were global generic concepts. But within the framework of the Integrative Accounting CARE Model (IACM), the preservation of this forest takes place in its own environment, in its own relational existence and according to a particular type of operation of this company. With this micro-economic accounting instrument we refocus the debate on the reality of this forest and we get out of inoperative abstractions. It is therefore certain squirrels, certain climates, certain trees, certain foresters, etc. speaking through spokespersons and concerned with the essence of the forest which will 'appear' on the liabilities side with regard to ecological capital. The squirrels of this forest, in particular, will be called upon to collectively 'debate' during the first two phases of the discussion on the essence of the forest with the foresters about what this forest is. It is therefore a matter of co-determining the ontological description of the forest. It is on this basis that the conservation of the capital of this forest and therefore the company's capital-debt to this forest can be defined, without this forest being a subject of law (see below). The company will therefore have new "capital" debts, for example with regard to squirrels and the climate, in the event of forest degradation as a carbon sink. Each type of spokesperson will be associated with a conservation cost center, the total of these different costs being estimated, as we have seen, at 1,500 for the first stage. This accounting vision makes it possible to 'repopulate the accounts' with subjects - existences which co-determine their existences. Forest F is therefore neither a resource (or a means or an asset) as in the orthodox economic perspective, nor an end in itself as in the perspective of environmental ethics, nor a subject that has power over objects: it is an existence to be studied attentively, in particular during its uses by E, and of course to be preserved. It is therefore liable for the costs of its preservation, and not for its price value or the costs of damages inflicted, as is generally the case in orthodox views or even in environmental ethics.

But, in some cases, there may not be a capital. Take the case of a mining company that exploits part of the mountain. If this mountain is taken as a candidate to be a capital from a static perspective then it is clearly impossible to use it. On the other hand, in a more dynamic perspective, we can consider the conservation of a capital with a progressive and limited flow of material to be collected, in agreement with the spokespersons of the mountain, without calling into question the existence of this temporalized being. And this amount will depend, for example, on other types of mountain attachments, particularly with ecosystems or certain communities. This has nothing to do with 'rational' attitudes which consist in fixing 'optimal' levels of mining operations, which amounts to presupposing a certain relation to reality (notably orthodox reality) which denies the ecological character of it. It is indeed because the modern attitude does not discuss what the mountain is (which becomes de facto a determinable object, support of the 'natural capital' of the orthodox approach) that it is necessary to have to determine eco- politically the quantities of materials that can be extracted

.At the end of this reflection, we see that it is possible with relational ecology to take into account environmental entities for themselves in a very different way from modern approaches, in particular those of orthodox 'environmental' economics (based on the concepts of objective natural capital and existence value), and environmental ethics (based on objective intrinsic value).

In this new philosophical and accounting view there is a knot (nexus) between capital(in the classical accounting sense of capital-debt) and entities whose existence is to be taken into consideration for themselves. Let us again underline that, in this context, non-human entities are not considered as legal entities endowed with a personality: in this approach it 'suffices' to lay down the general legal principle that any company has the obligation to take into account the costs of conserving natural capital in its balance sheet. This in the same way as in the balance sheet of a sole proprietorship which does not have a legal personality: there is however an obligation to include on the liabilities side of the balance sheet a 'debt' of financial capital following any contribution by the founder of the company.

More generally, whether it is a business (entity) which has a personality or not, it is a decision taken by an 'adult' society to impose, in a new accounting law, the preservation of human and natural capitals, just as classical capitalist accounting law has imposed this obligation on financial capital. This in the same way that the right to drive a vehicle requires its owner or user to drive correctly on the right (or on the left for the English). No intention either, in this pragmatic and efficient legal approach, to enter into a "natural metaphysical, virtual and unsigned contract" with nature as proposed by Serres[19] (1990, 78). There is no need in this construction to invoke obligations towards future generations, as Jonas (1973) does. There is no need either to turn nature and its non-human components into legal persons as already proposed in 1972 by the jurist Christopher D Stone[20] and ecologists like Claude-Marie Vadrot (1973) in his "Declaration of the Rights of Nature." These proposals, which are currently being relayed by the jurist Marie Angèle Hermitte (2011), are quite commendable, defend a just cause and can provide elements to resolve part of the ecological problem we are facing. But besides that they proceed from a problematization which, curiously, amounts to extending modernity to nature, insofar as it is a question of creating new subjects,[21] they are not linked to a management practice, such as CARE's capital-centered approach, capable to provide concrete elements for the daily conservation[22] of nature for all ecological problems (see below). Likewise, the beautiful principles of Arne Naess' deep ecology platform (2009, 61) on the intrinsic value of nature and the critique of its destruction do not provide any concrete solution for a new economic practice. CARE, for its part, tackles directly the source of the

[19] What use can such a type of contract be if it is virtual? Capitalist accounting, on the other hand, has been imposed by law on all companies: there is nothing virtual in this type of "contract."

[20] This jurist invokes in support of his reasoning the fictions that the law knows how to create, in particular that of the legal personality of boats.

[21] Our argument against the creation of rights to nature differs entirely from that of Ferry (The New Ecological Order, 1992, 39). It is not a question, like him, of preserving humanism from ecologism (in particular a return to animism) but of laying down general rules for the preservation of non-humans and humans in the interest of these latter.

[22] Rather than multiplying lawsuits for non-preservation of nature, it is better to prevent them with the help of correct management. We must not put the cart before the horse.

problem: the management of the pernicious production of capitalist companies and not the general behavior of consumers.

In this regard, we can only agree with Foucart's thesis (Le Monde, June 21-22, 2020, p30) who courageously asserts, by referring to the Hummingbird movement, that "a modification of individual behavior is not in a position to change quickly "[the situation] and who, relying on the geopolitical specialist and member of the IPCC François Gemenne, underlines that" climate change is largely due to the functioning of the large structures which form the basis of the world economy, in particular energy production and food production which emit greenhouse gases." As he points out "doing your part [as an individual] is undoubtedly a great idea, but it is also a dangerous idea.. it can lead to the impression that a sum of small individual actions..might be enough." He adds, referring to an article by Jean-Baptiste Malet in Le Monde Diplomatique of August 18, 2018 that "many big bosses...and even officials from the most liberal right... appreciate the ideas of the Hummingbird movement, or even openly court its leader." He concludes, with reference to the Covid-2 crisis, against this generous liberal idea of doing your part individually, that even" the confinement of nearly half of the humanity will ultimately have only a limited impact" in terms of improving the ecological situation[23].

The CARE model, on the other hand, aims to attack capitalist structures of production as a priority and not small consumers. It is a matter of obliging multinational firms as a priority to conserve natural and human capital by extending the accounting concept of capital-debt to types of capital other than financial capital. We have shown that it is an accounting law that allowed the creation of modern capitalism,[24] the cause of the social and environmental crisis we are going through. It is another ecological accounting law which will make it possible to effectively emerge from this crisis through a general obligation of immediate conservation which is

---

[23] He quotes climatologist Corinne Le Quéré who says that "The drop in daily carbon dioxide emissions [..]following the confinement [..] only corresponds to the level of emissions in 2006."

[24] At least its primitive expression as it emerges towards the end of the Middle Ages in the cities of northern Italy such as Florence, Siena, Genoa and Venice (Lemarchand, 1992).

imposed on present generations, without needing to invoke the problematic respect of future generations or the recourse to sacred respect of nature[25]. In the context of this ecological accounting law, unlike what main stream economists generally propose, the fundamental notion is not that of value, whether it is an existence value, intrinsic, or economic one but, as in the case of classical accounting, that of the cost of conserving what we want to conserve. It is this conservation cost which expresses, as Rambaud demonstrates in his thesis (2015), the true 'value of existence'. In summary, what radically differentiates this approach from others is on the one hand the systematic consideration of the interrelationships between the various natural, human and financial capitals and the focus on their conservation costs, with reference to ecological limits and human rights, to the exclusion of any idea of valuation with the help of market selling prices. In this perspective, the capitalist concepts of dominant subject and of the value-price of things completely disappear (Richard, 2013). It is then possible to present concretely (but schematically) the typical structure of the CARE balance sheet as follows (the costs of using the capitals to be conserved or preserved being designated by "CU"[26] and the costs of their preservation, by "CP"):

Assets (CU of related entities)	**Liabilities (CP of related entities)**
Natural assets(CU of forests X, Y...)	Natural capitals(CP of forests X,Y ...)
Human assets(CU of employees)	Human capitals (CP of employees)
Financial assets (CU)	Financial capitals (CP)

Table 13-1 *Typical balance sheet of a company according to CARE / TDL*

While, as we have shown, the traditional capitalist balance sheet only treats financial capital as capital-debt, we see here an 'explosion' of capital - debts located in three distinct areas of natural (non-human), human and financial capitals. These three groups (types) of capital are to be kept separately in accordance with what is called 'strong sustainability' (Neumayer, 1999).

[25] For examples of recourse to this type of solution see Goldsmith (1992) and Hainard (1972) in Flipo (2014a, 284).

[26] The costs of use (CU) being dictated by the costs of preservation are equal to the latter. It is neither more nor less than the application of the rules of the classical double entry accounting that distinguishes liabilities (to be kept) and assets (to be used).

CARE is thus an accounting system that achieves real (non-formal) equality of treatment of the three types of capital which are all essential to the conservation of life on earth. It is therefore not possible in this conception, as the World Bank does in its accounts of the Wealth of Nations (2006),to compensate for a loss of biodiversity by the construction of new buildings, according to the so-called weak sustainability framework (Richard, 2012,192-7). Note that this rule of non-compensation applies in principle also within human and natural (non-human) areas. In the human zone one cannot compensate, as is currently done in the capitalist measurement of the Gross Domestic Product (GDP), the miserable wages of some by the exorbitant incomes of top executives linked to financial capital. In the natural zone, for example, losses of forests cannot be compensated by gains in meadows. On the other hand, it is generally the opposite principle that operates in terms of financial capital: nothing prevents a priori from replacing a production tool by another more efficient if this replacement does not call into question the preservation of human and natural capitals. It should be noted that this last remark is fundamental. In the CARE model technological progress is constrained by the strict conservation of human and natural capitals while in modern capitalism it is constrained by the conservation and a certain level of profitability of financial capital. Thus with the CARE model this new and major constraint should lead to a totally different type of technological progress. As shown by this new use of the double entry accounting system, a technique may accommodate to various possible uses: the main problem of techniques is that of the uses that one makes of them. In itself a technique is not more dangerous and problematic than another. As we show with the case of double entry accounting, this major weapon of destruction of modern capitalists can be turned against them: like some martial arts which use the strength of the adversary to fight him. What is problematic is the conception that human beings have of the type of capital to keep and, in particular, of the possibility or not of making compensations between the different types of capital: the choice of the concept of capital-debt is therefore essential.

It should be noted in this regard that in the CARE model the effective achievement of the separate preservation of the three types of capital will be verified by new auditors who will no longer be paid by the companies themselves but, given the crucial importance of this control, by a state body under the direct control of parliamentarians. Controlling the conservation of financial capital will be relatively straightforward. If we except the problem of taking inflation into account, it will only be a question of checking whether the financial capital stakes are well conserved.[27] The control of the preservation of human capital will be carried out both by spokespersons for this type of capital and by auditors specialized in labor law (see below). The most difficult task will be, as we will see, controlling the conservation of natural capital: for this type of capital, given its current "dilapidated" state (to put it mildly) if improvements are made to it rather than simple preservations we will not complain.

This new structure of the balance sheet of companies based on an integration of three types of capital on an equal basis will have drastic consequences. First, the establishment of a new type of corporate governance: ecological co-management. Second, a new way of calculating production costs and, third, the emergence of a new concept of 'ecological' profit common to the three types of capital. Let's start with the first consequence.

Towards ecological co-management in companies

Monsieur Jourdain used to say "I live on good soup and not on beautiful languages." But the human being, if he must be nourished in order to live, cannot really live his life and go towards his "Sein," to borrow the language of Heidegger, if he is simply nourished as a rabbit in a cage: he also wants to decide his fate at all levels of his political and economic life, especially in the capitalist enterprise, the 'box' where he spends a good part of his life, where he finds himself confronted especially to problems of hierarchical relations[28]. Simmonet (1979, 89) therefore quite rightly asserts the principle

---

[27] But it will be impossible for financial contributors to want to maximise their capital by relying on its potential value: the CARE model is in fact based on the cost 'value' of financial capital, a 'value' very easily identifiable since it most often corresponds to the sum disbursed for investing this financial capital. This, unlike the 'fair values' of IFRS, which often require very complex calculations to discount future flows of services rendered by assets, such as financial assets.

[28] Lévinas (Totalité et infini, 1994) takes up this formula of the "good soup" to add other elements to it, but does not mention the problem of freedom (Pelluchon, 2015, 36). See, however, his interesting thesis on "the ruin of representation" in his work of 2001 written against the philosophies of Husserl and Heidegger.

that "power relations are at the center of the concerns of environmentalists." Likewise, just as rightly, Eva Sas (2010, 119) insists on the fact that one of the central values of ecology is to ensure that each human being can "take his affairs in hand and, ultimately, assume his responsibilities," this within the framework of an" ethics of solidarity." These declarations seem to be in line with the denunciation by the sociologist Linhart (2021) of the "unsustainable subordination of employees."

But, oddly enough, it is difficult to find among environmentalists models of concrete application of this principle to business, the fundamental organism of life in society, the one that has the most impact in ecological and human matters. Among ecological philosophers, rare are those who like Grange and Stengers clearly denounce the capitalist model. Pelluchon (2011) has the merit of criticizing the "race for profit" and "profitability" (172-237-239-245) and of wanting to oppose a new philosophy to it. But even this committed philosopher does not offer a close analysis of the capitalist system, nor of the elements of its concrete transformation. She does not, in our opinion, sufficiently address the precise causes of ecological problems, those which mainly derive from the characteristics of the capitalist system, such as its type of accounting and its system of governance in the hands of shareholders. If she leads a fight it is rather, visibly under the influence of 'managerialists', 'rationalists' and 'anti-techniques', against very general, if not vague, things. This is particularly the case with the "managerial conception of work" (229), the "over-valuation of management" (238), the "technocracy" (238), the "managerial logic" (239), or, without more precision, with the "economic rationality" (246) or the "quantification" (248), the "rationalization and instrumentalization of reason" (247), or even quite simply with the "system" (244). How can we deal with such things where we do not know where they come from, or what they really consist of, or especially by whom they are actually controlled and used and in whose favor? As has already been shown there are many types of management and economics possible, even within the modern capitalist family. This does not prevent Pelluchon from saying, influenced by the theses of Arendt (1951) on the origins of the totalitarian system, that the capitalist actors are ''not the only culprits'' and" would not exist without the men who, for defend themselves individually, reinforce them "(103-244). How then is it possible to fight against such an enemy both invisible[29] and, moreover, supported by its victims?[30] No wonder she can't even come up with guidelines for a new type of business. Although we can broadly subscribe to her goals, we cannot as to her means, especially when she states that "it is by being resolutely modern that we can actualize the wisdom of the ancients" (247). One can also doubt that, as she asserts, the mere fact of "thinking of jouissance as an existential" (42) and the "removal of certain goods from the laws of competition" (173) are enough to change things. In fact our proposals are not incompatible, on the contrary, with her objectives. We only have the weakness to think that the CARE model, by directly attacking the roots of evil, makes it possible to reach them more effectively, especially by going beyond the current modern democracy which has never penetrated the management of companies.

The philosopher Stengers (2013,109), pictorially, asks the question "who is the chicken and who is the egg?" Our answer is clear. In the modern capitalist system the decisive role is played by the capitalist caste of the large multinational firms which brings together both the providers of financial capital and their allies the big managers, highly paid for their dirty work. Protected by an iniquitous legal system, this caste has proliferated practically since the Renaissance. CARE in a true humanist perspective therefore wants to free not only nature, but also citizens from the clutches of capitalism, supported by the liberal-socialists.31. Given the influence of capitalists and their experts, specialists handpicked to endorse their decisions, both in business and in political spheres, one cannot conceive of a new ecological society without the most rapid possible establishment of this ecological co-management in firms, especially big corporations with considerable power. This will prevent a huge amount of financial resources from being spent by the capitalists to control the press and opinion organs

---

[29] Pelluchon even asserts that this system "is only a mirage" (242): we think we see it but it does not exist! Even more difficult to fight against him!

[30] Pelluchon passes a little quickly, in our opinion, on the trade union struggles in France, as Arendt passes on those which enamelled the workers' struggles against Hitler, who was supported on the other hand by the big German capitalists.

[31] We have shown that both socialist and right-liberal governments have unabashedly supported the development of international capitalist accounting standards in all countries (Richard 2017, Richard and Rambaud 2020,2022 abc).

and 'buy off' numbers of politicians, economists and scientists. It will also bring the power of these often gigantic groups to a standstill and allow to consider their fragmentation into human-sized units that are less dangerous for other companies.32. Their financial resources have become so enormous that they can, in the absence of a credible alternative to capitalism, not only finance their political supports, but even manage to convince, through the media at their service, large parts of the populations of the lesser evil represented by their aberrant economic system. It is therefore necessary as a priority to show that another system of management is concretely possible and to use it to radically change the situation. This task is urgent and essential. Considerable time, of the order of 50 years, has been lost since the warnings of the famous Meadow report (1972) in prevarications organized by the capitalist caste: we must finally take the necessary measures to break this caste.

In this context, our thesis is that we will not quickly and sustainably change the current state policy without a drastic reform of the governance and management of large companies, in particular their accounting system. Against the Marx of the Grundrisse and the Gorz of the 1970s who believe that capitalism provides the weapons of its own destruction (Flipo 2014a, 197) we think that we must quickly get out of the current formal humanism and democratism which stop at the doorstep of companies, in which human beings as objects spend most of their lives, often suspended from the decisions made by subjects who live thousands of kilometers from these companies. One of the strengths and flaws of today's financial capitalism is that its agents decide the fate of people without even perceiving the dramatic consequences of their actions. Unlike Datini who could see the damage caused by his actions in his companies, at least those of his northern Italy, these financial capitalists can sleep peacefully: their victims are invisible. We must therefore change this inhuman system and massively relocate decisions to the level of firms. Unfortunately the corporate ecological revolution is largely forgotten by environmentalists, especially promoters of environmental ethics. The focus on the notions of intrinsic value and the rights of nature should not obscure the fate of human beings who are in companies. CARE therefore aims to relocate the

[32] But this will not prevent coordination agreements from being made between them.

power of citizens in companies and give it to all the representatives of capital who cooperate there: not only to financial capital, whose representatives will have to be profoundly transformed (see below).

With this "ecological co-management," contrary to the case in the famous American "Stakeholder Theory" inspired by Freeman (1984), it is not a question of offering a jump seat to scattered "stakeholders" while the effective power practically remains in the hands of financial capital providers (Richard, 2016-33). It is a matter of ensuring that the three types of capital are placed on a footing of strict equality in terms of decision-making power, within the framework of a precise legal structure. The very condition of an effective participation of citizens in the management of their businesses requires that they should not be taken for fools, as is the case today in all attempts at 'co-management' or 'co-determination' including the most advanced of these, German-type co-determination. In fact, in all these experiences, structurally, everything has been done to ensure that financial capital has the last word: how can we then imagine that discussions between the representatives of the various types of capital are serene, even possible, whereas in the event of disagreement the outcome of the 'debates' is predictable? To represent this crucial problem of the structure of debates, we can refer to the situation of citizens, in the context of their participation in political life, when there was censual suffrage, before the establishment of parliamentary democracy.

CARE thus wants to build a third generation of law with a new egalitarian right of citizens in societies and businesses: a strictly legal remedy that establishes new structures of egalitarian participation (Richard 2016). There is no solution, therefore, in CARE of the type proposed by Jonas with his "benevolent tyranny" and his "heuristic of fear": on the contrary, ecological change must emanate from beings who are masters of their decisions and lucid in the face of their responsibilities and not of frightened beings. The transformation of salaried personnel into real capital holders appearing on the liabilities side of the balance sheet on equal terms of power with

---

[33] This text provides in particular a description and a precise analysis of the theses of Freeman (1984), the main founder of the "Stakeholder Theory."

financial investors will change their fate of simple means. [34] Their representatives or,better, themselves, in the context of smaller companies, will be able to speak out on all company decisions, whether financial or not, especially those concerning new techniques or technologies.[35]

As such, these representatives in the decision-making bodies (General Assemblies, boards of directors, management, specialized committees) will have one third of the powers (votes). At first glance, this weight of votes may seem low, but it must be considered taking into account the other changes concerning other types of capital: we will show subsequently that if the employees of this new type of company use the methods of representation planned for natural capital and (new) financial capital in an intelligent way they will be able to acquire a considerable force of influence. Let us already underline that this representation, in terms of power, is independent of the importance of the contributions of these new partners, including those made by the employees under their "human capital"[36]. Indeed, in the CARE model, as in the family societies of antiquity, the size of human capital, whatever its nature, is taken into account only at the level of its preservation[37] and not at the level of its participation in the life of the company: at this last level it is not the dimension of the capital that is taken into account but the motivation and the capacity for innovation of its owner or its representative. With regard to human capital, this means that the power of new employee-partners is not linked to the size of their pay or their grade (see below): their power is based on the one woman/man one voice principle.

---

[34] The philosopher J.Grange (2012, 33) quite rightly speaks of "disposable employees." See also Ogilvie's Disposable Man (homme jetable) (2012).

[35] In this context, we should see radical changes in techniques in the service of humans and nature and not just financial capital. There is then no need to ask, as Anders suggests to engineers, to take the Hippocratic oath (Grange2012,84).

[36] The concept of "human capital" in CARE has nothing to do with that of the neoclassical school, in particular with the positions of Becker (1964). One human capital can hide another! See for more details on this point Rambaud and Richard (2017).

[37] This systematic preservation is not insignificant whether it concerns human capital or financial capital (see below).

The second drastic change made by CARE is that the pay of these associated workers will no longer be a salary[38] assessed in a labor market and dependent on its fluctuations, as is currently the case in most countries of the world, even of those who have instituted a minimum wage. This pay will be calculated on the basis of an amount which allows the possibility for these worker-associates to lead a dignified or decent life, having regard to the economic conditions of the time and of the country concerned and the locality concerned[39]. This fact alone will lead to a revaluation of the pay of a large number of employees as part of a drastic tightening of the pay scales, preferably of the order of one to five. This "conservation or preservation pay" will be established with the participation of the interested parties themselves, but also with the help of spokespersons such as unions, ergonomists, etc., this in compliance with the collective agreements that may be drawn up within the framework of re-conceptualized national or international agreements (see below). Such a pay is very different from the concepts of minimum income,[40] or universal income[41].

Indeed, on the one hand, it aims to ensure a decent and correct life and not a survival income and, on the other hand, it is part of the systematic participation of these people in the management of their business. On all these points it seems that we are in agreement with the proposals of Gorz (1990,54-74) who wanted for workers "a form of guaranteed income for life-normal and not basic or minimum" in a context of self-determination. It

---

[38] The word salary comes from the Latin sal -salis (salt). It refers to the salaries made in salt that Roman soldiers received within the framework of hierarchical relationships. This term of salaries is no longer suitable, neither etymologically nor practically in a conception of human relations in the company as envisaged by the CARE method.

[39] Our conception of a correct pay seems to join that of Nussbaum (2007) who speaks of the possibility of a "valid" and "flourishing" life (Frontiers of justice). See also Nussbaum and Sen (1993) and especially Corning (2011) and Anker et alii (2011).

[40] As the name suggests, this type of income is generally subsistence income and not proper pay.

[41] The universal income concerns, as its name suggests, everyone, employed or not. The CARE model, for its part, establishes for those who have a job a decent pay and for those who are involuntarily unemployed a subsistence pay which is systematically guaranteed and financed by the corporate community.

may also seem to agree, if we disregard the terminology, with the proposals of Friot (2012) of a "salary for life."

The third radical change comes from the fact that the very reason from their new status as partners the employees will be entitled to a participation in the common profit of the new company. Moreover, it is only at the level of this distribution of profits that we can consider that these new types of employees will receive real remuneration (or income) for their contribution as human capital. This in the same way that providers of financial capital receive dividends only after the conservation of their financial capital is ensured[42]. Obviously this co-management will not only concern the issue of pay but also that of working time. The ecological tradition is that of the reduction of working hours to "work to live and not to live to work" (Simmonet, 64). But how to achieve this goal without real ecological co-management in the company and, at the national level, without a new ecological constitution?[43]To achieve this goal it is absolutely necessary to break the capitalist dictatorship in the companies. In this regard, we share Gorz's (1990, 69) wish for free time to be allowed for family life. These questions of working hours will have to be the sole decision of the associated workers and their answers may vary from company to company, thus promoting great freedom in the choice of the alternative amount of pay-working time, given different pay levels[44].

Let us end this overview of the prerogatives of associated workers by invoking the case of company bankruptcies and the resulting layoffs. CARE's basic principle is to hold the corporate community responsible for the economic difficulties that arise in the context of their new ecological co-management and to institute a levy that will weigh on them to finance the

---

[42] In general, following J.B. Say, shareholders' dividends are compared to employee salaries. But this comparison is totally biased. A dividend automatically assumes the conservation of the financial capital invested (except distribution of fictitious dividends). But a salary covers, most often, at best, only the preservation of employees: this simple compensation is therefore not, in the proper sense of the term,a remuneration or an income.

[43] See the chapter 13-4 on this point.

[44] This means that those who prefer it will be able to have a lower pay than the preservation pay (as we understand it here). Different philosophies of life will thus be made possible.

payments of the workers concerned while waiting to find work. It is therefore a form of collective insurance managed by firms, which will make them responsible for their dismissal practices, whereas in the capitalist system, thanks to the flexibility of the capitalist labor market, they are generally not responsible for their actions. As Kapp (1950) said, firms currently are not obliged to pay the real price of their activity, which leads to their asocial practices.

Turning now to non-humans and therefore natural capital, we have already specified how their spokespersons will intervene, including at the level of the company, for determining their ontology and the conditions and costs of their preservation. But this type of capital will also have a say in the decisions of management to avoid, in particular, that they are taken to the detriment of its preservation. We could have entrusted this task to staff representatives only, but we considered it preferable to institute a specific representation of non-humans. As Flipo (2014, 190) quite rightly says, "even admitting that production is under workers' control, what tells us that the ecological objective will be achieved?." The experiences of really existing socialism have not demonstrated a break with productivism of the employers. Let us underline that the simple objective of 'gaining use', as Jacques Bidet and Gérard Duménil put it (2007, 256), in the sense of giving priority to use value over exchange value - a watchword that is widely taken up in Marxist literature-, remains too general an objective. We have shown that the urgency is not so much that of a theory of the mode of use by humans as of a theory of the mode of their preservation. In other words, the preservation value takes precedence over the value in use. In our opinion, ecological preservation therefore requires a particular representation. Indeed, recent experience has shown that including in Germany, a country with strong ecological traditions, representatives of the employee world do not necessarily have an ecological attitude, although they fight against capitalism. Our thesis is therefore that to anchor ecological issues even more within the company, we must add a specific ecological representation that will ensure the effective defense of the particular interests of non-humans. In this regard, we have opted for a broad solution that brings together representatives from different backgrounds: not only members of staff particularly noted for their concern for ecology, but also activists of ecological NGOs, scientists knowing the region and the company well, and especially the local residents who are victims of pollution (in the broad sense) of companies: as such, for example, the representatives of Amazonian tribes struggling with financial capitalism which destroys the forests where they live will have finally a voice in the matter, regardless of whether or not they own the land on which the companies concerned are located[45]. Like the staff representatives, these non-human representatives will have one third of the votes, to be shared equally in all decision-making bodies. Let us stress once again that the representatives of human and natural capital should not be confused with their spokespersons. The latter, as we have shown in the case of the example of the forest, intervene in matters of ontological order, while the former deal with management issues: strategy and allocation of financial results in particular.

Let us now discuss the case of representatives of financial capital providers. Many current proposals in left-wing circles tend to completely exclude this type of representation of firms: we generally remain in the 'self-management' logic, in the sense that the workers have (at least theoretically) all the power. This is the case, for example, with the proposals of Friot (2012) and Borrits (2018,2020), the latter, in a very suggestive way, wanting to "fire the shareholders." We understand the motivations of these authors who reason by taking into account the traditional and current behavior of capitalists, especially big financial capitalists. But we believe it is a mistake to attempt to fix this problem in this way, for several reasons. The first reason is that this attitude seems to derive from an erroneous Marxist conception which makes the private property of the means of production the cause of all current evils. Haro therefore on any ownership of assets or of shares in companies. We dispute this view. For us, already, the case of small family businesses, particularly agricultural ones, must be treated separately: their characteristics are very different from those of large modern capitalist firms and are more like, in terms of state of mind, of those of the pre-modern antiquity. But this problem of private ownership of the means of production does not appear to us to be the case either in large enterprises, generally in the form of companies. A precise legal

[45] This would not prevent their members from also being able to act as employees of companies.

analysis of modern capitalism shows that the "biggest" and the most powerful capitalists are precisely those who, in stockholders companies (SHCs), *no longer own the means of production of these companies*. In fact, in an SHC, as, notably, Thaller (1904), then Ripert (1952) and, more recently Robé (2011)[46] have shown, because it has legal personality (as wanted by the capitalists themselves to escape the seizure of their personal patrimony), it is the company itself which owns the means of production. Consequently, the shareholders, legally, are no longer proprietors of the means of production, but only, in respect of their shares of capital, creditors of this type of company.[47] But this situation of non-owner of the means of production does not in any way prevent them from really having power in the SHCs: it was enough for the jurists to declare that it is only the holders of (financial) capital-debt who have the power in the fundamental bodies of the SHC (in particular its General Assembly) and that accounting law is exclusively oriented according to their interests. Berle and Means in 1932 claimed in a famous book that the capitalists kept property but lost power. This managerialist thesis was then taken up by many political scientists,[48] sociologists, philosophers and even economists. But, from a corporate and accounting law perspective, at least, it is, as we have shown (Richard, 2015a), a baseless thesis. In truth, the exact opposite has happened in SHCs: the capitalist shareholders have lost ownership of the means of production but, despite the dispersion of their capital, kept power, notably thanks to their accounting system.[49] Consequently, it appears that lawyers have been perfectly capable of granting the power of management (and of undoing it) without any question of property, whether it is a question of property of means of production or claims on these production means. If this is so there

---

[46] The great merit of Robé is to have recalled this evidence often forgotten, in particular by economists, who, with Friedman and the school of agency theory, base the power of shareholders on the ownership of the means of production.

[47] This legal recognition of capital-debt in public limited companies, which dates from the 1860s in Europe, in no way detracts from the credit of an unknown accountant from northern Italy for having invented this concept at the end of the Middle Ages.

[48] The latest being Musso (2020).

[49] Concretely, they will first of all pay the top managers very well, whom they appoint, so that they follow their wishes. But above all they will content themselves with looking each year if the last line of their income statement shows a sufficient profit and vote with their feet (sell their shares on the stock market) in the opposite case: this will generally be enough to influence the decisions of the so-called all mighty managers.

is no need to eliminate shareholders to resolve the question of the power of the capitalists: it is enough to reduce their rights and power in the company as we do with the CARE method. This reduction of rights and power concerns four fundamental elements. First, in CARE, holders of new financial capital will no longer have any right to demand a systematic dividend. Their only fundamental right will be that of the conservation of their capital contribution, which is by no means negligible. The reader will probably object that he does not see how shareholders could be interested in an investment which does not necessarily pay off. But this is the situation of the millions of people who lend their money in banks at almost zero interest rates with the sole concern of keeping that money. Capitalism fully accepts this situation for these types of investors.

Secondly, these new shareholders will only represent a third of the votes in the administrative bodies, while specifying that they will have to share this power not only with the states and the communities which provide funds to the firm but also with all the money lenders.

Third, they will be on an equal footing with one woman/man, one vote with each other, just as in family businesses of antiquity.

Finally, fourth, they will be forced to share a common profit with the other types of capital due to a new accounting law (see below). These are the main elements of this first type of argument against the suppression of shareholders.

Now we come to the second type of argument. While it turns out naïve if not impossible to imagine that we can transform the attitudes of current shareholders, we can nonetheless foster the birth of a new "breed" of shareholders who would readily accept the rules of the game proposed by the CARE model. We can think first of all of those who nowadays invest their savings resulting from their work in production cooperatives. In this regard, the CARE model could appear as a proposal for the generalization of production cooperatives,[50] at least in an established and specific form. Instead of remaining within the optional framework of the current

[50] But without the partner-employee dualism which is totally contradictory with the CARE model

cooperatives, their application would be generalized with, however, an ecological connotation that these cooperatives do not have today. CARE is indeed aiming for an effective cooperation of the three types of capital through a drastic transformation of the mentality of financial providers. This would probably attract a much larger number of people, especially "little people," who would be more willing to entrust their savings to companies, whereas they are reluctant to do so in the model of current financial capitalism. Let us add that these 'new small shareholders' would be at an advantage compared to the 'big ones' because, as we have just seen, in CARE/TDL, the right to representation is not proportional to the size of the invested capital: once again it is the rule a woman (or a man) a voice which is applied. We would therefore be heading towards an 'explosion' of the number of associates and a radical transformation of the shareholder structure. If we accept this type of reasoning, we can all the less deny these new shareholders the right to participate in the decision-making bodies of companies as this right is already granted to members of production cooperatives who have contributed their savings. Company employees, in particular, will thus have an additional incentive to invest in their companies, especially since a company solidarity mechanism will make it possible to insure the losers in the event of non-tort bankruptcy (see below). In short, the new employees of these new firms will then have the opportunity to be able to participate in the decisions of the companies for three different reasons: as contributors of human capital, as contributors of financial capital and even, although at a smaller level, as defenders of non-humans. Under these conditions, if they 'manage' their strategy well, they will be able to have a major influence in the firms where they are present.

The third type of argument relates to the solutions advocated by supporters of the total foreclosure of shareholders. As, for them, direct recourse to private savings is impossible or at least unwanted,[51] they only have two solutions left: either a withdrawal of companies' savings by the state (Friot's solution), or the centralization of private savings in state-owned banks whose managers will decide how to use them (Borrits' solution). In the first case, the company is practically no longer an institution responsible for its

[51] It should also be emphasized that, paradoxically, this recourse is accepted within the framework of production cooperatives.

management. In the second case one risks witnessing the re-emergence of a class of bureaucrats with powers similar to those held by the masters of the Gosbank of the USSR or the directors of the banks in the former Yugoslavia, supposedly self-managing[52]. It should be noted, moreover, that these two types of solutions paradoxically result in strengthening a kind of management based on indebtedness, which is in contradiction with the requirements of company stability and more generally of the principle of prudence. The tragedy of certain hard-line Marxist theorists, including Kardelj (1975) the father of the Yugoslav self-managed economy, is to have excluded any individual financial participation of citizens in firms, which prevents the possibility of a real economic democracy. It therefore seems clearly preferable to us to play on the solutions of the CARE model which are based on external financing in the form of capital contributions to companies 'by the people,'[53] with advantages granted to shareholders who really participate in decision-making, which should encourage those who are close to these companies and thus favor local financing provided by many new small shareholders. Charb (2009, 52) has written que "the big shareholder is a dangerous predator..".while the small shareholder is a failure who thinks he can one day find himself in the shoes of a big shareholder...And finally a ruined idiot who finds himself in underpants in the middle of the street" (2009, p.52). Admittedly, this is often the case at present, but we must remain optimistic and think that new, more social, more intelligent and more present shareholders will be able to emerge.

This will make it possible to have companies less dependent on the international, in particular on the big capitalists who impose their will thousands of kilometers away. This aspiration to independence from

[52] It is practically impossible to conceive of a non-bureaucratic management solution for centralizing banks of public savings, whether private or public. Experience has proven this even in the so-called "popular" banks. Better is a real popular capitalism in which citizens put their savings directly into their companies (or others) managed within the framework of ecological co-management.

[53] We are aware that this expression may shock because of the confusion with the slogans that capitalism has always wanted to formulate in favor of a "people's capitalism." But, in fact of 'popular' capitalism, it was rather a question of trying to capture a fraction of the savings of the people to better strengthen the power of the "big capitalists," and to reduce to the maximum the powers of the employees and, more generally, citizens, in the company. CARE's popular capitalism has nothing to do with that, especially since it is coupled with a totally different accounting law.

anonymous shareholders will be all the more reinforced as, in the CARE model, self-financing is possible on the basis of the common profit generated by the companies. This last point leads us to the question of cost and profit concepts in this model.

Towards new concepts of full cost, fair price and ecological profit

Kapp (1950) rightly asserted that capitalism is an economic system that does not fully pay its human and natural production costs. We have shown how it systematically protects only one type of capital, financial capital. In this world of truncated costs we are witnessing a gigantic distribution of fictitious dividends widespread on a global scale. On the contrary, the CARE model aims at the systematic conservation of the three types of capital that underpin the activity of any business: natural capital (at the base of others), human capital and financial capital. These three types of capital, as we have shown, are 'valued' on the basis of a new 'ecological economic value', that is to say their cost of conservation or preservation, and not on that of a capitalist economic or financial value. This new type of costing results in the formation of a full ecological cost of the various products produced by the companies and, on this basis, in 'fair' ecological selling prices. The history of religions and philosophy is marked by the quest for the fair price of products, a question without a practical solution in most cases. This quest is even more important today in a world marked by capitalist globalization. CARE's concept of full ecological cost can be precisely the foundation for a new kind of fair product pricing. The systematic imposition of such prices at the national and international level would make it possible to put an end to the ecological and human dumpings which characterize the capitalist system, a situation still today not only approved but also favored by great world institutions such as the World Trade Organization(WTO)[54] and the World Bank (see Richard and Rambaud, 2022ab and Richard 2022d).

---

[54] The World Trade Organization has instituted a legal procedure to fight against companies which underestimate their production costs, in particular against those which do not expense all of the depreciation of their machines. But this does not concern the question of depreciation of humans and nature.

It is this legal dumping, sometimes accentuated by aid to large capitalist firms, especially in times of crisis, which 'kill', in particular, small peasants throughout the world and relegate them to shanty towns, or even lead them to suicide, as this is shown by the works of agronomists such as Parmentier (2007) and Dufumier (2012).It is also these dumpings that contribute to the torture of millions of animals transported in appalling conditions, after a short life, to be delivered and slaughtered thousands of kilometers from their place of birth[55]. Systematic application of the CARE model, coupled with measures to tax the human and ecological surplus profits of recalcitrant capitalist firms would allow small farmers to sell their products at their real production costs, thus promoting agriculture that is mindful of the condition of men, animals and nature in general. In this context, there would no longer be any need to resort to subsidies or hidden aids such as payments for ecosystem services. These capitalist 'solutions' are only palliatives to avoid a fundamental questioning of an aberrant economic system which leads farmers to ask for alms in order to be able to sell their products. It is therefore imperative that prices, especially agricultural prices, take into account the full burden of human, non-human and natural capitals [56] if the current type of catastrophic globalization is to be avoided under the aegis of financial capitalism. African food crops have been completely destroyed due to the fact that its productivity is apparently lower than that of European exporting countries and its production costs much higher. But this productivity and these European costs are fictitious because they are based on a systematic destruction of the soil and the living conditions of small farmers, not to mention transportation costs unrelated to their real ecological costs. It is this type of destruction, often aided, moreover, by subsidies, linked to the ravages of global warming, which are often at the origin of human migrations around the world. But, generally, the Western political classes ignore these root causes of migration and

[55] Although this problem cannot be adequately addressed in this short work, CARE's position is to promote vegetarianism by all possible means and, simultaneously, to introduce a drastic overhaul of the conditions for raising, transporting and slaughtering animals that can deliver them from suffering and stress. This reform should in particular include strict regulations on the maximum length of transport distances for the animals concerned.

[56] We will not deal here with the problem of differences in purchasing power parity but these should also be taken into account in anti-dumping actions.

prefer to accept, willy-nilly, to receive these migrants on minimal conditions, with the blessing of the employers who are delighted to find a docile and cheap workforce. These migrations must absolutely be stopped by establishing fair agricultural prices and by helping farmers in the countries affected by these tragedies to be able to stay at home, which they generally want. This is not to mention actions to end dictatorships which only exacerbate these problems. It is also imperative that the development of techniques, particularly agricultural techniques, be under the constraint of the conservation of the three types of capital as proposed in the CARE model and that these technical innovations be widely disseminated for the benefit of all. This will not prevent even globalized trade if the entire world economic system respects ecological and human conservation limits. Contrary to what is often asserted, it is not Globalization (with a capital G) which is in itself a problem but a particular globalization, of the capitalist type. It is therefore a matter of finding another form of globalization that makes it possible to re-establish the conditions for competition or, better, for healthy emulation, based on the systematic conservation of men and nature everywhere on the planet. Contrary, also, to the theses of Postone (1986-2009) exposed in particular by Flipo (2014a, 192-193) or of the German situationist movement Wertkritik,[57] specifically of an author like Jappe, the problem is not that of the 'abandonment of value' but its replacement by a new ecological value based on the concepts of conservation costs of the three types of capital.[58] This is possible within the framework of the CARE model which establishes new rules of the competitive game and which ensures the assumption of responsibility by the community of companies of the vagaries of economic activity.

As part of this new conception of ecological costs and prices some companies, thanks to innovations, will manage to have lower costs than others, which will lead them to have justified profits and, thus, greater

[57] See the site www.palim-psao.over-blog.fr (cf Flipo 2014a, 193).

[58] It seems to us that an author like O'Connor (1988, 11-38), who claims to follow a "Marx-Polanyian synthesis," aims for this objective but without the possibility of concretizing his approach due to ignorance of the concept of capital-debt. (See Flipo 2014a, 195-196).

chances of economic expansion than others[59]. CARE therefore recognizes that there can be a 'green profit' and recognizes that this type of profit that stimulates economic activity has its place. By affirming this we are aware that we are going to make certain left ecologists "howl," more especially those who claim to be followers of Marx or of Illich, qualified by Flipo (2014, 237) as 'Marx of the ecologists'. But, except to abandon all the terms that capitalism has used and polluted (-and there are many-), which seems to us a tactical error, if only on the educational level,[60] we prefer to address ourselves to a reader who is not entirely held up by a literal dogmatism and which admits that the same word can have several meanings, in particular an initial meaning which has nothing to do with the later meanings which will be, often abusively, given to it, in particular by the capitalists[61]. CARE is not an anti-scientific and technical progress system, quite the contrary: it 'only' considers progress under the constraint of respect for the three types of capital and the calculation of an ecological and human profit: as what the concepts of progress, of scientific policy, just like those of economic value or productivity (productivism), of wealth and even of profit, mean absolutely nothing on their own. There is in particular a capitalist productivism and a non-capitalist one. It all depends, once again, on the concepts of capital to be preserved (conserved) which are implemented.

In the case of CARE three types of capital are now conserved (preserved) and a profit obtained under these conditions, which is not a priori a bad thing. In this context, more efficient ('productive') firms will have a possibility of faster growth than other firms, on condition that they respect not only CARE's accounting rules but also those of the wider ecological society in which they operate: in particular rules for sharing scientific and

[59] The issue of the transmission of knowledge of new management methods and new technologies will not be addressed within the restricted framework of this book. Let's just say that it will take both a reward for innovators and at the same time wide access to their discoveries.

[60] It seems fundamental to us to show that all the terms with an economic vocation have evolved in history according to the ideologies which animate the different economic models which have followed one another (see notably Richard, 2010).I

[61] In this case CARE refers to the initial meaning of the term capital in the Greeks as an important thing and profit in the Latins as a good thing for the human being. What is wrong with using these words with this meaning? For the term accounting, the reader may refer to Richard (2010).

technical information and for the systematic conservation of the three types of capital. Contrary to Illich's thesis according to which any accumulation of means and wealth can only lead to regressions, it seems even to us that, within the framework of this new approach to profit, a growth of these companies is possible which can be a vector of progress for all firms and beneficial to all citizens. It's all about respecting constraints, particularly ecological and human ones. It should be noted in this regard that CARE is based on the same principles of respect for ecological constraints as those mentioned by supporters of degrowth such as Latouche (2006). But, unlike the latter it does not make degrowth (a vague concept) an objective but a consequence of the constraint of respect for ecological and human limits and the conservation of the three types of capital. Within the framework of these new constraints there will surely be a sharp decrease in current (largely fictitious) profits but a growth in the weakest pay. There will be a decrease in the production of cars and planes but an increase in public transportation and bicycles or walking. Difficult to make an exhaustive catalog of decreases and growths. In our examples (in the Appendix) we show how there are strong declines in profit and GDP, for complex reasons that are both conceptual and operational. That said, with regard to this last 'operational' point, it is almost certain, as Bihouix (2013, 95-116) convincingly shows that recycling, often presented as a panacea, will not be a sufficient solution to resolve the current crisis. It is also likely that production of unrepairable and disposable products will have to be discontinued. This in favor of repairable and long-lasting products as was the case in the 'old days'. It is also likely that we will have to favor thermal solar energy with small installations to the detriment of gigantic nuclear power stations and a revival of little towns and villages to avoid long transportation and massive road or even rail infrastructure.

But all this comes under concrete solutions of growth or decrease that are not the domain of CARE. The main thing, again, in CARE, is the 'ecological and human' constraint of all economic activity with adequate accounting instruments.[62] This in the same way that the capitalist system did not need to enumerate the activities that he was going to develop: it contented itself

[62] It is perhaps at this level that we will not agree with Bihouix who plans to eliminate accountants and lawyers (2013, 114). He does not see at all their major role in the preservation of capital.

with putting the economic activity under the constraint of the conservation of (only) its financial capital. These are the concrete modes of this constraint that unfortunately do not propose the authors of degrowth. But the objectives of this "degrowth" movement are common with those of the CARE model, which should allow an alliance and a common struggle against capitalism.

It remains that in our vision if firms can have a growth of their ecological profit within the framework of these constraints why prevent them? There is, let us be clear, no religion of growth any more than a religion of degrowth. We can even say that in our new model of accounting there may be a certain ecological accumulation, an expression which should startle all Marxists and even ecologists who do not know the possible variations in the management of firms according to the concept of capital used.

The type of profit that results from the application of the CARE model will have two basic characteristics. On the one hand, it assumes covering the costs of preserving humans and nature and can thus be qualified as both 'human' and 'ecological'. On the other hand, it is a *'common profit'* resulting from the common use of the three types of capital. Indeed, contrary to Marxist theses, we adopt here the theses of the Proudhonian economist Cornelissen (1913, 152-3) [63] who maintains that past (dead) labor contributes, as well as living labor, to the result of companies. Marx indeed made a drastic distinction between living labor and dead (past) labor, the latter being for him a vampire who sucks life from living labor, the exclusive source of wealth creation. But why focus only on the case of capitalists who have monopolized the work done by others? Why not take a different look, in a cooperative type of enterprise, at the past work of workers of previous generations and even of current generations. We do not see why a retired employee who saved and invested them in a cooperative of production would not be considered as participating in the wealth creation of this cooperative and, therefore, allowed to be a representative of the financial capital in its administrative bodies.

---

[63]. We thank the philosopher Jourdain (2019) for pointing out this important author and for taking an interest in the CARE model.

Let us add that, for us, non-human nature is also a contributor to the common result. It is therefore logical, under these conditions, that these three types of contribution will all be represented and that the result of the firm will be considered as a common good. During the general assembly which will decide on the distribution of this kind of ecological profit, the three types of representatives will therefore have to agree: first on the choice between the retention[64] or the distribution of common profits, and, then, on the modalities of the distribution of a part of profits. But CARE does not fall into naivety or utopianism: the existence of a new common profit will not make the new ecological firm a fraternity in the sense of Gierke (1868) or a community linked by a common ethos in the sense of Hegel (Pelluchon 2015, 215). However this common profit is likely to reduce the antagonisms that automatically result from the selfish conception of current financial accounting. We have seen previously that while in the capitalist accounting model wages are expenses which weigh on the profit of the capitalist, in the CARE model the three types of depreciation expenses corresponding to the three types of capitals *weigh together* on the new type of common profit. In the context of this new type of revolutionary profit calculation, we can estimate that the three types of new 'investor-associates' will be keen to harmonize their views in order to have real human and ecological profit. We will thus have the basis of a better cohesion of the various providers of capitals: they will be obliged to discuss among themselves on the basis of a common ecological benefit to be improved. Dividends may be awarded collectively or individually to employees but also to particularly deserving financial capital contributors (for example in the case of stability of their stake and their active and face-to-face participation in decisions). But, once again, let us underline that, unlike the current system, there can be no clauses (statutory or not) providing for a systematic distribution of dividends as is currently the case. The constraint of the famous 'cost of capital' therefore disappears completely in the case of the CARE model. Thus, in this context, the end of the annuitants that Keynes dreamed of should be assured. Normally, if the new co-managers are vigilant, we should see the end of the concentration of power and wealth in the hands of a minority of private or public

[64] This reserve can be used to finance ecological investments (reconstruction of wetlands, for example), as well as human (new training) or financial investments.

capitalists and overpaid executives at their command. Gone are the quasi-divine powers of an 'elite' of private or public capitalist managers who pays themselves exorbitant salaries and dividends. Gone is their ability to control the media and politics. Contrary to Rousseau's famous thesis,[65] the problem is not that of the enclosure of land by a private (or public) owner but a problem of power and of management model.[66]

In this conception of control 'at the source' of the distribution of wealth no need, as most Keynesian progressive economists advise, of a tax on wealth. There is also no need, as Rawls (1987) suggests, for 'alms' to keep the weakest from dropping out, while allowing capitalists to continue to dominate the scene. There is no need either for an illusory expectation of a collapse of capitalism which would deprive itself of outlets by compressing wages and dig its own grave. Moreover, it is naive to believe in the famous 'ruse of history' which would automatically destroy the capitalist economy because of the unequal distribution of productivity gains and the deprivation of outlets due to the compression of wages.[67]

It remains to examine the case of losses, a situation that could be a major obstacle to the implementation of ecological co-management. We know that, for the most part, the power of capitalists in companies is justified by the existence of this risk of losses. To put it simply, according to the capitalist vulgate, employees do not take risks and do not have power, while shareholders do take this risks, and therefore 'logically' have power. A first response to this type of argument would be to say that employees, consulted nationally on this issue, for example with the help of 'popular initiative referendums', also decide to want to take the same risks as shareholders in stockholder companies. This would make sense in the

---

65 We know the famous formula of Rousseau (1754, 91): "he who first, having enclosed a piece of land, took it into his head to say, this is mine, and found enough simple people to believe him, was the true founder of civil society..be careful not to listen to this impostor, you are lost if you forget that the fruits belong to everyone and the land to no one."

66 In the Alps, nowadays, small or medium-sized farmers enclose their fields to prevent their cows from disappearing: are they going to be banned or even, following the Soviet example, dekulakized?

67 It suffices for this that the capitalist class itself consumes in sufficient splendor the product of the wealth it has extorted, while also paying for the pleasure of having minions in its service. This is clearly demonstrated by the work of Piketty (2012, 2014).

context of the CARE model with the transformation of capitalist societies into 'three-capital-debt' societies. In addition, more generally, this would make it possible to make citizens more responsible: they would finally have the possibility that things depend on the choice of their actions, including in companies. But, until now, these citizens have never been consulted on this point by national or international political bodies. Another type of argument, in favor of a change of the system, consists in proving that the risks taken by the capitalist shareholders are not as great as the defenders of the capitalist system want to say. We have already pointed out that modern capitalists have invented a type of accounting which in principle protects their capital. Obviously, this protection does not prevent the occurrence of contingencies, especially in the context of capitalist competition and the economic crises that characterize it[68]. But it can be shown that the entire history of large capitalist corporations is marked by a constant and successful desire to avoid, or at least limit, the liability of capitalists for losses (Richard, 2015a). Undoubtedly, in Datini's time, the capitalists assumed the risks they take and, in the event of bankruptcy, not only respond to their personal property but are often covered with opprobrium: the bankrupt who cannot repay his debts is a dishonored man and if fraudulent bankrupt becomes excluded from society[69]. We can therefore consider that in a certain way they are totally and truly responsible for their actions, with regard to their financial capital, both in their way of acting (principle of prudence) and also legally (financial sanctions, even criminal ones). This situation will last until the beginning of the 19th century: it is the era of classical capitalism which remains in a family configuration. But around 1850, with the creation of public limited companies (notably SHCs), things changed. In fact, as we have seen, in this new legal context, the capitalists, including the big ones, are no longer responsible in the event of bankruptcy on their own assets for debts that

[68] The fact that the capitalist system has instituted a principle of systematic conservation of financial capital is an 'enormous' event that allows capitalists to enrich themselves globally in the long term. But this global and long-term evolution obviously does not prevent fluctuations, or even disasters for some.

[69] The term bankruptcy comes from the Italian "banca rotta." In the brotherhoods of Italian merchants of the High Middle Ages, when one of them made a fraudulent bankruptcy, the bench (banca) in his name on which he sat was symbolically broken and he most often had to leave his town.

exceed their investment in capital: this is a first legal, fundamental, loss of responsibility unthinkable at the time of Datini[70].

Subsequently, the capitalists, mainly in the SHCs, will invent a whole series of techniques which make it possible to reduce their responsibility even more. First they will endeavor to reduce their capital stakes as much as possible to favor the maximum recourse to financing by debts (at the lowest possible rate). So, in the event of bankruptcy, they will tend to make bear the losses by their lenders, while not paying them to increase their profitability: this is the famous technique of 'leverage' taught in all the 'good' finance textbooks. In the same spirit, instead of favoring self-financing (in particular the reinvestment of profits) as their ancestors did, they will tend to distribute these profits massively in order to be able to invest part of them in less risky investments than companies (for example in real estate): this will allow them to have substantial reserves in the event of problems with their businesses. Another process, which goes in the same direction, but in a more systematic way, will consist in ' not putting their eggs in the same basket' with what is called the diversification of the equity portfolio (while capitalists like Datini invested heavily in companies that they founded themselves). As part of this prudent management, a policy of diversified long-term investments often makes it possible to overcome economic crises. But other means are still available in the case of very large companies. One tactic for them is to have the most risky investments, such as research costs, financed by governments. This is remarkably illustrated by an author like Mazzucato (2014). Finally, last resort, for really the biggest SHCs, that of the financial assistance of the state as we could see it more and more during the financial crises of the 21st century (like the crisis of 2018) and, more recently, during the last ecological and health crisis of the 'corona virus' in 2020.

In conclusion on this point the capitalists who lead the world in the large limited companies have imagined a whole panoply of recipes which allow

[70] At the time, this disempowerment was highly criticized by certain jurists who saw in it the end of capitalism or at least those of the values of prudence and foresight (Richard 2012b).

them to considerably reduce their risks[71]. It is therefore a little simplistic, to put it mildly, to say that capitalists assume the coverage of all risks in the company: their tendency is to take less and less risks.

Now consider the other 'side' of classical reasoning which is to say that employees do not take any risks. This assertion is false. We have already pointed out that on a global scale a large part of these employees are subject to the vagaries of unemployment and this without guarantee of permanent pay if this unemployment is of long duration. Even in a country like France, unemployment subsidies only last for a relatively short, fixed period of time. If we put aside the very special case of artists and sportsmen who have succeeded in amassing fortunes, the fringe of the biggest capitalists and their allies, the big managers who run the big SHCs who have also amassed considerable fortunes, is, with the senior officials and the great political leaders who support them, the only social fraction which is really sheltered from serious crises: this explains why they have no interest, well on the contrary, for this system to change and why they tend to be allied to make it sustainable.

The CARE model takes this situation into account and proposes a radical change in the law of SHCs and, more broadly, of big companies. Instead of opposing social categories in companies between those who have power and those who do not, between those who take risks and those who do not, it considers that all providers of capital are investors 'in the same boat,'[72] who share the successes and misfortunes of entrepreneurial activity.

This within the framework of the overall responsibility of these companies regulated by the states, a regulation which allows systematic coverage of classic risks (notably unemployment) and survival insurance in the event of very serious crises. The vast majority of the world's citizens would have a great interest in opting for such a model against which a fringe of capitalists will obviously struggle with all their might. They should impose

---

[71] This is not the case for most small and medium firms where investors continue, traditionally, to have a type of management very centered on the companies they found: they run them personally with significant risks.

[72] Capitalism has the art of capturing flattering terms. Thus, under IFRS, only contributors of financial capital are investors: employees and nature invest nothing.

on the various states referendums in which the innovations which have been described above would be offered: one could thus submit to their decision the choice between the current capitalist model of companies and an ecological management model of the type of CARE. In addition, to support this new deal through permanent democratic bodies, it should also impose the formation of a special tripartite ecological parliamentary chamber (investors of natural capital, labor and financial capital) whose approval would be necessary for any decision concerning companies. (Richard and Rambaud, 2020; Rambaud and Richard, 2022b). This seizure of economic power by citizens in large companies would make it possible in particular to review the gigantism of these firms by playing on the transformation of subsidiaries into more autonomous units, and thus rebalance their difference of power with SMEs[73].

After having acquired, not without difficulty, political democracy, citizens would obtain economic and ecological democracy within the framework of a certain market economy which retains private property. Most environmentalists want a "re-enchanted man" (Simmonet 1979, 86; Flipo2014a, 257) in a manner that is himself re-enchanted. This first requires a transformation of the power relations in large companies with in particular the abolition of the global dictatorship of shareholders who impose their economic and accounting rationality. Any other solution, such as for example a simple appeal to the authenticity of the being or at a spiritual retreat in the wilderness is just romantic gossip with no practical effect. It remains to be seen how to achieve this goal at the political level.

Towards generalized ecological co-management at the economic and political level

In her book on ecologism, Simonnet (1979,84) explains that ecologism will pass through " gentle greening of society" [74] "and not through legislative

---

[73] On the contrary, this would not prevent, in certain cases, using the centralization/decentralization game to impose, for example, on large commercial firms the relocation of their subsidiaries in all the villages associated with a single price policy. We would thus get out of an absurd policy of gigantism which has led to the desertification of the countryside and the loss of life in the villages.

[74] She refers in particular to Lalonde who says that "ecologism is not upheaval but a multiplicity of imperceptible steps aside."

reform or revolution." His argument is that "both are using the state too much to have the strength to take away its power" (idem). While respectable, this belief is not ours. History, for the moment, has shown, particularly with the movement of workers' cooperatives, that capitalism can live very well without being hampered, perhaps even on the contrary, with deviant forms which allow it to show its 'liberalism' while being assured that these spontaneous forms are not dangerous for him. This is also the opinion of a specialist in social and solidarian economics like Laville (2010). In any case, the significant changes which led to a reduction in the powers of the capitalists, in particular before and after World War II, were obtained thanks to legislative initiatives supported by strong forces (unions and political parties in particular).This is how labor law was born in Europe. We believe, from a pragmatic perspective, that all opportunities must be seized: spontaneous actions certainly, but also legislative, parliamentary or even, more original, in the form of referendums imposed by powerful peaceful popular movements.

Another point of disagreement with Simmonet (1979, 77-78) no longer concerns the means of the targeted change but rather that of the goals. Referring on this point to a work of Bourdet (1974), she cites the self-management experience (autonomous management of a company by its workers or, in a broader sense, generalized self-management without private ownership of the means of production and decision-making) as a possibility while specifying that "the ecological meaning of the word self-management refers more to everyday life than to the world of production" (77-78). Obviously her focus, inspired by the theses of Michel Bosquet (André Gorz), is more that of the cooperatives of residents of buildings, neighborhoods, municipalities, regions, etc., than that of business cooperatives. She thinks she can reduce the power of the state thanks to this strategy of revitalizing civil society with, as Michel Bosquet also recommends, "relations based on reciprocity and voluntary service, not on law and legal obligation" (ibid45). Here again, while not excluding this proposal at all, we nevertheless believe that it is also necessary to play on laws carrying ecological co-management to put an end to the power of capitalists in firms: it is not only the possibility of extending the participation of citizens in the context of their working life but also the very condition of the reduction of the power of the capitalist state that Simmonet demands. It is also the condition of a true realization of the ideals of the enlightenment and, for those who claim to belong to the personalist current, the condition of stopping the mutilation of the human person, reduced in the big business to a pawn who obeys injunctions from shareholders.

It is very curious that, for the moment, the various environmental movements are not interested in this question of the reform of the business constitution, in particular of its heart, the company law, of which the accounting law is a part. Perhaps the reasons for this 'withdrawal' should be sought in the general inability of political movements to break away from the Capitalism / State Socialism alternative which has dominated the scene so far? But another track is also in order. As Flipo (2014a, 102-107) shows, for at least the case of France, "the great environmental leaders have often been located in the center" and this center-right ecologism "is therefore caught in a contradiction that prevents a coherent speech; it believes in ecological threats... but it does not see how to change society. It wants to believe in the impossible: a change that takes place within the established order, without disturbing him... ideally a change that is not one." Flipo makes particular reference to Bourg (1996) and to the fact that capitalism "is hardly criticized by him" (107). He believes that this center-right ecologism is of no practical use on the road to corporate reform. Indeed, the best way to perpetuate the power of the capitalists is to give up being interested in the sphere of production and to hold all populations responsible for current ecological problems, in particular because of their inveterate consumerism [75]. But aren't consumption and lifestyles also conditioned by the sphere of production?

The thesis often defended is that the state, by definition, is an instrument of oppression, including and above all a social state. But why would a state respectful of the principles of ecological co-management at all levels and anchored in a new constitution be an automatic enemy? If the current state can be an oppressor, it is because it is dominated by a legal constitution in the service of capitalism and not because of an essence specific to the state.

[75] See on this point Mireille Dobré (2002) quoted by Flipo (2014a 105).

Should the two enemies of environmentalists always be technology and the state? Isn't this a wrong target?

Throughout this comparative survey on the fate of the three types of capital which are the basis of any business, we have not only dismantled the neoliberal mirage of the spontaneous 'benefactor' market but also shown that only the financial capital is the object of systematic protection backed up by national and international laws. It is time to abolish this global economic constitution in the service of selfish private interests and replace it. For this, it is necessary, as the economist René Passet[76] (1979) proposed, "to reverse the process and prioritize respect for fundamental standards." The politicians in power, until now, have refused to discuss openly in front of the people of the economic constitution which governs nations even though economic questions, which deal with the conservation of nature and of human beings, that is to say of their very existence, are capital questions. They have always sought to prevent people from deciding basic economic structures. In a country like France, a political constitution ensures citizens equal rights to participate in elections from time to time, at regular intervals, while a true economic constitution, [77] not explicitly ratified by the people and supported by precise accounting laws, accompanied by sanctions, confirms the permanent inequality of the types of capital in companies and a gigantic distribution of fictitious dividends for the benefit of a small minority.[78]

It is time to put an end to this situation which is leading to ecological and human disaster. We need a new comprehensive social contract including the economic one. This is why we propose to include in the constitutions of the countries and in the future world constitution of the United Nations the following two basic principles specifically aimed at all business accounting and any form of economy. First, company accounts and national accounts

[76] L'Économique et le Vivant, Paris, Payot, 1979. See also L'Illusion néo-libérale, Paris, Fayard, 2000.

[77] We can consider that the conceptual framework of the IFRS which appears in the preamble of this financial code plays the role of such a constitution on an international scale (since validated by practically all the States).

[78] The French Constitution guarantees the right to work but it is rather a right to work if one finds work. The preservation of human beings is by no means obligatory whereas that of financial capital is, as well as the repayment of financial debts.

will have to endorse equal protection of the three types of natural, human and financial capital: this is the essential basis for achieving real societal justice leading to a reasonable economy. It is also what makes it possible to rebuild the current system on moral foundations acceptable to all. Second, equal rights of participation in the deliberations on the management decisions of companies will be granted to the representatives of the three types of capital.

Privileges of financial capital will be abolished by introducing the same rules of the game for the three types of capital: such a 'tri-capitalism' will cause a mutation of capitalism, with a disruptive financing system in which the new shareholders, who may be the new employees themselves or retired employees, will have to respect rules different from those of financial capitalism. Finally, Parliaments will have to ratify these positive principles that can be universalised by appropriate laws, in particular accounting laws, accompanied by severe sanctions in the event of failure to respect these rules.

This approach has nothing to do with that of the "benevolent tyranny" of which Jonas (1979) speaks in his work devoted to the "principle of responsibility" nor with a patchwork of liberalism. We also underline that, contrary to the Marxist approach, it is not a question of wanting to plan or regulate all economic activity, but rather of laying down the basic principles of a new market economy in which private or public initiatives remain free to develop but subject to respecting these principles. If this approach is accepted, it is clear that all the action of parliamentarians will be totally modified by the fact that an economic, social and ecological contract will be imposed on them, this in the tradition of what the founders of the theory of "social contract," including Hobbes, Rousseau and Locke, but with the fundamental difference that the economy is concerned by this contract: it is treated as a political issue, as it should be. Thus the new parliamentarians will exercise their mandate within a pre-constrained framework which will guarantee the fundamental rights of the three types of capital providers who found a company and, more globally, a nation. Humans and nature will emerge from the clutches of capitalism and its organized fight against each other. In addition, citizens will then be able to develop their "communicational action," as recommended by Habermas

(1987), but within a very precise and much more effective framework. Indeed this German philosopher defends a problematic dualist thesis. On the one hand, one cannot, according to him, avoid the presence of an economic rationality in the private sphere (practically that of the capitalist market economy for lack of an alternative proposal on his part). And, on the other hand, this influence of capitalist rationality could be counterbalanced by the effects of the extension of a "communicational rationality of citizens" (-in practice, in particular, the massive development of citizen forums-) leading to a sort of public planning aimed at correcting the problems generated by economic rationality. On the contrary, we believe that we cannot envisage a profound transformation of the current system without a total questioning of the rationality of the capitalist mode of management.

In conclusion on this presentation of this ecological co-management, we can compare this approach with other conceptions defended by philosophers, in particular those of Rawls and Sen. Rawls, in his famous work Justice as Equity (2003) does not deal with the ecological question. On the other hand, he wants to solve the social problem of a fair distribution of the wealth produced. It puts forward a general principle with which one can only agree: to provide citizens with the things they need "as free and equal people living a full existence." Unfortunately this beautiful principle is not accompanied by any proposal for reform of the capitalist system, a system which prevents the assurance of the good life of which it speaks. There is not the slightest hint of a reform of the governance of capitalist companies in his proposals that would allow employees to become subjects who co-manage the companies in which they invest their workforce. The only constraint he introduces is that of the famous maximin: in any production of additional wealth the poorest should receive a share which would allow them to see their income increase more than that of the most rich. It is therefore far for them to ensure the "complete existence" of which he speaks: they remain second-rate subjects. This is neither more nor less than the current capitalist-liberal approach: raising the standard of living of the poorest enough to prevent them from transforming their lives. On the other hand, the proposals of Marta Nussbaum and Amartya Sen (1993) for an index of primary goods to be respected[79] are more interesting because they are more concrete and broader. However, they are not accompanied by proposals for reforms of power in capitalist enterprises and only speak of the ecological question in very general terms. It also seems to us that this new type of ecological co-management could enable the concrete implementation in companies and administration of Ostrom's proposals (1990) aimed at establishing governance of the commons. The same goes for the more recent proposals of Rifkin (2019) who wants to make a third industrial revolution based on a Green New Deal with "peer assemblies": the CARE Model seems to us to be a good solution to actually achieve this Green New Deal to which he aspires.

We are now going to devote a special chapter to proposals which emanate from jurists, philosophers, ethnologists, and religious who are interested in a reform of capitalist law: it is about the approach of the "common goods," of the theory of the gift of Mauss and of the vision of an ecological and human society of Pope Francis.

[79] 1. To be able to live as much of a full human life as possible: to avoid dying prematurely or to be able to die if life has become too difficult and no longer seems worth living. 2. Adequate nutrition and good health. Decent home. Opportunity for sexual satisfaction. Being able to move. 3. Being able to avoid pain. Knowing the existence of pleasure. 4. Being able to use your five senses to imagine, think and reason. 5. Being able to feel an attachment for people and things. To be able to help those who love us, to be able to love and to feel desire and gratitude. 6. To be able to forge a conception of the good and to engage in critical reflection on the goals of our life. 7. To be able to live harmoniously with others, to be respected, not to suffer humiliation. 8. Relations with nature and other species. 9. Being able to play, laugh and enjoy leisure activities. 10. Being able to participate in political choices and have access to property, including in terms of real opportunities.

Chapter 14
Comparison of the CARE approach with that of the "commons"

A major stream of jurists and philosophers who are contesting the current world order, in particular capitalist multinationals, are currently trying to influence national and international law to orient them towards more humane and ecological management.1. Let us immediately point out that we fully share their goals and that we salute the courage of these jurists and philosophers to tackle clearly the dominant capitalist forces. Grange, in particular, is particularly clear in this respect: "capitalist logics... are the real adversary" (2012, 36-7).

This legal current is therefore in search of a new anti-capitalist law. It goes against the theses of Murray Bookchin (1976) and Illich (in numerous works spanning 1971 to 1977 cited in bibliography), authors who believe that the law, by nature, stifles freedoms, as Simonnet also seems to think (1979, 55). We adhere to the convictions of these jurists, but we nevertheless ask questions about the relevance of *the means they use* to achieve their ends. Their basic proposal is not, as proposed by the proponents of biocentrism or Serre and Latour (the latter with its Parliament of things), to give political rights to non-humans with a transposition of the social contract between men to human / nature relations but, within the framework of political ecology, to "protect humans from themselves" (Grange 2012, 17), this essentially on the basis of laws that regulate the economy.

In practice, the main idea which will be the basis of these new ecological laws is to make certain goods, known as 'primary goods', either public goods (such as health, knowledge) or common goods,[2] such as air, water

---

[1] In the legal field, we can cite Mr. Delmas Marty, in particular her works of 2004 and 2010 (bibliography). In that of philosophy J. Grange.

[2] Grange (2012, 26) specifies in this regard that "it is not a question of rediscovering the commons or communal prior to the appropriation by individuals (enclosures of the 17th century) but of constructing, for reasons of safeguard, another category of property."

(groundwater, rivers, seas), the subsoil, the forests. The main weapon[3] is therefore to remove from private property and from economic logic certain basic primary goods which would have no price but "a value in the sense of civic duty, an intrinsic value, an absolute value in themselves." (Grange, 2012, 27-28). It is therefore above all, as Grange underlines, a "work of a legal nature,"[4] in particular within the framework of international law, a work which she compares to that of labor law in social matters, in Europe, with the laws on workers and peasant pensions (idem, 35-39). We find similar proposals in the work that the jurist Chauvier (2006) devotes to "Justice and rights on a global scale:" that of generalizing common property (res communis) for non-exclusive natural goods (Pelluchon, 2011, 71).

These considerations deserve respect. However, they seem to us to have the following limits. First, their scope cannot be general. Essentially, it is only a question of goods which have not yet been or only slightly reached by private property such as the sky, seas, rivers, ground water, the subsoil. However, in this enumeration, a fundamental good is missing: the land. Obviously, as Grange herself says, it is not a question of excluding private property and of imposing communism but only "of putting beyond the reach of the logic of financialized capitalism a certain number of great goods" (2012, 28). But what then of the 'small goods'[5] which generally come under this private property of the land? How, in particular, with such principles, concretely protect the sky, forests, waters and biodiversity of the billions of acts of these private land properties? We know very well that attacks on these common goods come from these private properties and also from public properties (in communist states). Even the sky is affected by their actions, although it may be thousands of kilometers away: every piece of land, every factory emits greenhouse gases. Are they going to be completely excluded from the question on the pretext that they cannot be made public or common goods? Or are we going to have to consider all

---

[3] Other means such as the taxation of capital income and the use of new indicators such as the ISH are mentioned in particular by Grange (2012, 94).

[4] Note that the economist Stiglitz is one of the few of his brotherhood to use such reasoning. In a report (2012, The Links that Liberate, 105) he believes that to solve the problem of the planetary commons [..] the only remedy is a form of global public management of global natural resources."

[5] Small all relative goods which can concern very large agricultural, mining or industrial operations.

these private or public goods as common goods? This hypothesis is apparently rejected by these authors. So what to do with this theoretical and practical impasse which aims only at securing certain goods when there should be a system of general scope?

This is where, in our opinion, the second flaw in the reasoning of these authors occurs. For us the problem that is posed is not a problem of the type of property but a problem of the type of management, which is totally different. Viewing the sky as a common good is not going to change the practices of destruction on its own. It seems to us in this respect that we are faithful to the theses of Ostrom (1990), who has repeatedly stressed that, for her, the problem of the type of ownership is not the main problem. The thesis of perfection in itself which would result from the use of the commons seems to be as absurd as that defended by Hardin (1968), who saw in private property the automatic solution to the problems of soil conservation. In fact, the real way to have a real change is to modify the management of all these companies that pollute, whether they come under private, public or common property: we must therefore move towards generalized ecological and human co-management which associates the three types of representatives of capital providers in decisions. Let us underline, in this connection, once again, that the expression 'managerial logic,' which is generally stigmatized by most critics of capitalism, means absolutely nothing: there can be totally different types of management, including one management which takes into account ecological problems and on the contrary capitalist management.

The third flaw in the reasoning, which follows from the second, is that in matter of law the concepts of good or patrimony (either public, private or common) generally refer to a problem of use[6] and hence cannot be useful for questions of conservation: all type of good is in principle intended to be worn out. However, in order for it to be kept permanently at the same time, within the limits of inevitable entropy, one must resort, as modern capitalist experience has shown, to another concept: the accounting concept

[6] This is why the German accounting lawyers, who have a richer vocabulary on this point than the French, clearly distinguish, for a long time, the Vermögen (goods to be used or heritage or assets) from the Kapital, which indicates a thing to be kept (see, in particular, Passow, 1910).

of capital-debt. Consequently, any change in management, including and above all that which will make it possible to go from the capitalist economy to an ecological economy, must pass, as we have shown, through a radical transformation of the concept of accounting capital-debt in companies' law: we must broaden the restrictive conception of current capital-debt to systematic protection of natural and human capitals (capitals in the sense of things to be preserved).

To conclude on all these points, it seems to us that all these problems come from a focus largely inherited from the errors of Marx and his followers who see private property as public enemy number 1: as if we could not do a distinction between private properties managed in a way that conserves nature, as African smallholder farmers do[7] for example, and those of multinational private agrobusiness firms that destroy the "life" of the soil and the Amazonian forest, or the firms of Chinese state capitalism which pollute the rivers, in particular within the framework of the mining activity.

The solution of ecological problems does not therefore necessarily lie in actions of collective responsibility, with recourse to public or common goods: it can just as easily "nest" in individual and family solutions anchored in private property, which must be rehabilitated. Certainly Proudhon said that "property is theft." But, as Jourdain (2019) recently reminds us, this well-known quote has been unreasonably detached from a complement: it is theft if it is not regulated by law, which changes everything. Still, for us the solution of all these problems is fundamentally within accounting law, a law unfortunately ignored, with rare exceptions,[8] by jurists, in particular international law jurists and even private law jurists[9]. However, this accounting discipline belongs in principle to the

[7] This is eloquently shown by the agronomist Dufumier (2012): he says he learned the principles of good soil management from African peasant women, while the agronomist training he had received at "Agro" in Paris encouraged him rather to propose methods that are said to be productive but which tend to destroy the soils.
[8] Among these notable exceptions, we must mention Bardy's landmark thesis (2017) under the supervision of Professor Martin and the publications of Professor Pasqualini which promote the question of the evolution of accounting law within the framework of the Center Français de Droit Comparé (Richard, 2016)
[9]It is interesting in this respect to note that the concept of capital (capital-debt) of accounting law does not appear in the work, moreover remarkable, that Rochfeld (2011) devotes to the main concepts of private law: accounting law is really a separate

branch of law and provides major lessons. The big lesson it gives in particular is that it is impossible to preserve something on the basis of the consideration of goods, (that is to say of assets in accounting language and patrimony often in legal language) whether it is of private, public or even common goods[10]. That said, these criticisms that we address to the theory of the commons do not at all prevent the possibility of a common action (it is indeed the case to say it) between these jurists and these philosophers and the 'CARE movement': the basic and common idea is to settle the ecological question through politics and, mainly through its armed wing: the law. The latter, and in our opinion first and foremost accounting law once transformed, will become human[11] and ecological. It will then be the basis of a new economic paradigm.

Capitalism has made such an impact on people's minds that it is equated with economic logic, as if there could only be this capitalist economic logic. Many works by philosophers and political scientists speak in particular of "escaping from economic logic" or of economics as an "inhuman science"[12] testifying to a conceptual inability to conceive of an economy other than the one that has dominated since the Middle Ages. As we have shown, this impotence is the consequence of a deficiency, even of an absence of analysis of the concrete functioning of the capitalist system: one cannot change a system without having studied it thoroughly.

---

right practically reserved, both in law and in politics, to a caste which has seized it, this to the great satisfaction of the capitalists who have no interest in people sticking their noses in their business (see Richard and Rambaud, 2020, 2022abc).

[10] Ostrom, who defends an economy of the commons, was right to affirm that a management in common which ensures the preservation of goods has nothing to do with questions of ownership of goods, including common goods. On the other hand, as a member of the community of economists, she has not seen at all the practical aspects of this question of conservation: another striking example of the regrettable traditional caesura between economists and accountants.

[11] As Savatier wished (1969)

[12] To use an expression of the philosopher of science Fagot-Largeault.

Chapter 15
Comparison of the CARE approach with proposals from the gift economy and the Catholic church

Due to its use of the double entry and its focus on capital other than finance capital, the CARE accounting system has, in our opinion, some commonalities with the theories of economics that have been developed by sociologists like Mauss or leading personalities of the Catholic Church like Pope Francis. We will successively study the positions of these outstanding personalities to compare them with those who underlie the CARE model.

CARE and the gift economy

The ethnologist Marcel Mauss is well known for having presented a theory of the gift on the basis of practices observed in peoples whose economic 'laws' are very different from those observed in the modern West. In his famous book "Essay on the gift" 1925), Mauss, based on Malinowski (1922), shows that certain Melanesian societies which practice 'kula' have non-commercial exchanges of gift and counter-gift which allow them to ensure the cohesion and the conservation of their type of society: these societies exchange but without a system of trade totally dominated by the law of supply and demand and the rational calculation of the capitalist type. We believe that we have a similar situation in the case of the CARE / TDL model, in particular in the case of its application to the problem of human capital. In fact, in this accounting model, employees make the (temporary) 'gift' of their person to a firm under the promise of a counter-gift 'return': that of the strict preservation of their person. The donation received by the firm is recorded in its balance sheet as an asset to be used while the counter gift, the obligation to return, is recorded by the firm as a liability: an employee's preservation debt. Thus the double-entry mechanism is put at the service of a non-market economy insofar as the human person is not treated as a commodity (a simple means) but well as a capital to be systematically maintained, which more a capital who is the co-manager of the firm in question. The CARE / TDL "Maussian balance sheet," applied to the case of human capital, can appear schematically as follows[1]:

Balance sheet of the firm (date X)

Gifts received (assets received)	Counter gifts (debts)
Gift of a person P for use of this person	Human capital P to be preserved

In this example, unlike the cases studied by Mauss and Malinovski, the gift concerns people themselves and not exchanged objects. But the ethical goal is similar: a focus on the non-instrumental character of relationships. More generally, the general goal is to found a type of company within the framework of co-management for a common goal with, in particular, a common profit. In this context, our conception is broader than that of Mauss: it aims not only at individual exchanges made by people but also at the creation of an economic-accounting constitution, approved by the citizens, which governs all of their actions, including their mode of participation in society. Another difference is that there is normally a strict equality between the gift and the counter-gift, which is not always the case in the practice of Kula or other types of 'primitive' exchanges[2]. As Chanial (2008) shows, with reference to articles by Gouldner, cases of disproportion between donors and recipients are often sources of problems. Caillé (2014,45) observes thus: "the danger is that the donation suffocates the receiver"[3]. Florence Weber in her introduction to the work of Mauss (2007,7-58) emphasizes the political issues behind the positions of the "father" of

[1] In the case of nature, natural capital has no personality, yet the firm borrows resources and must return them because of its declaration to respect their conservation. If this accounting constitution is applied unilaterally, then we can consider that it is possible to apply the theory of the gift to (non-human) nature without resorting, as Caillé does (Flipo 2014a, 329), to the concept of quasi-subject. The gift and the counter-gift become commitments of the firms made obligatory in accounting law by the human community. There is also no need to appeal to the concept of responsibility towards future generations (Jonas, 1979) or to a personification of Mama Pasha.

[2] Sahlins (1972,164-168) also speaks of unequal exchange within the framework of Maori customs. He even asserts that a benefit ("hau") had to be given in addition to the gift capital ("mauri").

[3] In general we know, as the German language says, with its word Gift, that any gift can be a poison!

the gift economy. She shows that Mauss wanted to find a solution to get out of the traditional system of patronage or charity which characterizes the capitalist world and to create a system of social security which would give each citizen the means to lead a decent life (10-11). This is exactly the goal of CARE/TDL. Note, however, that unlike Mauss, who seemed more interested in human than ecological issues, the CARE method also treats the gift of nature as something to be returned[4]. In addition, this whole donation system can be framed by a company law which sanctions those who do not respect the common social conventions at the base of this new gift economy: we are then moving away from a simple gift economy based on emotion and goodwill which would serve to compensate for deficiencies in public order. The experience of the history of the capitalists has shown that even this brotherhood, however united by very close links of interests, was obliged to ask the states for their help in 'forcing' their members to respect their own system: the simple working of routine was not enough. CARE, therefore, generalizes and institutes the gift / counter-gift economy by substituting pure social pressure for social pressure rooted in law. In a sense, it is an extension of the 'capitalist gift economy': we remember that, in the context of a kind of schizophrenia established by himself, the private capitalist donates his contribution to a company and intends that his capital be returned to him by this company. Note that this accounting law is part of a new political constitution ratified by all citizens (Richard and Rambaud, 2020,2022b): it is at this level that a sort of collective and 'sacred' oath by citizens for a new economic constitution protective of men and nature will intervene.

CARE and the ecological and social positions of Pope Francis

The Catholic religion has always taken a keen interest in economic problems and had the great merit during the Middle Ages of trying to fight against the development of modern capitalism, especially against its practice of lending at interest. We can consider that CARE is inspired by this struggle today to try to put an end to the evils of the famous 'cost of capital', a kind of paroxysm of idolatry of self-interest that leads to

[4] This is a request that Flipo (2014a, 230-4) had formulated, in a relevant way, in a development dedicated to the link between the gift economy and ecology.

ecological disasters. But, today, this traditional struggle of Catholics finds a revival in the person of a remarkable Pope: Pope Francis. In his encyclical letter 'Laudato Si'(2015) about the concern (care) of the common home the Pope underlines that certain passages of Genesis (Gn) invite to "cultivate and guard the garden of the world"[5] (cf. Gn 2,15). The Pope infers from this sentence that if the verb "to cultivate" refers to plowing, removing the weeds, or working the soil, the verb "to guard" means to protect, to safeguard, to preserve, to take care, to watch, which implies that " each community can derive from the goodness of the soil what is necessary for it to survive, but also has the obligation to keep and guarantee the continuity of its fertility for future generations "(53-54)[6].

This dualistic perspective corresponds to that of traditional accounting: that of the double entry which makes it possible to conserve a capital while using up the corresponding assets. This type of thinking is all the more in harmony with the CARE / TDL model as the Pope insists on respecting the limits imposed by the renewal of the soil. Indeed, he often uses the words "breaking points" and "limits" to be respected. This is particularly the case when he addresses very strong criticisms with regard to "financiers": he says against them that "the belief in the infinite availability of the planet's goods... leads to pressing it to its limits and even beyond limits "(83). In agreement with the declarations of the bishops of Portugal, the Pope concludes that "the environment is in the logic of reception. This is a loan that each generation receives and must pass on to the next generation "(122-123). The CARE / TDL model is also based entirely on these concepts of borrowing and debt. To conclude on these points, we can say that the CARE method is in phase with many conceptions of society, religious or not. CARE / TDL also offers the possibility of integrating these philosophies within the framework of a money-based economy. But can there then be a possibility of conciliating environmental philosophies? It is this last question that we will address before concluding our book.

---

[5] Note that the word 'garden' (garden in English, Garten in German) has the same root as the word guard (which comes from the Latin hortus).

[6] We see here that the ethical claims of Jonas (1979) had been anticipated by these old religious texts.

Chapter 16
Do we need a specific philosophy of nature?

Many natural philosophers, notably Routley (1973),argue that it is impossible to conceive of a philosophy suited to the problem of nature conservation within the framework of 'classical' philosophies. However, the philosopher Norton (1984) (in Afeissa, 192-196), for the sake of ecumenism, defends the opposite thesis of the possible convergence of environmental ethics. A thesis that Callicott (2007)denies. Norton, however, persists and believes that attempts to place an intrinsic value on nature only create tension among environmentalists. For him the conventional approach, limited to the intrinsic worth of human beings, is sufficient. But, according to Callicott, Norton is neglecting two points. On the one hand, a moral aspect: giving an intrinsic value to nature and in particular to animals makes it possible not to resort to repulsive economic arguments (such as those of the southerners who wanted to keep their slaves for economic purposes). On the other hand, a pragmatic aspect: giving nature an intrinsic value would make it possible to reverse the burden of proof. (196). Callicott's thesis, in fact, is that if the intrinsic value of tall forests were recognized the companies that want to destroy it should seek permission in court, which would resolve the issue. But Norton (see Afeissa, pp. 232 et seq.) continues to argue that the opposition of non-anthropocentric ethicists to anthropocentric ethicists is both damaging and sterile. Damaging because it divides environmental ethicists into two clans. Sterile, because this opposition is based on a false conception of the human interest: that of a utilitarianism which would be limited only to the consumption of the goods provided by nature, whereas the man is not totally stupid and knows that it is in his interest to maintain the ecological services provided by this nature. Man is then perfectly capable of understanding that this conservation takes precedence over the satisfaction of his short-term human interests.

Norton draws the conclusion that it is very possible to conserve nature on the basis of anthropocentric morality, which leads him to say that "the debate between anthropocentrism and non-anthropocentrism has not the importance that one generally lends to him "(250). Norton thus defends the thesis of an environmental pragmatism and favors a theoretical and metatheoretical pluralism (Light and Katz, Environmental pragmatism, 1996). He admits a multiplicity of theoretical models and several divergent morals that can work together within the framework of a single encompassing morality, a thesis that Stone (1972) had already defended. But he nevertheless poses as basic principles of agreement that an environmental ethic first "cannot be deduced from the rights or interests of non-human beings (which leads him to reject the concept of the intrinsic value of nature) and, secondly, that neither can it be the rights or interests of future generations of human beings" (249). As we have already seen, he then distinguishes two forms of anthropocentrism: one passionate (strong) and another, weak, reasoned or religious([1]).He believes that the latter, with its non-passionate vision of the world, makes it possible to "subject to criticism the systems of values which prescribe a relationship of pure exploitation of nature" and therefore to "live in harmony with nature" (Afeissa, 2007, 256). Under these conditions nature "also becomes an important source of inspiration as a creator of values" (idem, 257). This theoretical position allows him to affirm (against notably Regan) that various "ideals of human behavior" can lead to the conservation of nature "without attributing an intrinsic value to the objects conserved" (261).Another conclusion he draws is that the fundamental problem for human beings is not that of an anthropocentric type of position but that of an individualistic position (264). Now, according to him, individualism is the hallmark of contemporary standard ethical theories, at least in the United States and Europe (264). It is notably the mark of utilitarian theories based on the maximization of the greatest possible happiness for the greatest number of individuals and of modern deontological ethics (264-6). Norton emphasizes that his ethics, on the contrary, is not individualistic: it is concerned with the conservation of nature and includes the prohibition of behaviors that are likely to have negative long-term effects. For him all this implies that the individual interests of the people who will live in the future cannot be at the base of the decisions taken now because these condition the very existence of these individuals (268).[2] He takes the

[1] Norton specifically mentions followers of Hinduism or Jainism (261).

[2] For example a reduction in the number of births to avoid a later catastrophe.

example of a generation that decides to sterilize itself and consume and destroy all wealth. It is clear that in this case future generations would not be harmed since they would not exist. However, he condemns this decision in the name of his theory of weak anthropocentrism: "the present generations must care about the generations to come" (272-3). He therefore believes that it is up to the present generation to properly manage resources by maintaining "a stable flow of resources for an indefinite time... so that human life is perpetuated, this notwithstanding its individual demands" (274). This implies that these resources are not deteriorated and therefore that the current generations must not harvest more than what exactly corresponds to the maximum renewable yield of the resource "(276). In this regard, he considers that, ultimately, the central problem facing today's society is that of "felt preferences of the fundamentally consumerist type leading to a serious overexploitation of nature" and therefore that it is above all a question of "criticizing and to modify felt preferences "thanks to a" rationally justified worldview "informed by" scientific understanding of nature "(279-280)[3].He concludes that "it is by no means necessary to take up the highly debatable ontological theses that presupposes the attribution of an intrinsic value to nature... and that Occam's razor recommends... to favor the choice of weak anthropocentrism" to the detriment of non-anthropocentrism (283).

Norton's reasoning strikes us as reasonable and pragmatic, in the sense that it encourages practical solutions to the current ecological and human crisis based on an understanding of the problems and man's reasonable reason. But we can make two criticisms of his view. First, and we join here the position of Maris (2010, 185-8) it seems perfectly possible to postulate, like Norton, that human beings can adopt a position of weak anthropocentrism while thinking that they can also grant to nature a non-instrumental value. Secondly, Norton seems to us to underestimate the danger of a particular species of men, formidable for their power and their selfish interests: the modern capitalists.

---

[3]Norton particularly criticizes the neo-Kantians such as Rawls "who emphasize the most individualistic tendencies present in Kant and make it possible to consider his thought from the perspective of the contractualist tradition" which leads to a modern contractualist deontological ethics (265)

General conclusion

Before you act, you have to comprehend. This maxim is the basis of CARE's approach. The current urgency is first to comprehend what is happening on our earth with global warming, epidemics such as that of the coronavirus, the suicides of many farmers, the increase in human migrations and the growth of social inequalities in a very large number of countries, apparently very different phenomena, but linked. To comprehend (cum prehendere in Latin) is above all to take into account all of these related phenomena and to identify their fundamental causes. Currently a large number of studies indict characteristics common to all humans such as the egoism and lack of humility of modern man, or general problems related to the use of science, technology, markets, numbers, industrialization. On this basis, many philosophers of nature(but fortunately not all) will above all propose to change the human beings in general, in particular their relationship to nature in order to live more humbly and more peacefully. This in particular, by encouraging them, through an introspection on their attitude, to no longer consider the elements of nature as simple means but as real subjects. Some even want the human beings to change their relationship to death: in particular to accept the coronavirus crisis as a normal phenomenon. Still others, a little more concrete, inspired by old Marxist theses, would simply like to give the public sector a greater number of tasks of protecting their lives, believing that the causes of crises are essentially the question of the type of property at work. Most of the time, these fine exhortations stop there and are not accompanied by concrete proposals for reforms, in particular in the management of companies, entities which nevertheless play a crucial role in the current problems of humanity.

Our thesis is that these types of advice are both inadequate and ineffective. They are inadequate because they ignore the fact that in the emergence of current social and ecological crises some humans with economic power are more responsible than others. These are, as we have tried to demonstrate, the financial capitalists of the big firms who have succeeded in imposing a world economic constitution based on an iniquitous and destructive accounting system. They have also been able, until this day, thanks to the help of the Marxist-Communist scarecrow as well as to their considerable means of action, in particular the control of a large part of the press and the media, to persuade people to vote for the candidates they support in the classic parliamentary system inherited from the Enlightenment, a system that has shut down democracy at the gates of business while touting it under the name of liberalism. This advice is also ineffective because, without a precise analysis of the means of action of this financial capitalism, these philosophers cannot, as we have explained, not only understand the weapons of destruction of capitalism, but also find the ways to deal with it.

For us, therefore, the 'drama' of many philosophers of nature is to have conducted their reflections ignoring the real essence and practice of the modern capitalist system. They did not see the strength of its accounting management model and in particular the drastic accounting regulations that it imposes on all large companies, whether public (as in China in particular) or private, in order to systematically and efficiently conserve only the financial capital of capitalists, both of private and public type. Many of these philosophers further consider that regulations are unnecessary or at least ineffective in ecological matters, and that it is better to change the mindset of consumers first. But if they had analyzed the international accounting regulations of the capitalists and seen their terrible effectiveness they might have changed their opinion. They could have seen all the interest of the concept of capital-debt of these capitalists which makes it possible to force the company to systematically conserve its financial capital independently of any theory of the personification of this capital. They could have seen that in this 'capital-centered' approach there is no need to extend the notion of subject, a modern notion, to ecosystems to protect them. It 'suffices', as we propose in the CARE / TDL approach, to decide that these ecosystems will be a capital in the accounting sense of the term, that is to say something very important (capital) to preserve[4].

The fundamental question posed by the CARE model is indeed what is important to us, what is 'capital'? If the response of human beings, consulted and well informed of the reality and the misdeeds of the world capitalist system, is that the preservation of ecosystems is as important as

[4] As already mentioned, in ancient Greek capital means 1/ the human head 2/ something very important 3/ the main part of a debt (excluding interest).

that of financial capital then an ecological obligation will be imposed unconditionally on all managers by a new accounting law accompanied by criminal sanctions. This, without any reference to a relationship to a subject. This, within the framework of a new accounting system in which the existence value of this capital will appear concretely on the liabilities side of the balance sheets of a new ecological accounting in the form of a budget of preservation costs. We will then finally achieve a realization of the famous intrinsic value of the partisans of the ethics of the earth. And we will succeed in changing the economic system not on the basis of economic tools of secondary importance but on the basis of powerful accounting tools revised and corrected.

Thanks to this action, we will finally be able to get out of the endless discussions around the mysterious 'intrinsic value'. We will also come out of the palaver around the concept of sustainable development. CARE / TDL accounting makes it possible to concretize this notion with precise rules for the conservation or preservation of the three main types of capital. The decision to preserve ecosystems will be taken by autonomous human beings aware of their actions on the basis of a correct understanding of the current situation of the planet, and not of mere fleeting compassion. These human beings will thus bear witness to their full and entire responsibility vis-à-vis the Earth.

But this presupposes, as the CARE / TDL model proposes, first a complete reform of powers in big business and, more broadly, in the political sphere. This with the establishment of a generalized ecological co-management which puts an end to the economic and political dictatorship of the financial capitalists. We must therefore go beyond the philosophy of the Enlightenment which, de facto, ratified the capitalist system. With modern capitalism and its considerable forces of action we have indeed entered, at the end of middle-ages, the Capitalocene: the capitalist subject who has economic and even political power, has gradually become capable of destroying the ecological system which conditions the survival of humanity. The vast majority of the most 'advanced' economists, during recurrent economic and ecological crises, have no solution but to tax the rich, which in no way modifies the destructive power of action of the capitalists but only cuts down on their wealth. Many philosophers are looking for an exit from capitalism but have few solutions which can effectively thwart capitalist management. Some, like Grange (2012), propose the institution of a new sacred, relying in particular on Auguste Comte.[5] Others, invoking certain instruments of law, simply want to correct the shortcomings of capitalism with fiscal laws. Still others, who go further, want to reduce its sphere of activity, for example through the extension of the commons. But, practically, no one thinks of modifying its concrete mode of operation and its rationality: its accounting management. Changing your life and life for self-management involves reversing the type of nefarious and hidden accounting calculation that has dominated the world for centuries: tell me how you calculate I will tell you who you are could assert a philosopher who understands the importance of accountability. It is not the entertainment society that is the problem, nor the industrial or consumer society, but the society of capitalist accounting profitability which conditions all the ecological, economic and social factors.[6] Capitalist accounting is an extraordinary model for conservation of resources, but strictly limited to those relating to financial capital. Moreover accounting law is largely forgotten by environmental lawyers.

However, it must be recognized that some (very rare) scientists have sensed the importance of this discipline for rebuilding a new ecological economy: De Rosnay (2010), in particular, affirmed that "the true notion of sustainable development is depreciation of land capital."Indeed classical accountants (not modern IFRS accountants infected with the ideas of neoclassical economists) are specialists in depreciating and conserving financial capital. They can help ecologists turn their general principles into concrete realities. This help will be particularly valuable in resolving viral issues such as the current corona virus pandemic and others that are sure to arise in the future. Indeed these viral questions, in the opinion of most experts, are linked to ecological problems of conservation of forests and habitats of wild

[5] Comte, quoted in Grange (2012, 123 124), in his "Subjective Synthesis," wants a "just adoration of the Earth, set up as a Great Fetish, seat and support of the Great Being."
[6] This view should normally be shared by all ecologists since, according to Simmonet (113), they "have clearly affirmed their anti-capitalist position." But this, for the moment, has not been proven.

animals and more broadly of soil.[7] All current problems are therefore essentially problems of conservation, types of problems which fall within the scope of accounting management and not questions of economic tools or types of property as still believe many economists whether they are Marxists or not. And this question of the conservation (or preservation) of capitals, which is a capital one, is unfortunately exclusively dealt with by the capitalists and their accountants, which leads us to the current catastrophes. This situation must absolutely be changed as quickly as possible with an accounting revolution supported by a new ecological democracy. The first capitalists needed accountants to conserve their financial capital. Ecologists and, more generally, environmentalists will need other accountants to fulfil their ambition to move towards a reasonable society that respects people and nature. This new society will be based on a new economic policy coupled with ecological co-management at all levels. The urgency of the challenges facing us invites us to proceed as quickly as possible in this direction.

---

[7] We are referring to the risks of permafost thawing which could have catastrophic consequences due to the release of viruses "dormant" for millennia.

Annexure 1
Simplified example of the application of the CARE / TDL method to a company

Here we take up the case of accounting which served as a basis for explaining the capitalist management model. Recall that our capitalist had founded his company with an initial balance sheet which was as follows:

Assets (ressources to use)	Liabilities (debts)
Money in cash 100	Capital due to X 100

Table 1 *Annex 1: initial capitalist balance sheet*

During his first period of management he had been able to buy a commodity for 100 and resell it for 320 but had to pay his employees, depending on the labor market, for 50, which ultimately left him with 270 in cash. He then made a profit of 170 (320-100-50) which appeared as a debt to be paid on his balance sheet at the end of this first period:

Assets (ressources to use)	Liabilities (debts)
	Capital due to X 100
Money in cash 270	Profit due to X 170

Table 2 *Annex 1: final capitalist balance sheet*

The corresponding income measurement, which gives the details of the positive movements (revenues) and negative movements(expenses) generating the profit led to the following P&L statement:

Revenues (sales)	+ 320
Cost of use of wares	– 100
Cost of use of salaried people (wages)	– 50
Net profit	170

Table 3 *Annex 1: capitalist income statement (first period)*

We can see that these documents confirm the 'burden' that the employees represent for the capitalist: the latter had to sacrifice for their use around 12% of his gross profit (50/220). We are indeed in this terrible vision of accounting where the only capital that matters (which must be systematically kept)is the financial capital: employees, for their part, are not only simple means of this capitalist but also its enemies since they reduce his gross profit. We can say that this type of income statement is of a "Hobbesian" type: homo lupus homini.

But, now consider the perspective of CARE with its three types of capitals with equal fate. To this end, we introduce two additional data from ontological analyzes of the human and natural capital used by this new type of business. First, in order that the human capital can be effectively preserved, the employees of this company should receive a remuneration of 100 instead of 50. Second, this firm should have a budget of 70 to rent a special device allowing no longer to pollute the river which flows near its warehouse of goods. On the basis of these two data, we can reconstruct the initial assessment of this ecological and human firm to make a CARE / TDL type of accounting

Assets (ressources to be used)		Liabilities (debts of conservation)	
Financial asset (CU)	100	Financial capital	100
Human assets (CU)	100	Human capital	100
Natural asset (CU)	70	Natural capital	70
Total des assets	270	Total of capitals	270

Table 4 *Annex 1: CARE-TDL initial balance sheet of firm X* CU = cost of use.

In accordance with the propositions set out throughout this book, at the time of the foundation of the firm, three types of capital now appear under three different lines of liabilities. To these three types of capital correspond three separate lines of assets or, more exactly, three lines of cost of use (CU) of these assets. In this simplistic example which concerns only one period of activity, all the types of capital represent budgeted costs which must in principle be the subject of an expenditure in this single period, in order to preserve the three capitals considered. In the next phase, that of the purchase of goods, this balance sheet will not be fundamentally changed except that the cost of purchasing the goods will replace the money in the assets side. We therefore pass this step to examine the case of the balance sheet after the sale of the goods and reception of the corresponding cash but before any purchase of new goods, and even any payment of the employees and of the company that rents the equipment of ecological protection.

Assets			Liabilities	
Financial asset (CU)	100 – 100=	0	Financial capital	100
Human assets (CU)	100 – 100 =	0	Human capital	100
Natural asset (CU)	70 – 70 =	0	Natural capital	70
Common cash	320	320	Net common profit	50

Table 5 *Annex 1: CARE-TDL balance sheet of firm X after sale, before payments*

As can be seen, within the framework of this ecological and human accounting, the net profit, which is now a profit common to the three capitals, has been greatly reduced: it has fallen from 170 to 50. This is obviously due to the fact that the firm, to preserve its human and natural capitals, must plan for additional expenses: 50 for human capital and 70 for natural capital. One can also immediately see from the balance sheet that, despite a sufficient amount of money in 'common cash' (due to sales of goods),the firm has not yet taken measures to ensure the effective conservation (or preservation) of the three capitals. As can be seen on the left side of the balance sheet, the result is that the corresponding assets have been used up without being replenished. Thus, the stock of goods (financial asset) appears at zero on the balance sheet; likewise, the staff members were 'worn out' without receiving compensation for this wear and tear. Finally, as the firm has not yet paid for the service to ensure the non-pollution of the river, we must consider that for the moment this obligation of preservation of this river is not fully respected. All the assets corresponding to the three capitals have therefore been depreciated (that is to say reduced) by the accountant, which shows them for a net amount equal to zero.

Conventionally, these depreciations of the three types of assets give rise to an entry in depreciation expenses[1] in the profit and loss account which we reproduce below.

Revenues (sales)	+ 320
Financial depreciation expense (cost of goods sold)	– 100
Human depreciation expense (cost of use of employees)	– 100
Natural depreciation expense (cost of use of the river)	– 70
Net common profit	50

Table 6 *Annex 1: Care/TDL Profit and Loss statement period one*

We therefore see how a triple line of depreciation appear which allows us to have an estimate of the total cost of the period corresponding to the maintenance of the three types of capitals. Gone are the days when, as René Passet,[2] this visionary economist pointed out and deplored, only [financial] capital was subject to depreciation intended to allow its renewal. Of course, each of these depreciation expense lines can be made up of a large number of components as is the case here for human capital (we will not detail).

As can be seen, each type of capital has its own depreciation expense(s) and, in particular, employees are no longer a burden of finance capital. The balance of the income statement therefore indicates a real ecological and human profit after preservation of the three types of capital. And this profit is no longer that of financial capital alone, but a profit common to the three types of capital, a profit resulting from the joint action of the three 'commoners' that are these three types of capital providers. Ostrom dreamed of a generalization of the commons but could not design an economic and accounting model to match this ambition. The CARE / TDL model provides the basis for this generalization, globally, with an accounting system comparable in scope (but not content) to the IFRS.

But let's come back to this new ecological and human profit. We can clearly see, by comparison with the profit resulting from capitalist accounting,

[1] That is to say a potential reduction in capital if reinvestment in the assets concerned does not occur.

[2] See bibliography

how much the latter was a fictitious profit. In general, most of the profits currently distributed by firms, more specifically the large firms which dominate the world and which play on the competition of peoples on a planetary scale, are fictitious profits. It is already the case of our capitalist at the beginning of modern capitalism who has an undue profit of 120 (170-50). CARE / TDL accounting can therefore provide extremely useful information on the existence of these fictitious 'surplus profits' of financial capitalists. As such, it can be the basis of a tax policy by a state in the service of the ecological and human causes. These super profits would be heavily taxed and the proceeds of this taxation could go to subsidize those who have additional costs because of their commitment to the ecological and human causes, additional costs that the CARE method also allows to identify. This would be particularly useful in the case of agriculture and would encourage those who embark on organic while taxing those who make profits to the detriment of nature and their employees, especially in the case of large-scale monocultures with large recourse of pesticides. Surplus profits from supermarkets that destroy the life of small town centers and fail to pay farmers their fair cost of production could just as easily be identified and taxed.

Let us now return to our example by supposing that the firm performs the last normal step of the process which leads it to the effective conservation of the three capitals. We admit that it uses the amount available in common cash to renew its three types of capital. Here is the final balance sheet after this final operation.

Assets			Liabilities	
Financial asset (CU)	100 – 100+ 100=	100	Financial Capital	100
Human assets (CU)	100 – 100+ 100 =	100	Human capital	100
Natural asset (CU)	70 – 70 + 70 =70		Natural capital	70
Common cash		50	Common net profit	50

Table 7 *Annex 1: CARE/TDL final Balance sheet of firm X*

What happened? It is clear that the pooled money has fallen from 320 to 50, which implies an overall expenditure of 270. You can easily see the use of this sum by looking at the evolution of the various lines of the other assets. First we see that financial assets have increased by 100. This corresponds to the purchase of a new commodity, which makes it possible to renew the financial capital. We then see that human assets have increased by 100: this corresponds to the pays for conservation received by employees. Finally, the natural capital has also increased by 70. This is the consequence of the payment for the rental of the instrument for river protection. We can then see that all the types of capitals have been conserved (save effects close to the inevitable entropy[3]). This preservation can be verified immediately by comparing the level of "value" (accounting cost value for preservation, it is understood) of the capitals to be kept on the liabilities side and the 'value' of the assets. Normally, three types of auditors, respectively specialists in the custody of the three types of capital, should certify the reality of these conservations or preservations.

All these new calculations will lead to new ecological concepts of profitability, efficiency, effectiveness, competitiveness, productivity etc., which it is not possible to study within the limited framework of this text. Let us be content to say once again that it is wrong to speak of technical rationality or economic rationality in general: these rationalities are always conditioned by subjective choices which can be very diverse as far as the types of capitals to be conserved are concerned.

[3] Unfortunately, the preservation of human beings and nature is not total. Nothing will prevent the total degradation of human beings and even of the earth, but in the longer term (about three billions years).

Annexure 2
Towards new ecological national accounts based on the CARE/TDL mode

The purpose of national accounts is generally to give an idea of the creation of wealth in a given country during a given period; the most famous of its indicators is the gross domestic product (GDP), although the focus should be on the net domestic product (NDP) after taking into account the depreciation of machines and, more generally, of all assets that are used for production (in the broad sense) for several periods, which we will do here.

Basically, in all countries, the NDP is an aggregation of micro-economic data provided by companies in the country concerned, more precisely an aggregation of the income statements of companies, since national accounts are rarely able to give national balance sheets. To understand how this type of account is made, we will use the simplistic previous example used for the explanation of individual accounts.[1] We first recall the income statement of the capitalist firm X

Revenues (selling price of the goods sold)		+ 320
Expenses (costs of wares sold)		- 100
Expenses (costs of labour)		- 50
Net operating profit		170

Table 1 *Annex 2: Profit and loss firm X (period 1)*

Now imagine, at the cost of an outrageous simplification, that this company is the unique and gigantic firm of a country, which would live solely on the import-export of goods and which would have bought goods from abroad for 100 to resell them in the country concerned and in other countries for 320. What would then be the NDP of this imaginary country for the period

[1] For more information see Richard: Towards a new ecological and human type of national accounting for developing economies (The CARE/TDL model). (2020) BRiCS Journal of Economics 1/1.

considered according to the classic accounting rules of national accounts? Two different methods can be used.

The first one, known as the *deductive approach,* consists in taking the revenues (that is to say the sales) of the period and in deducing from them the consumption of all production or sales tools necessary to accomplish these sales. This calculation makes it possible to obtain what is called the 'added value' by the activity of the nation. In the case of our example, the product merges with the sales of goods, and the so-called intermediate consumption or depreciation merges with the cost of goods sold. This nation's NDP is therefore 320 - 100 = 220.

The second method, called *additive,* consists in summing all the types of income that have been distributed in the country. In our case, there are only two social classes, to which correspond two types of income: on the one hand the capitalists and their profits, on the other hand the employees and their wages. The additive calculation therefore consists in adding the salaries of the employees (50) and the profits of the capitalists (170) to again obtain the NDP of the nation equal to 220. It is clear that we cannot distribute more wealth than there has been no net produced value, it means added value. But this is incidental to our survey. What is more interesting is to compare the microeconomic view of the private accounting of the capitalist with the macroeconomic view of the national accounts. We note that while private accounting focuses, at the level of the balance of the income statement, on the profit of the capitalists of 170, national accounts, on the other hand, is interested in the overall income of all the two classes of employees and capitalists and gives a result of 220 (170 + 50). In other words, a nation's profit is, fundamentally, the sum of the "profits" of wage earners and their bosses, the capitalists. This macroeconomic reasoning can be represented by an income statement of the following type established on the basis of the preceding figures.

Revenues (selling price of goods sold)	+ 320
Expenses (cost of goods sold)	– 100
Net amount (national domestic profit or NDP)	220

***Table* 2 Annex 2: National income statement (period 1)**

Note that, nowadays, this type of macroeconomic measurement is published in all countries of the world and that economists generally take it as a basis for judging the evolution of the performance of nations and even of the globe: it is the indicator that dominates all current macroeconomic thought, even if this indicator is very open to criticism, and moreover criticized by certain (rare) economists and sociologists from an ecological and social point of view.[2]

In view of this account, the reader could say that insofar as he is interested in a macroeconomic magnitude, namely the value added by the 'labor' of capitalists and of their employees, this type of national income statement testifies to a conception of the result of the performance of companies more neutral than that established and published by the capitalists, who themselves see in their result only that of their financial capital alone. It is not, as we will show. Indeed, thanks to previous developments devoted to the CARE / TDL model, the reader knows that the capitalist figures of wages, profits and consumption do not give a true picture of the results of the firm. Indeed, they do not take into account the true cost of human capital and the true cost of preserving natural capital. And what is true for the accounts of capitalists as individuals is also true for national accounts which are based on the aggregation of the accounts of individual capitalist companies. All current national accounts are therefore incapable of giving a true picture of the reality of the performance of nations.

We will confirm this by showing what would be, in the case of this gigantic capitalist enterprise, the correct national accounts. To do this, we will start from the correct accounts of this capitalist company established by following the rules of the CARE / TDL method. Here they are again:

---

[2] See notably Paul Ekins, *Estimating sustainability gaps for the UK*, Forum for the future, London, (2000); Karl William Kapp, *op. cit.*; Roefie Hueting, *New Scarcity and Economic Growth. More Welfare Through Less Production?*,Amsterdam, North-Holland,1980; William D. Nordhaus et James Tobin, "Is Growth Obsolete?,"*Economic Research: Retrospect and Prospect*, vol. 5, National Bureau of Economic Research, 1972; Jean Gadreyet Florence Jany-Catrice, *Les Nouveaux Indicateurs de richesse*, Paris, La Découverte, 2005; Harold Levrel, *Selecting indicators for the management of biodiversity*, Institut Français de la biodiversité, 2007; Dominique Méda, *Qu'est-ce que la richesse?*,Paris, Aubier, 1999; Daniel Bachet (2019).

Revenues (sales)	+ 320
Financial depreciation (cost of goods sold)	– 100
Human depreciation (cost of preservation pays)	– 100
Natural depreciation (cost of preservation of the river)	– 70
Net common profit	50

Table 3 *Annex 2: national profit and loss statement (CARE/TDL)*

We can now resume our NDP calculations on the basis of these corrected figures for the true depreciation of all types of capital and obtain a correct NDP. Again, we will distinguish the deductive method and the additive method. According to the deductive method, we deduct all capital consumption (depreciation expenses) from the sales proceeds (320 - 270) and we get a NDP of 50. Why this huge difference with the 'official' NDP, which is 220? Because, contrary to the capitalist vision, to obtain a real added value, we no longer consider that there is only the depreciation of financial capital to be taken into account (that which corresponds to the use of commodities), but well three depreciations of three types of capitals. The overall depreciation expense for the period is therefore absolutely not 100, but 270.

With this type of reasoning, the NDP of 50 merges with the common profit of the CARE / TDL method, that is to say a real profit both of the company and of the country where the company is located. This is the true measure of a nation's wealth creation calculated at the macroeconomic level from 'sound' microeconomic data. It corresponds to a 'macro' version of the CARE / TDL model resulting in an ecological and human GDP or, better, NDP.

Bibliography

Adorno M., Horkeimer T. (1944). Dialektik der Aufklärung. New York und Amsterdam. Querido

Adorno M., Horkheimer T. (1944). La dialectique de la raison. Paris. Tel Gallimard (1974).

Afeissa H.S. (2007). Ethique de l'environnement. Nature, valeur, Textes réunis. Paris. Vrin.

Afeissa H.S. (2012). Nouveaux fronts écologiques. Essais d'éthique environnementale et de philosophie animale. Paris. Vrin.

Aglietta M. (2019). Capitalisme: le temps des ruptures. Paris. Odile Jacob

Aho J. (2005). Confession and bookkeeping: the religious, moral and rhetorical roots of accounting. Albany New York: State University of New York Press.

Aiken M., Lu W. (1998).The evolution of bookkeeping in China: integrating historical trends with Western influences. Abacus, 34 (2), 220-242.

Anders G. (2002). De l'obsolescence de l'homme t1.Edition de l'Encyclopédie des nuisances. T2. Paris. Fario.

Anker, R., and collaborators (2011).Measuring decent work with statistical indicators. Genève. International Labour Organization.

Arendt H. (1951). The origins of totalitarism. New York. Harcourt Brace.Co.

Arendt H. (1954). La crise de la culture. Paris. Gallimard. (1999)

Arrifin Y. (2012).Généalogie de l'idée de progrès. Histoire d'une philosophie cruelle sous un nom consolant. Paris.Editions du Félin

Arrow K.J., Fisher A.C. (1974).Environmental preservation, uncertainty, and irreversibility. The Quarterly Journal of Economics, 312-319.

Arrow K.J., Solow R., Portney P.R., Leamer E.E., Radner R., Schuman H. (1993). Report of the NOAA panel on contingent valuation. Federal Register (Vol 58). Citeseer.

Attfield R. (1998). Existence value and intrinsic value. Ecological Economics, 24 (2-3),163-168.

Attfield R. (1999). The ethics of the global environment. Edinburgh. University Press.

Aubenque P. (1963). La prudence chez Aristote. Paris. PUF. Quadrige.

Audard C. (2009). Qu'est-ce que le libéralisme? Ethique, Politique, Société. Paris. Gallimard.

Bachet D. (2019).Reconstruire l'entreprise pour émanciper le travail. Toulouse.UPPR Editions.

Barbault R. (2006). Un éléphant dans un jeu de quilles. L'homme dans la biodiversité. Paris. Seuil.

Bardout J.C. (2005). "Malebranche et la situation métaphysique de la morale. Note sur le déclin de la prudence" (12ème siècle). (cité par.Pelluchon, 2012,315)

Bardy J (2017). Le concept comptable de passif environnemental, miroir du risque environnemental de l'entreprise. Thèse de doctorat en droit. Nice. Université Côte d'Azur.

Barker R. (2010). On the definitions of income, expenses and profit in IFRS. Accounting in Europe, 7 (2), 147-158.

Baudrillart J. (1970). La société de consommation. Paris. Gallimard (2008).

Beadle R. (2006). MacIntyre on virtue and organization. Organizations Studies, 27 (3), 323-340.

Becker G. (1964). Human capital: a theoretical and empirical analysis with special reference to education. Chicago. University of Chicago Press.

Bénassy JP., Boyer R., Lipietz A. (1978). Approches de l'inflation. L'exemple français. Paris. Cepremap.

Benicourt E., Guerrien G. (2008). La théorie économique néoclassique. Paris. La Découverte.

Bentham J. (1789).And introduction to the principles of morals and legislation.

Benton T. (2003). "Marxism et limites naturelles: critique et reconstruction écologique", in Harribey J.M. et Löwy M.Capital contre nature. Paris.PUF.

Berger S. (2017). The social costs of neoliberalism. Essays on the economics of K.William Kapp. Spokane.Spokeman

Berger S. Foreword to Richard and Rambaud (2022a)

Berle AA, Means GC, (1932).The modern corporation and private property. New York. The Macmillan Company.

Bernanos G. (1946).La France contre les robots. Paris. Editions France Libre.

Bernstein P.L. (1998). Against the gods: the remarkable story of risk. Hoboken. John Wiley and Sons.

Berrier-Lucas C., Rambaud A. (2012). Ontological approach of corporate sustainability:proposal for a shift. In 8th Corporate Responsibility Research Conference 2012 (p18).

Bettelheim C. (1974). La lutte des classes en URSS.1ère période. Paris. Maspero.

Bidet J., Duménil G. (2007). Altermarxisme. Paris. PUF.

Bihouix P. (2013). Matérialité du productivisme. In A. Sinaï Ed: Penser la décroissance. Paris. Sciences Po Les Presses (95-116).

Birnbacher D. (1994).La responsabilité envers les générations futures. Paris. PUF.

Bloomfield P. (2003). Moral reality. Oxford. Oxford University Press.

Bommier S., Renouard C. (2018). L'entreprise comme commun. Au-delà de la RSE. Paris.Ed Charles Léopold Mayer.

Bookchin M. (1976). Pour une société écologique. Paris. Bourgeois.

Borrits B. (2018). Au-delà de la propriété. Paris.La Découverte.

Borrits B. (2020). Virer les actionnaires. Pourquoi et comment s'en passer. Paris.Syllepse.

Bourdet Y. (1974). Pour l'autogestion. Paris. Ed Anthropos.

Bourg D. (1996). L'Homme-artifice. Paris. Gallimard.

Bourg D. (1996). Les scénarios de l'écologie. Paris. Hachette.

Bourg D., Whiteside K. (2011). Vers une démocratie écologique. Paris. Seuil.

Bouriau C. (2000). Aspects de la finitude: Descartes et Kant. Bordeaux. Presses Universitaires de Bordeaux.

Braudel F. (2008). La dynamique du capitalisme. Paris. Flammarion.

Briot E. (2014). Manager l'entreprise au 19ème siècle-Organiser. In P. Labardin et A. Pezet (Eds), Histoire du management (48-80). Paris. Nathan.

Brower J.E (2001).Stanford Encyclopedia (http: plato.stanford.edu/entries/relations-medieval/).

Burgh G. (2006). Ethics and the community of inquiry: education for deliberative democracy. Stanford. Cengage Learning.

Caillé A. (2014). Anti-utilitarisme et paradigme du don. Pourquoi? Paris. Le Bord de l'eau.

Callicott J.B. (1989). In defense of the land ethic. Essais in environmental philosophy. Albany. State University of New York.

Callicott J.B. (1992). "La nature est morte, vive la nature. Hastings Center Report, 22, n°5, 16-23 (Traduction en français dans Ecologie politique, automne hiver 1993).

Callicott J.B. (1995). "La Valeur intrinsèque dans la nature: une analyse méta-éthique." In Afeissa (2007)(187-225).

Callicott J.B. (2005).The intrinsic value of nature in public policy: the case of the endangered species act. In A.I.Cohen et C.H. Welleman (Eds). Comtemporary debates in applied ethics (pp 279-297). Hoboken. Blackwell Publishing.

Callicott J.B. (2007). *La valeur intrinsèque dans la nature: une analyse métaéthique.* In Afeissa Ed Ethique de l'environnement (309-331). Vrin. Texte original: Intrinsic value in Nature: a metaethical analysis. Electronic Journal of analytic philosophy, 3 (1995).

Callicott J.B. (2009). Genèse. La Bible et l'écologie. Marseille. Wildproject.

Callon M., Lascoumes P., Barthe Y. (2001). Agir dans un monde incertain. Paris. Seuil.

Caradonna J.L. (2014). Sustainability: a history. Oxford. Oxford University Press.

Carlowitz H.C. (1713). Sylvicultura Oeconomica. Verlegts Johann Friedrich Braun.

Carolan M. (2013). The real cost of cheap food.London. Routledge.

Carton H. (2013). Une approche critique du concept de résilience. In A. Sinaï (Ed): Penser la décroissance. Paris. Presses Sciences Po (159-180).

Castoriadis C. (1976).Réflexions sur le "développement" et la "rationalité." Esprit. Mai. (897-920).

Castoriadis C. (2013). La "rationalité" du capitalisme.In "Quelle démocratie." Tome 2. Ecrits politiques 1945-1997,627-656. Paris. Editions du Sandre.

Castree N. (2003).Environmental issues: relational ontologies and hybrid politics. Progress in Human Geography, 27 (2), 203-211.

Chakrabarty D. (2010). "Le climat de l'histoire: quatre thèses" (traduction de the climate of history: four theses; Critical Inquiry,vol 35,N°2, 1/1/2009, 197-222) dans Revue internationale des idées et des livres, N°15, Janv -Fev 2010,22-31.

Chanial P. (ed) (2008).La société vue du don. Manuel de société anti-utilitariste appliquée. Paris. La Découverte.

Chauvier S. (2006). Justice et droits à l'échelle globale. Paris. Vrin.

Chiapello E. (2007). Accounting and the birth of the notion of capitalism. Critical Perspectives on Accounting (18),263-296.

Christophe B. (2007). L'entreprise et la décroissance soutenable. Paris. L'Harmattan.

Cliff T. (1955/74). State capitalism in Russia. London. Pluto Press.

Cochet Y. (2013). Trois modèles du monde. In A. Sinaï Ed, Penser la Décroissance.Paris. Presses de Sciences Po (49-71).

Comte.A (1830-42). Système de philosophie positive.

Comte-Sponville A. (2004). Le capitalisme est-il moral? Paris. Albin Michel.

Conrad J.M. (2010). Resource economics (second ed). Cambridge. Cambridge University Press.

Constant B. (1819). "De la liberté des anciens comparée à celle des modernes."

Cornelissen C. (1913). Théorie de la valeur. Paris. Giard et Brière.

Corning P. (2011). The fair society and the pursuit of social justice. Chicago and London. The University of Chicago Press

Cournot A.A. (1838). Recherche sur les principes mathématiques de la théorie de la richesse. Paris. Dunod. (2001).

Crowards T. (1997). Non use values and the environment: economic and ethical motivations. Environmental values, 6 (2), 143-167.

Crutzen P.J. (2002).Geology of mankind. Nature, 415 (6867), 23.

Dalsuet A. (2010).Philosophie et écologie. Paris.La bibliothèque Gallimard.

Daly H.E.et Farley J. (2004).Ecological economics. Principles and applications. Washington DC. Island Press.

Davidson M.D. (2013). On the relation between ecosystem services, intrinsic value, existence value and economic valuation. Ecological Economics, 95, 171-177.

Debaise D. (2007). Introduction. In D. Debaise (Ed). Vie et expérimentation Peirce, James, Dewey (pp.7-15). Paris. Vrin.

Debord G. (1967). La société du spectacle. Paris. Gallimard (1996).

Dedeuewaerdere T. (2014).Sustainability science for sustainability. Cheltenham. Edward Elgar.

Deegan C. (2013).The accountant will have a central role in saving the planet. Really? A reflection on "green accounting" and green eyeshades twenty years later."Critical Perspectives on Accounting, 24 (6),448-458.

Del Chiaro E. (1928). Le contrat de société en droit privé romain. Thèse de droit. Paris.

Deleuze G., Guattari F. (1972).Anti-Oedipus. Capitalism and schizophrenia. Minneapolis. University of Minnesota Press (2008).

De Libera, A. (2015). L'invention du sujet moderne. Paris. Vrin.

Delmas –Marty, M. (2004). Le relatif et l'universel. Paris. Seuil.

Delmas-Marty M. (2010). "Les biens publics mondiaux, le défi du droit face aux multinationales." Préface à l'ouvrage de W. Bourdon: Face aux crises du Marché. Paris. La Découverte.

Dépelteau F. (2013). What is the direction of the "Relational Turn"? In C. Powell and F. Dépelteau (Eds). Conceptualizing Relational Sociology, Ontological and Theoretical Issues (pp 159-181). London. Palgrave Macmillan.

De Perthuis C. (2013).Le capital vert. Une nouvelle perspective de croissance. Paris. Odile Jacob.

De Rosnay J. (2010). Le macroscope. Vers une vision globale. Paris. Seuil.

De Roover R. (1956). The Development of Accounting Prior to Luca Pacioli According to The Account-books of Medieval Merchants. In A. C. Littleton

& B. S. Yamey (Eds.), Studies in the History of Accounting (pp. 114–175). London. Sweet and Maxwell.

Descola P. (2005).Par-delà nature et culture. Paris. Gallimard.

Descartes R. (1637). Discours de la méthode. Ian Maire. Leyde.

Desjardins J.R. (2006). Environmental ethics: an introduction to environmental philosophy. Belmont. Wadsworth Publishing.

Dewey J. (1930). The quest for certainty. Crows Nest. Allen and Unwin Limited.

Dobré M. (2002). L'écologie au quotidien. Eléments pour une théorie sociologique de la résistance ordinaire. Paris. L'Harmattan.

Dufumier M. (2012). Famine au sud. Malbouffe au nord. Comment le bio peut nous sauver. Paris.NiL.

Dumont R. (1973). L'utopie ou la mort. Paris Seuil.

Dumont R. (1977). Seule une écologie socialiste. Paris. Seuil.

Du Pisani J.A. (2006). Sustainable development-historical roots of the concept. Environmental Sciences.N 3 (2), 83-96.

Dupuy J.P. (2010). Pour un catatrophisme éclairé. In J.P. Touffut (ed).Changement de climat, changement d'économie? (85-99). Paris. Albin Michel.

Eckersley R. (2004). The Green State. Massachusetts Institute of Technology.

Ekins P. (2000). Estimating sustainability gaps for the UK. London. Forum for the Future.

Ellul J. (1954). La technique ou l'enjeu du siècle. Paris. A. Colin

Ellul J. (1988). Le bluff technologique. Paris. Hachette.

Elkington J. (1997). Cannibals with forks: the Triple Bottom Line of the 21st Century Business. Minneapolis. Capstone.

El Serafy S. (1991). "The environment as Capital", in R. Costanza (ed). Ecological Economics (p 168-175).

Engels F. (1880).Socialisme utopique et socialisme scientifique (Anti-Dühring). Paris. Editions Sociales (1948).

Epstein R.A. (2003). The regrettable necessity of contingent valuation. Journal of Cultural Economics, (27), 259-274.

Everett J. (2004). Exploring (false) dualisms for environmental accounting praxis. Critical Perspectives on Accounting, 15 (8), 1061-1084.

Farinelli F. (2004).Map and territory. Retrieved May 17,2015 from http://www.amaze.it/AMAZE/node 41.

Faucheux S., Froger G., Noël J.F. (1995). What form of rationality for sustainable development? Journal of Socio-Economics, 24 (1), 169-209.

Favereau, O. (2014). Entreprises: La grande déformation. Paris. Parole et Silence.

Favereau O., Beaudoin R. (2015), Penser l'entreprise. Nouvel horizon politique, Collège des Bernardins Humanités.

Fayol H. (1916). Administration générale et industrielle. Paris.Eyrolles

Ferry L. (1992). Le nouvel ordre écologique. Paris. Gallimard.

Fieser J. (2000).Metaethics, normative ethics and applied ethics. Belmont. Wadsworth.

Finley, M. I. (2007). Economie et société en Grèce ancienne (2e ed.). Paris. La Découverte

Fisher I. (1906), The nature of capital and income. New York. Macmillan Company.

Flipo F. (2014a). Nature et politique. Contribution à une anthroplogie de la modernité et de la globalisation. Paris. Editions Amsterdam.

Flipo F. (2014b). Pour une philosophie politique écologiste. Paris.Textuel. Petite encyclopédie critique.

Foster J.B. (2000). Marx's ecology: materialism and nature. New York. Monthly Review Press.

Foster J.B. (2002). Ecology against capitalism. New York. Monthly Review Press.

Foucault M. (1994). Dits et Ecrits (ouvrage posthume). Paris. Gallimard (2001).

Freeman R. E. (1984). Strategic management. A stakeholder approach. New Delhi Cambridge University Press (reéd, 2010).

Friot B. (2012). L'enjeu du salaire. Paris.La Dispute.

Gadrey J., Jany Catrice F. (2005). Les nouveaux indicateurs de richesse. Paris. La Découverte.

Galbraith JK. (1967). The new industrial state. Boston. Houghton and Mifflin.

Gauchet M. (1985). Le Désenchantement du monde. Paris. Gallimard.

Gauchet M (1990a). "Peurs et valeurs. Sous l'amour de la nature, la haine des hommes." Le Débat, N°60, mai –août,247-250.

Gauchet M. (1990b). "La démocratie contre elle-même." Le Débat, n°60.

Georgescu-Roegen N. (1971). The entropy law and the economic process. Cambridge. Harvard University Press.

Gierke O.F (1868). Das deutsche Genossenschaftsrecht. Band 1. Elibron Classics Series. (2006).

Gimpel J. (1975). La révolution industrielle du Moyen Âge. Paris. Points Histoire.

Girard R. (1972). La violence et le sacré. Paris. Grasset.

Girard P.F. (1906). Manuel élémentaire de droit romain. Rousseau.

Gladwin T.N., Kenelly J.J., Krause T.S. (1995). Shifting paradigms for sustainable development: implications for management theory and research. Academy of Management Review, 20 (4), 874-907.

Gleeson-White J. (2014). Six capitals: The revolution capitalism has to have. Or how can accountants save the planet? Crows Nest. Ed Aleen & Unwil.

Godard O. (2010). La discipline économique face à la crise de l'environnement: partie de la solution ou partie du problème? In J.P. Touffut (Ed), Changement de climat, changement d'économie (pp13-38). Paris. Albin Michel.

Goetzmann W.N. (2005). Fibonacci and the financial revolution. In WN Goetzmann and K.G. Rouwenhorst (Eds), The origins of value: the financial innovations that create modern capital markets (pp.123-143). Oxford. Oxford University Press.

Goldsmith E. (1992). The way: an ecological world view. Athens. University of Georgia Press.

Goodpaster K.E. (1979). From egoism to environmentalism. In K.E. Goodpaster and K.M. Sayre (eds): Ethics and the problems of the twenty-first century. Notre Dame. University of Notre Dame Press (21-35).

Goody J. (2004). Capitalism and modernity. The great debate. Cambridge. Polity Press.

Gorz A. (1959). La Morale de l'histoire. Paris. Seuil.

Gorz A. (1967) Le socialisme difficile. Paris. Seuil.

Gorz A. (1975). Ecologie et Politique. Paris. Galilée. Réédition Seuil 1978.

Gorz A., Bosquet M. (1978).Ecologie et politique. Paris.Seuil

Gorz A. (1990). Le fil rouge de l'écologie. Paris. Editions de l'EHSS (2015).

Gowdy J.M. (1997). The value of biodiversity: markets, society and ecosystems. Land Economics, 73 (1), 25-41.

Grange J. (2012). Pour une philosophie de l'écologie. Paris. Agora.

Gray R. (1990). The greening of accountancy: the profession after Pearce. Certified Accountants Publications.

Gray R., Bebbington J. (2001). Accounting for the Environment. London. SAGE.

Grober U. (2014). The discovery of sustainability. The genealogy of a term. In J.C. Anders and M.Remig Eds: Theories of sustainable development (6-15). London. Routledge.

Groombridge B., Jenkins M. (2002). World Atlas of Biodiversity: Earth's living ressources in the 21st century. Berkeley. University of California Press.

Guerreau, B. (2013). "La mesure" au Moyen Âge: quelques directions de recherche. In Société des historiens médiévistes de l'Enseignement supérieur public (Ed.), Mesure et Histoire médiévale (pp. 17–38). Paris. Publications de la Sorbonne.

Habermas, J (1968). La technique et la science comme "idéologie." Paris. Tel. Gallimard (1973).

Habermas (1975) Raison et légitimité. Paris. Payot.

Habermas, J. (1987). Théorie de l'agir communicationnel, vol. 2.Paris.Fayard.

Hadot P. (1995). Qu'est ce que la philosophie antique? Paris. Folio. Essais.

Hainard R. (1972). Expansion et nature. Paris. Le Courrier du livre.

Harari Y.N. (2019). Sapiens. A brief history of humanity. London. Vintage.

Hardin G. (1968). The tragedy of the commons. Science N°162 (Dec), 1243-1248.

Hardouin –Fugier E. (2002). "La protection législative de l'animal sous le nazisme." Ecologie et Politique, n°24, 51-70.

Hargrove E. (2000). Toward teaching environmental ethics: exploring problems in the language of evolving social values. Canadian Journal of Environmental Education, 5, 114-133.

Harribey J.M. et Löwy M. Capital contre nature. Paris.PUF.

Harrison R. (1992). Forêts –Essai sur l'imaginaire occidental. Paris. Flammarion.

Hart S. (1995). A natural-resource –based view of the firm. Academy of Management Review, 20 (4), 986-1014.

Hayek F.A. (1941). The pure theory of capital. London Macmillan.

Hayek F.A. (1967). "L'entreprise dans une société démocratique: dans l'intérêt de qui devrait –elle être et sera dirigée?", in Hayek F (dir) Essais de philosophie, de science politique et d'économie, Les belles Lettres Paris, 2007: 433-449.

Heidegger M (1962). "Pourquoi des poètes," Chemins qui ne mènent nulle part. Paris. Gallimard.

Hendricksen E.S. (1970). Accounting Theory.R.D. Homewood. Irwin.

Hermitte M.A. (2011). "La nature, sujet de droit?." Annales, Histoire. Sciences sociales, vol 66, N°1,173-212.

Herre F. (1999). Die Fugger in ihrer Zeit. Augsburg.Verlag Dr Wissner.

Hess G. (2013). Ethiques de la nature. Paris. Presses Universitaires de France.

Hilaire J. (1986).Introduction historique au droit commercial. Paris PUF.

Hobbes T. (1651). Léviathan ou la matière, la forme et le pouvoir d'un Etat ecclésiastique et civil.

Hobson J.A. (1926). The evolution of modern capitalism: a study of machine production. Rev ed. London: Walter Scott: New York: Scribner's.

Hodgson G.H. (2015). Conceptualising capitalism. Chicago and London. The University of Chicago Press.

Holling C.S. (1973). "Resilience and stability of ecological systems." Annual Review of Ecology and Systelatics, 4: 1-23.

Holling C.S. (2001). Understanding the complexity of economic, Ecological and Social Systems. Ecosystems, 4 (5), 390-405.

Hudson M. (2000). How interest rates were set, 2500B.C-1000 AD: Mas,tokos and foenus as metaphors for interest accruals. Journal of the Economic and Social History of the Orient, 43, 132-161.

Hudson, M. (2000). How Interest Rates Were Set, 2500 BC-1000 AD : Máš, tokos and fœnus as Metaphors for Interest Accruals. Journal of the Economic and Social History of the Orient, 43, 132–161.

Hudson, M. (2002). Reconstructing the Origins of Interest-Bearing Debt and the Logic of Clean States. In M. Hudson & M. Van De Mieroop (Eds.), Debt and Economic Renewal in the Ancient Near East (pp. 7–58). CDL Press.

Hudson M. (2004a). The archaeology of money: debt versus barter theories of money's origins.In L.R. Wray (Ed), Credit and state theories of money: the contribution of of A Mitchell Innes,99-127. Cheltenham. Edward Elgar Publishing.

Hudson M. (2004b).The role of accounting in civilization's economic takeoff. In M. Hudson and C. Wunsch (Eds): Creating Economic Order: record – keeping, standardisation and the development of accounting in the Ancient Near East. (1-22). Lanham. University Press of Maryland.

Hudson M. (2010). Entrepreneurs: from the Near Eastern take off to the Roman collapse. In D. S. Landes, J. Mokyr and J Baumol (Eds): The Invention of Enterprise (8-39). New Jersey. Princeton University Press.

Hueting.R. (1980). New scarcity and economic growth. More welfare through less production? Amsterdam. North Holland.

Humphrey M. (2007). "Imagined Autonomy": or, any colour you like as long as it is green. Contemporary Political Theory, 6 (2),246-261.

IASB International Accounting Standard Board(2010). London.

IIRC Council. (2013). Integrated Reporting.

Illich I. (1971)Une société sans école; (1973 La convivialité; (1973) Energie et équité;(1975) Némesis médical; (1977) Le chômage créateur. Paris. Seuil.

Inglehart R. (1977). The silent revolution: changing values and political styles among Western publics. New Jersey. Princeton University Press.

Ingold, T. (1980). Hunters, Pastoralists and Ranchers. Cambridge. Cambridge University Press.

Ingold, T. (2013). Marcher avec les dragons. Bruxelles. Zones Sensibles.

Jabareen Y. (2008).A new conceptual framework for sustainable development. Environment, Development and Sustainability, 10, 179-192.

James, W. (1968).Le pragmatisme. Paris. Flammarion.

Jeanneney J.N (2020). Virus ennemi. Paris. Tracts Gallimard.

Jensen M.C., Meckling W.H. (1983). "Reflections on the Corporation as a social invention." Midland Corporate Finance Journal I, n°3 (Autumn):1-21.

Jezdimirovic M. (1974). Teorija i tehnika knjigovodstva. Beograd.Savremena administracija.

Joas H. (1993). Pragmatism and social theory. Chicago and London.The University of Chicago Press.

Jonas H. (1979). Das Prinzip Verantwortung. Frankfurt. Insel Verlag.

Jonas H. (1979). Le principe de responsabilité. Une éthique pour la civilisation technologique. Paris.Le Cerf. Collection "Passages."(1990)

Jones G. (2004). People and environment. London. Pearson.

Jorion P. (2018).Les règles comptables une constitution implicite. Le Monde 4 juin.

Jourdain E. (2019). Quelles normescomptables pour une société du commun? Paris. Charles Léopold Mayer

Kant E (1785). Fondements de la Métaphysique des Mœurs.

Kant E. (1788). Critique de la raison pratique.

Kapp W. (1950). The social costs of private enterprise. New York. Schoken Books (1971).

Kardelj E. (1975). Les contradictions de la propriété sociale dans le système socialiste. Paris. Eds Anthropos.

Katz E. (1997). Nature as Subject. Lanham. Rowman and Littlefield.

Koza M.P., Thoenig J.C. (2003). Rethinking the firm: organizational approaches. Organization Studies, 24 (8), 1219-1229.

Krebs A. (1999). Ethics of nature. Berlin and New York. Walter de Gruyter.

Krutilla J.V. (1967). Conservation reconsidered. The American Economic Review, 57(4), 777-786.

Laborit H. (1974). La nouvelle grille. Paris. Robert Laffont.

Larrère C. Larrère R. (1997). Du bon usage de la nature. Pour une philosophie de l'environnement. Paris. Champs essais. Flammarion (ed 2009).

Latouche S. (2006).Le Pari de la décroissance. Paris. Fayard.

Latour B. (1997). Nous n'avons jamais été modernes: Essai d'anthropologie symétrique (2ème ed). Paris. La Découverte.

Latour B. (1998). From the world of science to the world of research?Science, 280, 208-209.

Latour B. (1999). Politiques de la nature. Comment faire entrer les sciences en démocratie. Paris. La Découverte.

Latour B. (2007a). Turning around politics. A note on Gerard de Vries' paper. Social Studies of Sciences, 811-820.

Latour B. (2007b). L'espoir de Pandore (3ème ed). Paris. La Découverte.

Latour B. (2010). Cogitamus. Six lettres sur les humanités scientifiques. Paris. La Découverte.

Latour G. (2012). Enquête sur les modes d'existence. L'enquête écologique: du mode d'existence des objest sociaux. Paris. La Découverte.

Latour B. (2014) Another way to compose the common world. HAU: Journal of Ethnographic Theory,4 (1), 301-307.

Lavelle L. (1950). Traité des valeurs, tome 1. Paris. PUF.

LavilleJ.L. (2010). L'économie sociale et solidaire. Pratiques, théories, débats. Paris. Points.

Leary R.A. (1985). Interaction theory in forest ecology and management. Leyde. Martinus Nijhoff.

Leary R.A. (2012). Interaction theory in forest ecology and management. Heidelberg. Springer Science & Business Media.

Le Goff, J. (2010). Le Moyen Age et l'argent. Paris. Perrin.

Lemarchand Y. (1993).Du dépérissement à l'amortissement. Enquête sur l'histoire d'un concept et de sa traduction comptable. Nantes. Ouest Editions.

Lenoir Y. (1977). Technocratie française. Paris. Pauvert.

Leopold A. (1949). A sand county almanac. New York. Oxford University Press.

Lévinas E (1994). Totalité et infini. Paris. LGF.Bilio "Essais."

Levinas E. (2001). En découvrant l'essence avec Husserl et Heidegger.? Paris. Vrin.

Levi-Strauss (1962). La pensée sauvage. Paris. Plon.

Levrel H. (2007). Selecting indicators for the management of biodiversity. Paris. Institut Français de la Biodiversité.

Lewis S.L., Llewellyn-Jones L. (2018). The culture of animals in antiquity. London. Routledge.

Light A., Katz E. (1996). Environmental pragmatism. London. Routledge.

Linhart D. (2021). L'insoutenable subordination des employés. Paris Erès.

Lipietz A. (2012). Green deal. La crise du libétal productivisme et la réponse écologiste. Paris La Découverte.

Locke (1690) Second traité du gouvernement civil. Paris. Flammarion "GF" (1992).

Lusk J.L., Norwood F.B. (2011). Animal welfare economics. Applied Economic Perspective and Policy, 33 (4), 463-483.

Lynn White Jr (1967). The historical roots of our ecological crisis. Science, vol 155, issue 3767, 1203-1207).

Mc Connel K.E. (1997). Does altruism undermine existence value? Journal of Environmental Economics and Management, 32 (1),22-37.

Machiavelli (1571).Le Prince. Paris. Folio classique. (1980).

Mac Intyre A. (1981).The nature of the virtues. The Hastings Center Report. April

Mac neely J.A. (1994).Lessons from the past: forest and biodiversity. Biodiversity and Conservation., 3 (1), 3-20.

Maier D.S. (2012). What's so good about biodiversity? Heidelberg. Springer.

Makarov B.G. (1966). Teorija byxgalterskogoytcheta. Moskva.Izdatelstvo "Finansi."

Mäki U. (1985). Issues in redescribing business firms. in problems in the redescription of business entreprises (pp 121-129). Helsinki Scholl of Economics.

Malinowski B. (1922). Les argonautes du Pacifique occidental. Paris. Gallimard (1989).

Maris V. (2010).Philosophie de la biodiversité. Petite éthique pour une nature en péril. Paris. Buchet Chastel Ecologie.

Marquis S. (2022). On est foutu. On pense toujours trop. Paris Flammarion.

Marx K. (1847). Misère de la philosophie. Paris. Petite Bibliothèque Payot (2002).

Mauss M. (1925). Essai sur le don. Réedition avec introduction de florence Weber. Paris.PUF. 2007

Mazzucato M. (2014). The entrepreneurial state. Debunking public vs.private sector myths. London New York. Antheem Press.

Meadows D.H., Meadows D., Randers J., Behrens W.W. (1972).The limits to Growth. New York Universe Books.

Méda D. (1999). Qu'est-ce que la richesse? Paris. Aubier.

Meiksin Wood E. (2002). The origin of capitalism. A longer view. London. Verso

Migeotte L. (2007). L'économie des cités grecques. Paris. Ellipses.

Mill J.S. (1863). Utilitarism. Parker, Son and Bourn.

Mill J.S. (1909). Principles of political economy with some of their applications to social philosophy. (seventh ed). Longmans, Green and Co.

Minteer B.A and Manning R.E. (2005). An appraisal of the critique of the anthropocentrism and three lesser-known themes in Lynn White's "The historical roots of our ecological crisis." Organization and Environment, 18 (2), 163-176

Morin E. (1981). Pour sortir du 21ème siècle. Paris. Fernand Nathan.

Moscovici S. (1968) Première édition Essai sur l'histoire humaine de la nature. Paris. Flammarion.

Moscovici S. (1972). La société contre nature. Paris. Coll 10/18.

Moscovici S. (1977). Deuxième édition Essai sur l'histoire humaine de la nature. Paris. Flammarion.

Most K. (1976). How wrong was Sombart. Accounting Historians Journal. Vol 3, Issue 1, N°1-4 Winter Fall.

Mounier E. (1936). Manifeste au service du personnalisme. Paris. Seuil.

Mounier E. (1948). La petite peur du 20ème siècle. Paris. Editions de la Baconnière.

Mumford L. (1934). Technics and civilization. San Diego. Harcourt Brace and Co.

Mumford L. (1950). Technique et civilisation. Paris. Seuil.

Murphy D.F., Bendell J. (1997). Business environmental groups and sustainable development post Rio. The Policy Press.

Musso P. (2019). Le temps de l'Etat-Entreprise. Berlusconi, Trump, Macron. Paris. Fayard.

Naddaf G. (1992).L'origine et l'évolution du concept grec de phusis. In Lewinstone, Queenstone, Lampeter, The Eswig Mellen Press (cf LL Pp315)

Naess A. (1973). The shallow and the deep, long range ecology movement. A summary. Inquiry, 16,95-100.

Naess A. (1989). Ecology, community and life style: outline of an ecosophy. Cambridge. Cambridge University Press.

Naess A. (2009). Ecologie, communauté et style de vie. Paris. MF Editions.

Nanda M. (2003). Prophets facing backward: postmodern critiques of science and Hindu nationalism in India. New Brunswick-London. Rutgers University Press.

Neumayer E. (1999), Weak versus Strong Sustainability. Exploring the limits of two opposing paradigms. Cheltenham. Edward Elgar, USA.

Nietzsche F. (1887). Zur Genealogie der Moral. Kritische Gesamtausgabe. Abteilung 6. Band 2

Nitzan, J., Bichler S. (2009). Capital as Power. A Study of Order and Creorder. Abingdon. Routledge.

Nobes C. (2012).On the definition of income and revenue in the IFRS. Accounting in Europe, 9(1)85-94.

Nobes C. (2014), Accounting for capital: the evolution of an idea. Online (21/11/2014).

Nordhaus D., Tobin J. (1972). "Is growth obsolete?." Economic Research: retrospect and prospect, vol 5, National Bureau of Economic Research.

Norgaard R.B. (1994).Development betrayed. London. Routledge.

Norton B.G. (1984). Environmental ethics and weak anthropocentrism. Environmental Ethics, vol 6 (2), 131-148; traduction française in Afeissa Ed 2007, 249-283.

Norton B.G. (1992). Epistemology and environmental values. Monist, 75, 208-227.

Norton B.G. (2005). Sustainability. Chicago and London. The University of Chicago Press.

Nussbaum M.C. (2007). Frontiers of justice: disability, nationality, Species membership. Cambridge. Boknap Press.

Nussbaum M.C., Sen A. (1993). The quality of life. Oxford. Oxford University Press.

O'Connor J (1988). "Capitalism, Nature, Socialism: a theoretical introduction, Capitalism, Nature, Socialism, vol 1, N°1 p 11-38 reproduit in Ted Benton (dir): The greening of Marxism. Guilford Publishers, 1996.

OECD. (1999). Manuel de protection de la biodiversité. Conception et mise en œuvre des mesures incitatives. OECD Publishing.

Ogilvie B. (2012). L'homme jetable. Essai sur l'exterminisme et la violence extrême. Paris. Ed Amsterdam.

Olivier L (2006). Le 'briquetage de la Seille'" (Moselle): bilan d'un programme de recherche de cinq années archéologiques. Les cahiers Lorrains, 6-21.

Olson M. (1965). The logic of collective action. Public goods and the theory of the groups. New York. Shocken Books

O'Neill J. (1992). The varieties of intrinsic value. Monist, 75, 138-161.

Onfray M. (2006). Les Sagesses antiques. Contre-histoire de la philosophie t.1 Paris. Le livre de Poche.

Ornaf J., Rambaud A. (2012). From CSR to a genuine political CSR: corporations and global governance rethought through a reflexive, dialectical and dynamic model. In 7ème Congrès du RIODD (21). Nantes.

Osborn F. (1949). La Planète au pillage. Paris. Payot.

Ostrom E (1990). Governing the Commons: the evolution of Institutions for Collective Actions. Cambridge.Cambridge University Press.

Pacioli L. (1494). Summa de arithmetica, geometria, proportioni et proportionalita

Pacioli L. (1494), Traité des comptes et des écritures, Paris, Ordre des Experts-Comptables. Ed. Comptables Malesherbes (1995).

Packard V. (1957). La persuasion clandestine. Paris Calmann- Levy. (1979)

Paine R. (1971). Animals as capital: comparison among northern nomadic herders and hunters. Anthropological Quarterly, 44 (3), 157-172.

Parmentier B. (2007). Nourrir l'humanité. Les grands problèmes de l'agriculture mondiale au 21ème siècle. Paris. La Découverte. Cahiers libres.

Passet R. (1979). L'économique et le vivant. Payot. Paris.

Passmore J. (1980). Man's responsibility for nature. Ecological problems and western traditions. (second ed). London. Duckworth.

Passow R. (1910).Die Bilanzen der privaten Unternehmungen mit besonderer Berucksichtigung der Aktiengesellschaften. Leipzig. Verlag von Teubner.

Pearce D. (1976). The limits of cost benefit analysis as a guide to environmental policy. Kyklos 29, 97-92.

Pearce D., Markandya A., Barbier E.B. (1989). Blueprint for a green economy. London. Earthscan.

Peaucelle J.L. (2003). "Saint-Simon aux origines de la pensée de Henri Fayol."EskaEntreprise et Histoire. N°34:69-83.

Pellegrin P. (2011). In Lloyd G and Brunschwig J: le Savoir grec, Dictionnaire critique. Paris. Flammarion.

Pelluchon C. (2011). Eléments pour une éthique de la vulnérabilité. Les hommes, les animaux, la nature. Humanités. Paris. Cerf.

Pelluchon C. (2015). Le nourritures.Philosophie du corps politique. Paris. Seuil.

Perroux F. (1982). Dialogue des monopoles et des nations. Grenoble. Presses Universitaires de Grenoble.

Perroux F. (1991).L'économie du 20ème siècle. Grenoble.PUF Grenoble.

Petrazucky L. Von. (1893). Die Lehre vom Einkommen V1 Grundbegriffe.Berlin. Verlag von HW Müller.

Pickering A. (2009). The politics of theory. Journal of Cultural Economy, 2 (1-2), 197-212.

Pigou A.C. (1920). The Economics of welfare. London. Macmillan and Co Ltd (1938)

Piketty T. (2012).Le capital au 21ème siècle. Paris. Seuil.

Piketty T. (2014). Capital in the Twenty-First century. Cambridge, MA: Belknap Press of Harvard University Press.

Piper E. (1978). Der Aufstand der Ciompi. Berlin.Wagenbach.

Pisani-Ferry J. "Il faut réussir l'emprunt européen" (Le Monde du 21-22 Juin 2020 p.29).

Pister P. (Ed) (1985). Desert pupfishes: reflexion on reality, desirability and conscience. Fisheries, vol 10, 6 (10-15).

Platon. La République. Paris GF Flammarion.

Poirier S. (2014). Reproduction of hunters-gatherers' ontologies. In J. Boddy and M. Lambek (Eds): A Companion to the Anthropology of Religion (50-60).John Wiley and Sons.

Polanyi, K. (1922). "Sozialistische Rechnungslegung." Archiv für Sozialwissenschaft und Sozialpolitik. Separat Abdruck aus Band 49, Heft 2, 377-416.

Polanyi. K. (1944). La grande transformation. Paris.Tel Gallimard (1983).

Ponting C. (2007). A new green history of the world (second edition). Vintage.

Pope François. (2015). Lettre encyclique "Laudato si." Paris.Parole et silence

Porter M.E., Van Der Linde C. (1995). Green and competitive: ending the stalemate. Harvard Business Review, September, 120-134.

Postone M. (1986).Temps, travail et domination sociale. Paris Mille et une Nuits (2009).

Proudhon F.J. (1846).Système des contradictions économiques ou philosophie de la misère. Tome 1. Paris. Guillaumin et Cie. Libraires.

Pruner J. (2005). Missing the boat with Exxon Valdez and missing the mark with BMW is guideposts. An analysis of punitive damages under law and economics theory and the road to environmental ruin. Vermont Journal of Environmental Law, 606 (605-6).

Rambaud A. (2015), La valeur d'existence encomptabilité:pourquoi et comment l'entreprise peut (p)render encompte des entités environnementales pour "elles-mêmes", Thèse de Doctorat en Sciences de Gestion. Université Paris-Dauphine.

Rambaud A. (2018). "Aux origines du capital: Le capital chez Luca Pacioli, entre comptabilité et économie, entre mondes Ancien et Moderne." Working Paper – March 2018 presented at AFC.

Rambaud A., Richard J. (2015a), "The Triple Depreciation Line (TDL) instead of the Triple Bottom Line (TBL): towards a genuine integrated reporting." Critical Perspectives on Accounting, vol 33: 92-116.

Rambaud A., Richard J. (2015b), Sustainability, Finance and Accounting: From the today's Fisherian- (Falsified) Hicksian perspective to a traditional accounting approach. Working Paper. Presented at the ACRN Oxford Session 10/6/2015.

Rambaud A., Richard J. (2016) "La prise encompte d'éléments environnementaux dans la mesure de la performance," 6ème

Étatsgénéraux de la recherche comptable. Autorité des Normes Comptables (ANC). Paris. (French version).

Rambaud A., Richard J. (2017).The "Triple Depreciation Line" Accounting Model and its application to the Human Capital. In S. Alijani & C. Karyotis (Eds.). Finance and Economy for Society: Integrating Sustainability. Emerald Group Publishing: 225-251.

Rambaud A., Richard J. (2018). Vers une cogestion écologique fondée sur la comptabilité: le "capitalo- centrisme" du modèle CARE –TDL." Working Paper. Cercle des Bernardins. Paris.

Randall A. (1997). Whose losses count? Examining some claims about aggregation rules for natural resources damages. Contemporary Economic Policy, 15(4),88-97.

Randall A., Stoll J. (1983). Existence value in a total valuation framework. In R.D. Rowe and L.G. Chesnut (Eds): Managing air quality ans scenic resources at national parks and wilderness areas (265-274).Wentview Press.

Rawls.J (1987). Théorie de la justice. Paris. Seuil. "Empreintes."

Regan T. (1985). The case for animal rights. In P. Singer (Ed). In defense of Animals (13-26). Blackwell.

Reich W. (1933). La psychologie de masse du fascisme. Paris. Payot. (1972).

Reichel. F (1901). Der Begriff der Frucht im Römischen Recht. In Iherings Jahrbücher für die Dogmatik des bürgerlichen Rechts Bd 42.

Renouard Y. (1949). Les hommes d'affaires italiens au Moyen Âge. Paris Armand Colin.

Richard J. (1980). Comptabilité et systèmes économiques. Thèse Université Paris 1.

Richard J. (1983). "Comptabilité pour l'autogestion: la comptabilité des enterprises yougoslaves." In Cahiers Français de la Documentation Française n°210.Paris.

Richard J. (1995). "The evolution of accounting charts models in Europe from 1900 to 1945." The European Accounting Review, vol 4, N°1: 81-124.

Richard J. (2001). Histoire de la valeur dans les réglementations allemande et française de 1673 à 1914; In Casta JF et Colasse B Editeurs Juste valeur enjeux techniques et politiques. Mazars: pp 17-45.

Richard J. (2005a). "The concept of fair value in French and German accounting regulations from 1673 to 1914 and its consequences for the interpretation of the stages of development of capitalist accounting." Critical Perspectives on Accounting, 16 (6): 825-850.

Richard J. (2005b). "Hermann Simon, Eugen Schmalenbach et Fritz Schmidt: les trois "S" de la pensée comptable allemande"in ColasseB.ed, Les grands auteurs encomptabilité,2005:73-90.

Richard J. (2009). Comptabilité environnementale. In Colasse B. (Dir).Encyclopédie de la comptabilité. Paris. Economica. 2009

Richard J. (2010). Origines du mot comptabilité. Journées d'histoire de la comptabilité et du management (halshs- 00465984v2).

Richard J. (2012a).Comptabilité et développement durable. Paris. Economica.

Richard J. (2012b), "The victory of the Prussian railway "dynamic" accounting over the public finance and patrimonial accounting models (1838-1884): an early illustration of the appearance of the second stage of capitalist financial accounting and a testimony against the agency and the market for excuses theories," Accounting Historians Journal, 39 (1): 89-124.

Richard J. (2013). "La nature n'a pas de prix...mais sa maintenance a un coût." Revue Projet N°332: 81-87.

Richard J. (2015a). The dangerous dynamics of capitalism. From static towards IFRS futuristic accounting. Critical Perspectives on Accounting,30:9-34.

Richard J. (2015b). "La théorie économique de Fisher et la comptabilité américaine", in Mélanges enl'honneur du Professeur Christian Hoarau: Comptabilité, Finance et Politique (coordonnés par A. Burlaud). Paris.Ordre des Experts-Comptables: 65-80.

Richard J. (2016). "Refonder l'entreprise, la Société Anonyme et l'intérêt social par la comptabilité environnementale." In Vers un nouveau cadre conceptuel pour la comptabilité internationale? Centre français de droit comparé, Volume 19: 175-216.

Richard J. (2017). "The need to reform the dangerous IFRS System of Accounting" In: Which accounting regulation for Europe's economy and society, by R. Avi-Yonah, Y. Biondi and S. Sunder eds. Accounting,Economics and Law: A convivium, Vol 7,Issue2: 93-103.

Richard. J. (2023) Radical economics and accounting to save the planet. The failure of main stream economists. London. Routledge

Richard J., Bensadon D., Rambaud A. (2018).Comptabilité financière. Paris. Dunod.

Richard J., Plot E. (2014). La gestion environnementale. Collection Repères. Paris. La Découverte.

Richard J., Rambaud A. (2020).Révolution comptable. Pour une entreprise écologique et sociale. Editions de l'Atelier. Ivry sur Seine. Les éditions ouvrières.

Richard J., Rambaud A. (2022a).Economics, Accounting and the true nature of Capitalism. Abingdon. Routledge.

Richard J Rambaud A (2022b). Humanitarian ecological economics and accounting. Abingdon. Routledge.

Richard J. Rambaud A(2022c). Capital in the history of accounting and economic thought. Abingdon. Routledge.

Riesman D., Glazer N., Denney. (1950). The Lonely crowd. New Haven. Yale University Press.

Ripert G. (1946), Aspects juridiques du capitalisme moderne. Paris. LGDJ. 1951.

Robé J.P. (2011). "The legal structure of the firm." Accounting, Economics and Law I, N°1, Article 5.

Robert, A. (2013). La latitude de l'humanité dans la médecine et la théologie. In Société des historiens médiévistes de l'Enseignement supérieur public (Ed.), Mesure et Histoire médiévale (pp. 41–52). Paris. Publications de la Sorbonne.

Robertson H.M. (1959). Aspects of the rise of economic individualism. New York. Kelley and Millman Inc.

Rochfeld J. (2011). Les grandes notions du droit privé. Paris. Thémis droit.PUF.

Roddier F. (2013). Thermodynamique de l'évolution. In A. Sinaï Ed: Penser la Décroissance. Paris. Les Presses Sciences Po (73-94).

Rolstom III H. (1988). Environmental Ethics: duties to and values in the natural world. Philadelphia. Temple University Press.

Rolstom III H. (1994). La valeur dans la nature et la nature dans la valeur. In H.S Afeissa (Ed). Ethique de l'Environnement (153-186). Paris.Vrin (2007).

Rousseau J.J. (1754). Discours sur l'origine et les fondements de l'inégalité parmi les hommes. Paris Flammarion. "GF." (1971).

Routley S., Routley V. (1979). "Against the inevitability of human chauvinism." In K.E. Goodpaster and K.M. Dayre (eds): Ethic and the problem of the twenty first century. Notre Dame. University of Notre Dame Press (36-59).

Routley R. (1973). Is there a need for a new and environmental Ethic? In Proceedings of the Fifteenth World Congress of Philosophy, Sophia. Sophia Press (205-10).

Roxbee Cox J. (1997). The relations between preservation value and existence value. In J.Foster (Ed) Valuing Nature?(103-118). London. Routledge.

Rühle O. (1932). La crise mondiale ou vers le capitalisme d'Etat en URSS. Paris. Gallimard.

Sahlins M. (1972). Stone age economics. Aldine. Alherton, Inc.

Sahlins M. (2009). La nature humaine, une illusion occidentale. Paris. Edition de l'Eclat.

Saint-Simon H. (1823). Catéchisme industriel. In H. Saint Simon œuvres complètes tome 4. Paris. PUF (2012).

Samary C. (2017).D'un communisme décolonial à la démocratie des communs. Paris. Editions du Croquant.

Sas E. (2010). Philosophie de l'écologie politique. Paris. Les petits Matins.

Savatier R. (1969). Le droit comptable au service de l'homme. Paris. Dalloz.

Savitz A.W., Weber K. (2006). The Triple Bottom Line: how today's best run companies are achieving economic, social ans environmental success-and how you can too. Hoboken. Jossey-Bass.

Say J.B. (1803) Traité d'économie politique (ed de 1826). Paris. Calmann-Lévy (1972).

Schmidheiny S., Business Council for Sustainable Development. (1992).Changing course: a global business perspective on development and the environment. Cambridge. MIT Press.

Schmidt A. (1962-1994). Le concept de nature chez Marx. Paris. PUF

Schmitt C. (1922). Political theology.Four chapters on the concept of sovereignty. Chicago. University of Chicago Press (2005).

Schmitt C. (1927). The concept of the political. Chicago.University of Chicago Press. (1996).

Schopenhauer A. (1859). The world as will and idea. Garden City. Double Day (1961).

Schrödinger E. (1992). La nature et les Grecs. Paris.Seuil.

Schweitzer A. (1923). Philosophy and civilisation. A&C Black.

Sen A. (2003). L'économie est une science morale. Paris. La Découverte Poche.

Serres M. (1990). Le contrat naturel. Paris. Flamarion.

Serres M. (2008). La guerre mondiale. Paris. Le Pommier. Essais et documents.

Sidorkin A.M. (2002).Ontology, anthroplology, and epistemology of relation. Counterpoints, 173, 91-102.

Simmonet D. (1979). L'écologisme. Paris. PUF.

Sinaï A. (2013). Penser la décroissance. Politiques de l'anthropocène. Paris. Presses de Sciences Po

Singer P. (1975).Animal liberation: a new ethics for our treatment of animals. New York.New York Review.

Slife B.D. (2004).Taking practice seriously:toward a relational ontology. Journal of Theoretical and Philosophical Psychology, 24 (2), 157-178.

Smith A. (1776). An Inquiry into the nature and causes of the wealth of nations.Collier &SonUSA. (1909)

Sombart W. (1902). Der moderne Kapitalismus:historisch –systematische Darstellung des gesamteuropäischenWirschaftslebens von seinenAnfängen bis zur Gegenwart. München und Leipzig. Duncker & Humblot, Zweiter Band, erster Halbhand. (1969).

Stengers I. (2013). Au temps des catastrophes. Résister à la barbarie qui vient. Paris. La Découverte. Poche.

Stiegler B. (2008) Ars industrialis.Réenchanter le monde, la valeur esprit dans le populisme industriel. Paris. Flammarion. Champs Essais.

Stiglitz J. (2012) Rapport. Paris. Les liens qui libèrent.

Stiglitz J. (2010). Alternatives Economiques. (Avril).

Stone Christopher D. (1972).Should trees have standing? Towards legal rights for natural objects. Southern California Law Review 45, 450-501.

Strachan J.L. (1984).A synthesis of and inquiry in C. Bishop and D.R. Richards (Eds), The Academy of Accounting Historians-Working Papers Series-Volume 3 (28-44).

Tanuro D. (2005). "Marx, Mandel et les limites naturelles", intervention au colloque Ernest Mandel, Bruxelles, 2005. Disponible en ligne à l'adresse: www.ernest-mandel.org/fr/surlavie/txt/colloque/tanuro.htm.

Tanuro D. (2010).L'impossible capitalisme vert. Paris. La Découverte.

Taylor P.W. (1981). "The ethics of respect of nature." Environmental Ethics. Vol 3, (3),197-218.Traduction française in Afeissa (2007, 111-152).

Taylor P.W. (1986). Respect for Nature. A theory of environmental Ethics. Princeton. Princeton University Press.

Ten Have H. (2006).Environmental Ethics and international policy. UNESCO.

Thaller E. (1904). Traité élémentaire de droit commercial. Paris. Librairie A. Rousseau Ed.

Tisdell C. (2004). Property rights in non-captive widlife and biodiversity conservation. International Journal of global environmental issues, 4(4), 195.

Todeschini G. (2017). Les Marchands et le Temple. Paris. Albin Michel.

Trumpler (1906).Die Geschichte der römischer Gesellschafts formen. Berlin. Decker.

Turner R.K., Bateman I.J., Adger W.N. (2001).Ecological economics and coastal zone eco- systems' values:an overview. In R.K. Turner, I.J.

Bateman., W.N. Adger (Eds):Economics of coastal and water resources: valuing environmental functions (1-44). Springer Science and Business Media.

Turner R.K. (1999). The place of economic values in environmental valuation. In I.J. Bateman and K.G. Willis (Eds): Valuing Environmental Preferences (17-41). Oxford. Oxford University Press.

Turner N., Atleo R. (1998). Pacific North American first peoples and environment. In H. Coward (Ed). Traditional and modern approaches to the environment on the Pacific Rim (pp. 105-124). Albany. State University of New York Press.

Ulrich P. (1977). Die Grossunternehmung als quasi-öffentliche Institution. Stuttgart.C.E.Poeschel Verlag.

Vadrot C.M. (1973). Déclaration des Droits de la Nature. Paris. Stock.

Verhoef E.T. (2002). Externalities. In J.C.J.M. Van der Bergh (Eds). Handbook of Environmental and Resource Economics (197-214). Cheltenham. Edward Elgar Publishing.

Vidal Naquet P. (1990).La démocratie grecque vue d'ailleurs. Paris. Flammarion

Viveiros de Castro E. (2009). Métaphysiques Cannibales. Paris. PUF.

Vivien F.D. (2005). Le développement soutenable. Paris. La Découverte. Collection "Repères"

Walker, G., Holling, C.S., Carpenter S.R, Kinzig A. (2004). Resilience, adaptability and transformability in social –ecological systems. Ecology and Society,9 (2),5

Weber M. (1920). Die protestantische Ethik und der Geist des Kapitalismus. Ed Jokers (2009).

Weber F. (2007).Marcel Mauss Essai sur le don nouvelle introduction. Paris. PUF Quadrige.

Weisbrod B.A. (1964). Collective consumption services of individual consumption goods. The Quaterly Journal of Economics, 78, 471-477.

White M. (1996).Valuing unique natural resources: endangered species. Appraisal Journal: 64(6), 1-5.

Wieacker F. (1966). Societas. Böhlau.

Wildman W.J. (2010). An introduction to relational ontology. In J.Polkinghorne (Ed): The Trinity and an Entangled World (55-73). Wm. B.Eerdmans Publishing.

Williams M. (2006). Deforesting the Earth. Chicago. The University of Chicago Press.

Wood, D. (2002). Medieval Economic Thought. Cambridge. Cambridge University Press.

World Bank. (2006), Where is the Wealth of Nations? Measuring the Capital for the 21st Century. Washington DC. The World Bank,

Wunsch C. (2010). Neo-Babylonians Entrepreneurs. In D. S. Landes, J. Mokyrand W.J. Baumol (Eds), The invention of Enterprise (40-61). Princeton. Princeton University Press.

Yankelevitch (1972). Traité des vertus. Paris. Bordas.

Zhao, Y., Lou, E., Ge, J., Wu, C. (1979[1962]). Principles of accounting (kuai ji yuan li).Chinese House of financial and economic edition. (杨纪琬(主编), 赵玉珉, 娄尔行, 葛家澍, 吴诚之. 会计原理(高等财经院校试用教材).中国财政经济出版社,1979).

www.ingramcontent.com/pod-product-compliance
Lightning Source LLC
LaVergne TN
LVHW102009210926
848483LV00010B/232
9781804413388